Nietzschean Psychology and Psychotherapy

Nietzschean Psychology and Psychotherapy

The New Doctors of the Soul

Uri Wernik

LEXINGTON BOOKS
Lanham • Boulder • New York • London

Published by Lexington Books
An imprint of The Rowman & Littlefield Publishing Group, Inc.
4501 Forbes Boulevard, Suite 200, Lanham, Maryland 20706
www.rowman.com

Unit A, Whitacre Mews, 26-34 Stannary Street, London SE11 4AB

British Library Cataloguing in Publication Information Available

Library of Congress Cataloging-in-Publication Data

Names: Wernik, Uri, author. | Neitzsche, Friedrich Wilhelm, 1844-1900.
Title: Nietzschean psychology and psychotherapy: the new doctors of the soul / Uri Wernik.
Description: Lanham : Lexington Books, 2016. | Includes bibliographical references and index.
Identifiers: LCCN 2016002995 (print) | LCCN 2016005718 (ebook) | ISBN 9781498528672 (cloth : alk. paper) | ISBN 9781498528696 (pbk. : alk. paper) | ISBN 9781498528689 (Electronic)
Subjects: LCSH: Psychoanalysis and philosophy.
LCC BF175.4.P45 W477 2016 (print) | LCC BF175.4.P45 (ebook) | DDC 150.92—dc23
LC record available at http://lccn.loc.gov/2015034023

∞™ The paper used in this publication meets the minimum requirements of American National Standard for Information Sciences Permanence of Paper for Printed Library Materials, ANSI/NISO Z39.48-1992.

Printed in the United States of America

These pages are dedicated to you, my beloved Elanah. You are my answer to Nietzsche's question, "Do you believe that you will be able to converse well with this woman into your old age?"

But where are there psychologists today?
(*Human All Too Human*, Preface, 8)

Where are the new doctors of the soul?
(*Daybreak*, I, 52)

The good men of every age are those who dig
the old ideas deep down and bear fruit with them.
(*The Gay Science*, I, 4)

Contents

Bibliographic Note

For the sake of accessibility, I have used, when possible, printed translations of Nietzsche works, now in the public domain and also available online. Some quotations were amended in light of newer translations. All the translations used are mentioned in the *Selected Bibliography* at the end of the book. The italicized words in the following list will stand in the book for the full titles. References, applicable to all editions, will include a first level division (parts, essays or sections, according to the case) followed by numerals or literal headings.

The *Birth* of Tragedy Out of the Spirit of Music, 1872.
    An Attempt at Self *Criticism*
Untimely Meditations (or Thoughts Out of Season):
    David *Strauss* the Confessor and the Writer, 1873.
    On the Uses and Disadvantages of *History* for Life, 1874.
    Schopenhauer as Educator, 1874.
    Richard *Wagner* in Bayreuth, 1876.
Human, All Too Human: A Book for Free Spirits, 1878.
    Assorted Maxims and Opinions, 1878.
    The *Wanderer* and His Shadow, 1880.
Daybreak (also translated as *Dawn*): Thoughts on the Prejudices of Morality, 1881.
The *Gay* Science (also translated as The Joyful Wisdom): La Gaya Scienza, 1882.
Thus Spoke Zarathustra: A Book for All and None, 1883–1885.
Beyond Good and Evil: Prelude to a Philosophy of the Future, 1886.
On the *Genealogy* of Morality: A Polemic, 1887.
The *Case* of Wagner: A Musician's Problem, 1888.
Twilight of the Idols, or How One Philosophizes with a Hammer (completed 1888), 1889:
    Maxims and Arrows
    The Problem of *Socrates*
    Reason in Philosophy
    How the "True World" Finally Became a *Fable*
    Morality as Anti-Nature
    The Four Great *Errors*
    The "Improvers" of *Mankind*
    What the *Germans* Lack

Skirmishes of an Untimely Man
What I Owe to the *Ancients*
The *Antichrist*: Curse on Christianity (completed 1888), 1895.
Ecce Homo: How One Becomes What One Is (completed 1888), 1905:
Why I Am So *Wise*
Why I Am So *Clever*
Why I Write Such Good *Books*
Why I Am a *Destiny*
An Attempt at *Self-Criticism*
Nietzsche *Contra* Wagner: Documents of a Psychologist (completed 1888), 1895.
Dithyrambs of *Dionysus* (comp.1888), 1892.

POSTHUMOUS PUBLICATIONS

The *Greek* State (written 1871).
On *Truth* and Lies in a Nonmoral Sense (written 1873).
Philosophy in the Tragic Age of the Greeks (unfinished, written 1873).
On the *Future* of Our Educational Institutions (five lectures, delivered 1872).
We *Philologists* (written 1874).
The *Will* to Power (edited selection from Nietzsche's 1883–1888 notebooks), 1901.

Acknowledgments

Walter Kaufmann's *Nietzsche: Philosopher, Psychologist, Antichrist* was my first introduction to the commentary and interpretation of Nietzsche. Two thinkers inspired me later, Alexander Nehamas, the author of *Nietzsche, Life as Literature* and Leslie Paul Thiele's *Friedrich Nietzsche and the Politics of the Soul: A Study of Heroic Individualism.* Luke Rhinehart (George Cockcroft), the author of *The Dice Man,* influenced my thinking about Nietzsche, chance and therapy.

My ninety-nine-year-old mother Giza Wernik, always asked how the book is doing, never forgetting to mention the Polish play of words on Nietzsche and Kant "Jezeli przychodzisz do mnie z niczem, puszcze cie kantem," which translates as "If you come to me with nothing (niczem) I will break up with you (Puszcze cie kantem)." My children Haran and Dana, Edan and Neta, Sahar and Dan, and their families, surprised me at my birthday, arriving all dressed in black t-shirts with Nietzsche's picture and Über-Übermensch printed on it. I am wearing it right now, basking in their affection and support. Elanah Wernik, my life-partner, asked me many pertinent questions which made me reconsider my views.

Alan Rosenthal graciously read my book's different versions and suggested editorial changes. Raviv Meinrath granted me (and my colleagues) a supporting and pleasant work environment. Peter Raab, a pioneer and teacher of philosophical counseling, offered me important and different perspectives on Nietzsche. I enjoyed stimulating conversations with John Landau, Rafi Yungmann, and Ehud Kaufman. I was fortunate to have Amy King as my editor. She set high standards which I tried to achieve and always gave me good advice. I say to you colleagues, friends, and family, thank you, thank you from the bottom of my heart.

Introduction

I already know now how this book will end. It will be with Nietzsche's delightful meditation on endings; one of many passages that beg to be learned by heart, because, "whoever writes in blood and aphorisms wants not to be learned but to be learned by heart" (*Thus,* I, Reading and writing). This would never happen with plain descriptive or argumentative pedestrian texts. One also feels like quoting many paragraphs, finding it hard to paraphrase Nietzsche's beautiful phrases. Please accept this in lieu of an apology for the many Nietzsche quotes in this book. I must also ask you to bear with me, when I send you from one chapter to another—it is unavoidable because in Nietzsche, "all things are enlinked, enlaced and enamored" (*Thus,* IV, The sleepwalker song, 10).

I trust that you, my readers, will eventually find that Nietzsche is indeed "a psychologist who has not his peer" (*Ecce,* Books, 5). Not only is he a great and original psychologist and critic of psychology, but also one of the great teachers of the wisdom of life. I hope that you realize and agree that he is the predecessor and champion of action, chance, and acceptance-oriented self-help and therapy, far from being, as is often claimed a proponent of depth, dynamic or insight-oriented psychotherapy.[1] I will often show that an idea similar to Nietzsche's appeared years later and was expressed in similar terms, although there is not necessarily a causal link between them. Not only that, sometimes the later formulation clarifies or shows in a different light the earlier one, and in any case, it is esthetically pleasing to find that great minds think alike.

On interpretations: my book joins many other interpretations of Nietzsche. I will often use his name to refer to both the person and his writings, and I stand in relation to him as he stood in relation to his subject: the world we live in and more specifically the question of how to live our lives. A person stands like a prism between the world and its reflection in one's understanding and penning. This prism or perspective is made up of one's personality, health, talents, experiences, time, place, chance, and everything that makes humans who they are. In my case, Nietzsche became the world and I stand between this world and my book. You the reader, stand between my book and your understanding of it. Thus, we are all interpreting, as Nietzsche noted, "against positivism, which halts at phenomena—'There are only facts'—I would say: No, facts is precisely what there is not, only interpretations. We cannot establish any fact 'in itself': perhaps it is folly to want to do such a thing" (*Will,* III, 481).

Writing about Nietzsche, who wrote in different books and different periods different things about the same topics, creates a problem for his interpreters: should different takes be understood as developments of an idea, as revisions, or as contradictions? Should older versions be disregarded or discarded? My answer will have to be "all of the above," everything according to the case.

Academic discourse and aphorisms: Nietzsche intentionally wrote all his books in a personal tone, free of references, bibliography or footnotes, and thus turned them into a direct dialogue, not with other scholars, but with his readers. He argued that science is not estranged from belief and that scholarly works falsely pretend to be objective. Concepts, opinions, history, and other books and articles come between scholars and their subjects of study (*Untimely*, Strauss, 7). He did not wish to convince or prove a point by quoting "authorities" or assembling supporting facts; he never claimed that what he wrote is the truth or the whole truth, as for him, nothing like universal truth exists at all. The only question is whether an idea, Nietzsche's or the present author's, advances life; and each reader is sovereign, to decide on this point. Zarathustra said to his disciples, "Thou ask why? I do not belong to those who may be asked after their Why" (*Thus*, II, Poets), and in another place Nietzsche commented, "What must first be proved is worth little" (*Twilight*, Socrates, 5).

Most of Nietzsche's work consists of collections of short essays and aphorisms. It is possible to understand (that is to interpret) this fact in different ways: as an expression of affinity with sages who lived and taught in a pre-specialization world, such as the pre-Socratics and Heraclitus, "the dark one," in particular. This can also be understood as a reflection of his aversion to system building, and as a statement that there is no one unified and organized truth but rather, many fragmented and tentative perspectives. We should also take into account the fact that Nietzsche suffered from severe eyestrain, and could not read or write for lengthy periods of time. Nietzsche's *The Will to Power* is actually a collection of short entries in his notebooks, edited after his death, which suggests that this disconnected writing could have been a collection of notes towards a future comprehensive book. Being "hot," having one flash of insight after the other, it was a pity to arrest the flow of creativity for the sake of tedious mundane scholarly writing. These aphorisms are sudden insights, kernels or outlines of ideas that one suddenly hits upon and jots down in a notebook for future reference (*Gay*, II, 90).

Nietzsche was quite suspicious of the academic parlance, knowing that with the proper rhetorical (or statistical) maneuvers, one can defend or discredit almost any notion. "There is mistrust in me for dialectic, even for proofs," he wrote to Georg Brandes (December, 1887).[2] An aphorism, however, is delivered to the reader in a concentrated form, straight to the point, as if saying to its readers: "Love it or leave it." Similarly, Nietzsche talks to us in an unscholarly style, without the customary qualifications such as "one could argue" or "to a certain degree"; occasionally using outrageous extreme formulations, as if he enjoyed seeing us squirm in our seats.

Epictetus said that "everything has two handles,"[3] and we must decide with which one to pick Nietzsche's way of writing. I picked the handle of accepting his unique style as refreshing and stimulating, enabling me to decide what of it to accept and what to reject. Others pick the second handle of being frustrated by his many statements that can't be proved or disproved; feeling that he offers most of his insights and assertions as self-evident truths with little solid supporting evidence or arguments. His writings are therefore considered by them to be, at best, a collection of his personal beliefs, and at worst, his biased opinions.

It seems quite ironic to write about Nietzsche in a manner he himself shunned and I will, therefore, have only the barest necessary and customary academic apparatus. Most of the subjects discussed here were also treated by others; sometimes more extensively than I do here, often with different conclusions. Yet I am not going to discuss the secondary literature on Nietzsche, nor carry the customary disputations proving that some scholar totally misapprehends some issue while I, how surprising, really understand it. This can be construed as a lack of seriousness on my part. Academic reader, please try to swallow this bitter pill (or lifesaver to my taste) as good things might follow.

Writing about Nietzsche: I have been a clinical psychologist for almost forty years, and remembering that Nietzsche said that "every craft makes crooked" (*Gay*, V, 366), I cannot be too proud about this fact. I have been reading and rereading Nietzsche since my youth, in different periods of my life. I feel that he had, and continues to have, especially now in the process of writing this book, a strong influence on my life and work. From the beginning of my career, I had a dream of one day writing *The Nietzschean Therapist,* but it took many years until I sat down to the task. Reading quite a few scholarly books on Nietzsche, finding my thoughts expressed by others, and finding myself in total disagreement with the rest of them, ultimately enabled me to find my own voice. If I owe anything to these writers, it is that they were, as Nietzsche called it, my tongue-looseners. "The value of many books and people lies solely in their ability to constrain everyone to express what is most concealed and deeply buried within them" (*Human*, Assorted, 210). At this point, Zarathustra gave me the final push: "It is time for man to fix his goal. It is time for man to plant the seed of his highest hope. His soil is still rich enough for it. But that soil will one day be poor and exhausted, and no lofty tree will any longer be able to grow there" (*Thus*, Zarathustra's Prologue, 5).

Nietzsche did not write any textbook of psychology, but rather had many psychological topics interspersed in his writing. Thus the selection of segments, their interpretation and arrangement are mine, and it is obvious that another author would have ended with a different picture.

Shifting around and rearranging this material, necessarily involved, as Nietzsche detailed, "violating, emending, abbreviating, letting go, filling in the cracks, composing, forging, and the other actions which belong to the nature of all interpretation" (*Genealogy*, III, 24).

Books that are more than books: As we are encapsulated within a language and our unique past experiences, understandings, and prejudices, we have no way of conceiving what is really there, outside of us. I will later discuss this issue further. Here I will add that if there are no facts, "*Facta!* Yes, *Facta ficta*!" (*Daybreak*, IV, 307), if facts are fiction, there is no Nietzsche too, but only interpretations of him. Unlike most philosophers or thinkers, he is not linear, with one argument following another in some logical sequence and usually in a dry unequivocal style, but rather circular—referring to itself, returning to topics already discussed, multilayered and multi-faceted, changing opinions and styles. Unlike other scholars, he did not write in the customary format and even disregarded common punctuation rules. He wrote monographs, essays, poems, aphorisms, proverbs, parables, anecdotes as his moods moved him. His presentation is not a slide show, but rather one of shifting colored glasses in a kaleidoscope, each move changing the whole picture. This is why so many people write about him; this is why he cannot be summed up or nailed down once and for all. However, the "patchwork nature" of his writings can also be construed as lazy authorship, not in par with current standards of scholarship. This is a legitimate perspective, but ironically, had Nietzsche written otherwise, I am not sure that he would have been what he is.

Nietzsche's writings are not only a kaleidoscope but a mirror as well, an image he used himself: "When we endeavor to examine the mirror in itself we discover in the end that we can detect nothing there but the things which it reflects" (*Daybreak*, IV, 243). This holds true for Nietzsche, the person and his writings—who you are and what you know determines what you see, and as was quoted before, "in the final analysis one experiences only oneself" (*Thus*, III, The wanderer). Nietzsche is not a fascist or a libertarian, a feminist or a misogynist, a democrat or an antidemocrat, but an artist with a magic touch with ideas and words. He did not care much about consistency. What he wrote was true for a given moment in time and place, sometimes written down without giving it a second thought. Nietzsche moved on and in another moment, though, the same subject could be conceived differently.

Who you are and what your field of study is will determine what kind of Nietzsche you will find. The same aphorism can be approached from different points of departure: if you are an educator, you will write about his theory of education. If you happen to be a historian, you will probably consider his history of Europe. A Nazi supporter will zoom in on themes condoning racial supremacy and annihilation of inferior races, but disregard passages denouncing nationalism and anti-Semitism.[4] An anarchist will find anti-state rhetoric; a conservative will find law and order ideas. An excited optimist will discover a salutation of ecstasy; a naysayer will see only a commemoration of nihilism. A psychoanalyst will encounter a precursory depth psychology. I do not have to talk about myself, as you have before you the whole book to examine the question. Again, Nietzsche is not this or that, and following the subtitle of *Thus Spoke Zarathustra,* "a book for everyone and no one," we can say that Nietzsche is the sum of all his interpretations and none of them; he is a mirror. Here is the bottom line: if someone tells you that "this is the only way to understand Nietzsche," do not believe it; if someone says "this or that is not the way to understand him," do not believe it either. A text that has only one meaning must be trivial; and trivial (in most cases), Nietzsche is not.

Different approaches to Nietzsche: Granted that different readers or commentators have their own interpretation of Nietzsche, I would like to suggest that they all, nevertheless, vary on the following dimensions: Nietzsche himself differentiates between cold-detached and warm-personally involved approaches (*Gay*, V, 345). Students of Nietzsche are either down-to-earth and pragmatic or theoretical abstracters. The former descend to ground level, look for real concrete examples, ask about the practical implications of ideas, and examine how they contribute to life.[5] The latter climb up the ladder of abstractions, using philosophical-technical terms which Nietzsche hardly used (such as ontology or agency), discussing the work as a philosophical system, clarifying arguments, finding contradictions, comparing it with other systems, and checking for originality, consistency, and logic.[6]

Nietzsche can be read in a literal, prosaic, matter-of-fact manner; as opposed to poetic, non-literal and non-prosaic reading.[7] He wrote about Jesus: "It is only on the theory that no work is to be taken literally that this anti-realist is able to speak at all (*Antichrist*, 32). We do not lack for experts who approach Nietzsche's famed themes of the Superman and Eternal Recurrence (a.k.a. eternal return of the same) literally. They examine his writings as if he was suggesting a specific eugenics or bioengineering program to improve the human race or as if he was an astrophysicist describing a tangible cosmological event. However, it is possible to look at these themes poetically, and indeed Nietzsche saw himself as a poet (and psychologist, philologist, philosopher of life, physiologist, teacher, prophet, and hermit as well, and this list is not conclusive). His mocking critics wonder, "the suitor of truth—you?" and his answer was simply, "No! Only a poet!" (*Dionysus*, 1), and in the same vein he noted that Zarathustra, who stated that "the poets lie too much," was a poet himself, and that all gods were poetic images. "We set our motley puppets on the clouds and then call them gods and supermen" (*Thus*, II, Poets). Hence, the Superman and the Eternal Recurrence could actually be "motley puppets," poetic images—dreams and not realities. This is the place to comment on my use of Thomas Common's translation of

Übermensch into "Superman,"[8] rather than choosing one of the newer ones, which have their own shortcomings. Tradition and common usage won, and the allusion to Superman and Superwoman in the comics and movie, just adds some harmless zing to it. Superman will stand in this book, of course, for Superwoman too.

An additional dimension, to be considered here, is the opposites of lumping and splitting.[9] Lumpers prefer to cast nets with large holes, assuming that significant similarities are more important than differences; splitters, on the other hand, would rather use small holes, believing that additional categories should be invented and distinctions and precise definitions must be made. Splitters would claim and prove that "free spirit par excellence" is distinct from "we free spirits."[10] Lumpers, then again, would prefer to discuss the theme of overcoming rather than, in their eyes, the minute differences among the varieties of higher persons. To conclude, we can now map our approach to Nietzsche: my own profile would be warm, down-to-earth, non-literal and lumping. Reader, what is yours?

Nietzsche's most popular, and by many, his most esteemed ideas are the triad of the Will to Power, Eternal Recurrence and the Superman. They are the point of departure and the heart of some treatises on Nietzsche's psychology. Interestingly, his other original and far-reaching contributions to psychology and psychotherapy are unjustifiably much less known. My book deals mainly with these ideas, and extracts what is useful from the triad, discussing it in more down-to-earth terms. What is left from the three lofty themes is conceived as Nietzsche's meta-psychology, barely examined here. Do not be mistaken, the implications of these ideas are found throughout the book. Had these themes not been on Nietzsche's mind and soul, we would not have his psychology.

NOTES

1. A comprehensive discussion of Nietzsche's work from a psychoanalytical perspective can be found in, Graham Parkes, *Composing the Soul: Reaches of Nietzsche's Psychology* (Chicago: University of Chicago Press, 1994). A variety of interpretations of his psychology and influence on the "depth psychology" of Freud, Jung, and Adler can be found in Jacob Golomb, *Nietzsche and Depth Psychology* (Albany: State University of New York Press, 1999).

2. Oscar Levy, ed., *Selected Letters of Friedrich Nietzsche*, trans. Anthony M. Ludovici (London: Heinemann, 1921), 316. archive.org/stream/selectedletterso00nietuoft/selectedletterso00nietuoft_djvu.txt

3. Elizabeth Carter, trans. *The Enchiridion* (by Epictetus), Para. 43, http://classics.mit.edu/Epictetus/epicench.html, accessed November 26, 2015.

4. Nietzsche's impact on Nazi German scholars is discussed in Steven E. Aschheim, *The Nietzsche Legacy in Germany, 1890–1990* (Berkeley: University of California Press, 1992).

5. The practical implications for life of Nietzsche's writings are clearly presented in Robert C. Solomon and Kathleen Marie Higgins, *What Nietzsche Really Said* (New York: Schocken Books, 2000).

6. See as an example the highly technical and detailed approach in Robert B. Pippin, *Nietzsche, Psychology, and First Philosophy* (Chicago: University of Chicago Press, 2010).

7. See the personal, non-technical poetic-metaphoric approach in, Alexander Nehamas, *Nietzsche, Life as Literature* (Cambridge, MA: Harvard University Press, 1985) and in Leslie Paul Thiele, *Friedrich Nietzsche and the Politics of the Soul: A Study of Heroic Individualism* (Princeton, NJ: Princeton University Press, 1990).

8. Friedrich Wilhelm Nietzsche, "Thus Spake Zarathustra," in *The Complete Works of Friedrich Nietzsche: The First Complete and Authorized English Translation (CWFN)*, Oscar Levy, ed. and Thomas Common, trans., Vol. 11, (Edinburgh: T.N. Foulis, 1909–1927), archive.org/search.php?query=creator%3A%22Friedrich%20Nietzsche%22&and[]=mediatype%3A%22texts%22, accessed June 22, 2014.

9. Eviatar Zerubavel, "Lumping and Splitting: Notes on Social Classification," *Sociological Forum* 11 (1996): 421.

10. Jacob Golomb, "Can One Really Become a 'Free Spirit Par Excellence' or an Übermensch?" *The Journal of Nietzsche Studies* 32 (2006): 23f.

I

Psychology

ONE

The Queen of Sciences

Psychology, as an independent discipline, was founded in Germany. Johann Friedrich Herbart published his *Textbook of Psychology* in 1816.[1] Yet many commemorate 1879, when Wilhelm Wundt founded the first psychological research laboratory at the University of Leipzig. Historians of psychology do not give Nietzsche any significant place in the annals of modern psychology. Yet the first volume of *Human, All Too Human* published in 1878, a year before the founding of Wundt's laboratory, includes many psychological observations, especially in a section titled *Man in Society*. Even though Nietzsche anteceded the latest trends in psychology and psychotherapy, his contributions are mostly unlearned and unknown by psychologists and therapists. He forewent developments in cognitive psychology concerning language, consciousness, and the will; was a forerunner of psychobiology; was the first to describe and consider multiplicity (multi-selves) in personality theory; and made original contributions to the psychology of morality, social psychology, health and forensic psychology. He also studied self-actualization, coping, and happiness and is the precursor of action psychotherapy, acceptance therapy, narrative psychotherapy, and cognitive behavioral therapy.

AN UNACKNOWLEDGED PSYCHOLOGIST

Nietzsche saw himself as a psychologist, the first psychologist among philosophers: "Before me there was no psychology" (*Ecce*, Destiny, 6). He, for one, was not unaware of his importance: "The fact that my works bespeak a psychologist, who has not his peer, is probably the first discovery a good reader will make" (*Ecce*, Books, 5). The subtitle of *Nietzsche Contra Wagner* is "Documents of a Psychologist" and it has a section titled

"The Psychologist Speaks Up." He described himself as "a born psychologist and lover of a "big hunt," of exploring the intricacies of the soul (*Beyond,* III, 45). In 1888, in a letter to August Strindberg,[2] Nietzsche declared straightforwardly, "I am a psychologist" and he described Zarathustra as a psychologist too, "the first psychologist of the good man," "the over socialized domesticated modern human Being" (*Ecce,* Destiny, 5). He hoped for recognition as a psychologist and was disappointed when it did not arrive. In a letter to Karl Fuchs (July 29, 1888),[3] he wrote, "I have never been characterized, either as a psychologist or as a writer (including poet)."

How can we understand this lack of recognition? Why something did not happen, is a question upon which we can only speculate: his personal direct tone accompanied by an emotional show of likes and dislikes did not sit well with psychologists, who adopted a scholarly, objective and impersonal approach. Besides, current psychology is committed to politically correct liberal positions, touting multiculturalism, equal rights, human rights, and minority representation, all values he found objectionable. In addition, he was adopted by "depth psychology" as a precursor of their own theories, which made him redundant: why bother with Nietzsche if psychoanalysis and its different derivatives suggest a more up-to-date or a more clinically attuned version of his ideas? The first part of a quote is often mentioned[4] attempting to baptize Nietzsche as a depth psychologist: "All psychology hitherto has run aground on moral prejudices and timidities; it has not dared to launch out into the depths," although the second part of the quote shows that his and their "depth" is not of the same kind: "It seems as if nobody had yet harbored the notion of psychology as the Morphology and development-doctrine of the Will to Power, as I conceive of it" (*Beyond,* I, 23).

Moreover, Nietzsche used the metaphor of surface much more frequently than the one of depth, as in, "besides consciousness is a surface" (*Ecce,* Clever, 9) or "whoever has looked deeply into the world might well guess what wisdom lies in the superficiality of men" (*Beyond,* III, 59). Superficiality, stopping at the surface and adoring appearances, was the hallmark of the much admired Hellenic culture. "Those Greeks were superficial—out of profundity" (*Contra,* Epilogue, 2). I would like to offer here a "deep," rather than "depth" psychology, one anchored in an intellectual tradition and not in some rootless fads; one based on a deep text, which stood the test of time, and can be read more than once and more than in one way.

PSYCHOLOGY AND *PSYCHOLOGICA*

Nietzsche is not only an unrecognized psychologist; he is also an unrecognized critic of psychology. Escaping the examination of commentators, he used and distinguished between three related terms: psychology, *psychologica*, and *psychologicis*; the last two are simply the Latin equivalents of psychology, as found in titles of older textbooks. Nietzsche did not define these shades of meaning, leaving us the task of figuring out the differences between them. I understand that in his view, psychology is the naturalistic science that studies human behaviors and motivations as objectively as possible. *Psychologica* in contradistinction departs from a particular perspective with its own value-laden world view, desired ends and assumptions about humans. *Psychologicis* is the mostly speculative analysis of individuals and human conditions, in light of psychological theories, and in fact, Nietzsche found that the German depth psychology of personalities, in comparison with the French one, "lacked subtlety and divination in *psychologicis*" (*Will*, I, 107). The interpretation of historical figures, not in their own terms, but in terms of later biased commentators (*Antichrist*, 29) is "proof of a contemptible psychological frivolity." Nietzsche criticized in the strongest terms the Church's *psychologicis*, the psychological tendentious romantic-idealistic and moralistic interpretation of Jesus. Denying its far-reaching damage to humans is "in fact as an almost criminal fraud in *psychologicis*," a crime against life (*Ecce*, Destiny, 7). Nietzsche's *The Antichrist* is a direct attack on this fraud, aimed to unsettle Christian morality.

Psychologica is a biased system of thought, which uses mystification and distortion to hide its servitude to particular interest groups, ideologies or dogma. It is artful, presenting its notions as if they were self-evident facts and nothing less than the truth. The unmasking of *psychologica* and *psychologica*-based *psychologicis*, the two pseudo-psychologies, completed Nietzsche's task of debunking the received morality (chapter 4) and exposing the deficiencies of modern culture (chapter 5). *Psychologica*, however, is not only a historical relic. It is very much alive in current psychologies that aspire to circulate social and cultural "moral" values rather than analyze or expose them. It operates in any psychology or psychiatry that serves extraneous political or economic interests, including the interests of the corresponding professional associations.

Blunders and Crimes in Psychology

Psychologica invented and falsified the notions of soul, free will, and responsibility for the sake of inflicting punishment and taking revenge. "This whole psychology is a psychology of prevention, a kind of immuring out of fear" (*Will*, II, 296). *Psychologica* moralizes and narcotizes; it constructs a morality based on fictional ideas, lies, and sophistries. It connects all displeasure and misfortune with wrong-doing and guilt, and associates feelings of worth and pride with sin. It praises meekness, denounces selflessness, falsifies love as surrender and altruism, and sees life as punishment and happiness as a temptation (*Will*, II, 428).

Psychologica is the brain child of the priests, who in the name of God, the source of morality, invented the "psychology of will" and could thus monopolize the right of revenge, becoming the earliest agents of the penal law (*Will*, III, 765). Nietzsche saw this morality as the morality of breeding and taming; a morality which uses a holy lie, the *pia fraus*, proclaiming that those deemed immoral have "the unconditional resolve to act immorally." This is the typical psychology of all "improvers" of mankind, who never doubt their right to manipulate others and lie. Nietzsche concluded that "all the means by which one has so far attempted to make mankind moral were through and through immoral" (*Twilight*, Improvers, 5).

In Western culture, under the impact of Christianity, morality and religion promoted imaginary causes and effects. The causes, in addition to the free will, include God, soul, ego, and spirit; the effects consist of salvation, sin, grace, punishment and forgiveness. The presumed interactions of these fictions resulted in an "imaginary psychology," where the self and the emotions were misunderstood; where concepts like temptation and repentance were exclaimed; and an imaginary teleology, of the end of days and salvation, was proclaimed "with the help of the sign-language of religio-ethical balderdash" (*Antichrist*, 15).

An imaginary psychology was not the exception, but rather "the psychology existing so far." This psychology failed at understanding human phenomena because it "had placed itself under the dominion of morals, because it *believed* in polarities, oppositions of moral values, and saw, read, and *interpreted* these oppositions into the text and facts of the case" (*Beyond*, III, 47). Nietzsche had no sympathy for "the psychology of making men accountable," which is seeking to find guilt and punish people, and thus, "one has deprived becoming of its innocence of being." With this positing of will in order to find guilt, "the most *fundamental* falsification *in psychologicis* was made into the very principle of psychology" (*Twilight*, Errors, 7).

He summarized his criticism of psychology in three different occasions, writing about "naive blunders," "tremendous blunders," and "great crimes," listing six failures in each of them. The blunders are psychological misconceptions and their direct opposite make up his new psychology in a nutshell. He found fault with the false dichotomies of altruism and egoism, pleasure and pain, and attacked the degradation of egoism and the appreciation of altruism in love (*Ecce*, Books, 5). He saw the allurement and glorification of consciousness and spirituality as "tremendous blunders," in which they are erroneously seen as a concrete causative, thinking, feeling and willing unities. Similarly he debunked the ideas of, ego, soul and spirit, arguing that consciousness and conscious activity are not the only means to knowledge (*Will*, III, 529).

From blunders, Nietzsche moved to "great crimes in psychology," which include robbing pain of its innocence by falsely connecting suffering and misfortune with the idea of wrong-doing, and thus installing guilt feelings. The "psychology of prevention" is one that promotes anti-life attitudes, sees life as punishment and not as a celebration, and curtails happiness, passions, and self-confidence. This psychology opposes "strong feelings of pleasure" (such as elation, extroversion, triumph, pride, assertiveness, and happiness), and brands them as sins and seductions. It turns inhibition, timidity and weakness into esteemed desirable traits and attributes greatness and achievement to selflessness or self-sacrifice (*Will*, II, *296).*

The Science of Psychology

Psychology as a field came out of the field of philosophy and from being a branch of philosophy it became an independent discipline and moved from the humanities to the social sciences. The wandering did not stop here, and it is now trying to migrate to the natural sciences, sometimes under the names of behavioral sciences, brain or cognitive science.[5] And yet, unlike the natural sciences, it always has to remind its students and scholars in neighboring disciplines that it is a science. It is not a wonder that psychology aspires to be a science. From the end of the nineteenth century, science has enjoyed money, prestige, and respect, which only the Church used to have. If psychology is science, its pronouncements are not opinions and arm-chair speculations, as was the case in the pre-scientific area, but irrevocable facts, which society ought to take into account. Nietzsche's science of psychology and the current touting of psychology as science are two different things. The German word *Wissenschaft* used by him, translated as "science," combines the meanings of study, knowledge, learning and science, which unlike received dogma, are based on systematic critical investigation and teaching.[6] It is in this sense that he determined that psychology, compared with the likes of philosophy, philology or religious studies, is not merely a science, but "queen of the sciences" (*Beyond*, I, 23). In fact, the title of his *The Gay Science* was also translated as *The Joyful Wisdom.* Nietzsche tended to use the same word in more than one sense (like "morality" and "culture"), and he differentiated between narrow-minded science and knowledge promoting science; between science as a religion, an institution that claims monopoly on truth, and the scientific method, the scientists mode of operation. He rejected the former and appreciated the latter. "It is not the victory of science that distinguishes our nineteenth century, but the victory of the scientific method over science" (*Will*, III, 466). Psychology came out of philosophy and with Nietzsche, a philosopher and psychologist, it was returning home. It was returning to philosophy, according to the Online Etymological dictionary, to "love of knowledge, the pursuit of wisdom, and systematic investigation."

Nietzsche, the critic of culture, refused to accept the reputation and claims of science at its face value and took it (including psychology) out of its vacuum pack and showed it for what it was. His critique sheds light on the question of psychology as science (in the modern sense), and the answer matters, because if psychology is now a science, and science is what we assume it is, that is to say, a collection of hard objectively tested facts, then *psychologica* becomes merely a historical childhood disease that can be comfortably forgotten.

Science is not objective and not divorced from faith, and scientists are in a way religious persons who "still have faith in the truth" (*Genealogy*, III, 29; *Gay*, V, 344), and as such, became priests of a new religion which answers the need of "believers" for an orderly and sensible world, an illusionary escape from pessimism of strength into a decadent reassurance (*Birth*, 1). Is not faith a basic property of all psychologists who pledge allegiance to one school, who claim to understand the intricacies of the soul, who keep on quoting one seer?[7] What about the writer of these words, who keeps quoting Nietzsche? He too has faith in Nietzsche (who criticized faith in psychology). Science is essentially like other myths, something that can justify existence and make it more comprehensible (*Birth*, 15). Science, though, giving into simplification and reductionism, can also be a destroyer of myth and eliminator of poetry, making life more deplorable (*Birth*, 17). Science turns the world into something that can be measured and appraised, thereby eliminating the ambiguity of existence and losing a "taste of reverence for everything that lies beyond your horizon" (*Gay*, V, 373). Today this attitude would be captured by the word "scientism."[8] Thus, psychology can be seen as a myth-producing mill: the oedipal complex, the inner-child, and the rat in a Skinner box are primarily myths, metaphors, and images, making sense of living. This perspective can be applied to Nietzsches work as well: What are the Eternal Recurrence, the Will to Power and the Superman, if not myths, suggesting ways of understanding life and living?

Science is not objective and not divorced from faith, and scientists are in a way religious persons who "still have faith in the truth" (*Genealogy*, III, 29; *Gay*, V, 344), and as such, became priests of a new religion which answers the "believers" need for an orderly and sensible world, an illusionary escape from pessimism of strength, into a decadent reassurance (*Birth*, 1). Is not faith, a basic property of all psychologists who pledge allegiance to one school; who claim to understand the intricacies of the soul; who keep on quoting one seer?[9] What about the writer of these words, who keeps quoting Nietzsche? He too has faith in Nietzsche (who criticized faith in psychology). Science is essentially like other myths, something that can justify the existence and make it more comprehensible (*Birth*, 15). Science, though, giving into simplification and reductionism, can also be a destroyer of myth and eliminator of poetry, making life more deplorable (*Birth*, 17). Science turns the world into something that can be measured and appraised, thereby eliminating the ambiguity of existence and losing a "taste of reverence for everything that lies beyond your horizon" (*Gay*, V, 373). Today this attitude would be captured by the word "scientism."[10] Thus, psychology can be seen as a myth-producing mill: the oedipal complex, the inner-child, and the rat in a Skinner-box, are primarily myths, metaphors, and images, making sense of living. This perspective can be applied to Nietzsche's work as well: What are the Eternal Recurrence, the Will to Power and the Superman, if not myths, suggesting ways of understanding life and living?

Science does not discover truths; it can only offer interpretations (*Beyond*, I, 14). The main activity of doctors of the soul is interpretation. However, many of them are not aware that their "scientific theory," in whose light they understand reality, is in itself an interpretation. Nietzsche would expect them to know that they have no monopoly on truth, to realize that human beings are more complex than all their theories, to use psychological science as a source for tentative hypotheses and perspectives, and to ensure that the implications of their specific interpretation are constructive; in other words, practice with "subtlety and divination in *psychologicis*" (*Will*, I, 107). Yet despite his reservations about science, he considered scientific education to be advantageous, not because it furthers knowledge, but because it enhances abilities, "eventuate[s] an increase in energy, in reasoning capacity, in toughness of endurance" (*Human*, V, 256).

Modern persons with their scientific mindsets lost the "sure instinct," which is achieved by continued practice, making one's responses perfect and automatic. They find it difficult to create and set values independently, and their search for self-consciousness, divorced from action and from the experience of former generations, leads to stagnation and decadence (*Will*, I, 68). The loss of the "sure instinct," the buildup of science and the growth of psychology went hand in hand with modernity's flood of information and impressions. These are hard to digest, hinder spontaneous action and increase passivity and bewilderment (*Will*, I, 71). Subsequently, the role of the priestly scientist-expert was enthusiastically adopted by psychologists and therapists, who now take part in court proceedings, intervene in mass disasters, write advice columns in magazines and are often interviewed on news and television shows. From this perspective, people who seek therapy can be seen as suffering from decadence: their "sure instinct" is paralyzed, and they seek guidance from others. Fulfilling this expectation, however, will only reinforce their state of decadence and dependency. It would be more productive to point out that the answer lies within them and that they should listen to their own instincts. In conclusion, it is not necessary to jump to attention and salute the moment we hear that psychology is science, and we will have to continue to be on guard against our own blunders and crimes.

The New Psychologica

The mobilized psychology of will, guilt and punishment, still exists in societies and sectors of society which live under the influence of ascetic priests (and imams and rabbis). However in the second half of the twentieth century, it morphed into a new *psychologica,* this time spearheaded not by priests, but rather by professional mental health workers, among them psychologists, social workers, counselors, and psychiatrists. Like its precursors, although with different basic assumptions, it continued to serve ulterior interests, those of the state, big businesses (pharmacological industry) and the professions. Three aspects of the new *psychologica* stand out: rhetoric based on questionnaires and statistics, the medicalization of mental suffering by means of diagnosis and medication, and the proliferation of self-help books.

The Numbers Craze

Nietzsche, to use more recent terms, opposed the reduction of knowledge in the humanities to information or data, appropriate for the digital world and the physical sciences. His words bear directly on current studies of subjective feelings using verbal reports and their quantification and statistical analysis: "What? Do we actually wish to have existence debased in that fashion to a ready-reckoned exercise and calculation for stay-at-home mathematicians?"(*Gay,* V, 373). He went on to argue that it is naive to believe that an interpretation of the world is valid to the degree that it is based on counting or calculating some tangible quality, as it does not prevent the interpretation from being stupid. Nietzsche used music to make his point: "Supposing we valued the worth of a music with reference to how much it could be counted, calculated, or formulated how absurd such a scientific estimate of music would be!" (*Gay,* V, 373).

Would we accept a person's self-rating of her sense of humor, creativity or memory? And if not, why should we accept self-ratings of happiness, so popular in positive psychology?—not to mention that happiness has different meanings and implications, in different ages, periods and cultures: one person connects happiness with serenity, another with excitement; for a young Hassidic student or seminarian, happiness would be overcoming sexual temptation; for a teenager it would be finding a willing sexual partner. Thus, this kind of psychological science (as all science according to Nietzsche) cannot discover any truth, but only offer some interpretation with limited validity. So much of modern psychology is based on questionnaires, and yet the researchers who use this method of study do not pay attention to Nietzsche's remark on *The so-called Ego,* in which he explained, "language and the prejudices upon which language is based very often act as obstacles in our paths when we proceed to explore internal phenomena and impulses." Not all states of consciousness and feelings have corresponding words, and the existing words are very imprecise and describe only the extreme ends of feelings, mostly atypical states, such as love, hate, pity, and desire; disregarding the most frequent range of lower intensity feelings. It is these unrecognized feelings "which weave the cloth of our character and destiny." Thus insisting on a quantitative understanding (a score from 1 to 5), which measures only emotional "outbursts," makes understanding of the world practically impossible (*Daybreak*, II, 115).

About Evidence

The *dernier cri* in psychotherapy today is "evidence-based practice"[11] and we must look beyond appearances and examine what stands behind this beguiling notion. Psychotherapy research requires simple short interventions applicable to a class of problems or diagnoses, rather than ones custom-tailored for a unique person with a unique problem. The results can say something about a specific constellation of time, place, and participants, but not about different ones, and it disregards the issue of psychology and art. Therapy is an art, where sometimes the constructive definition of the problem, not in pathological terms, is more than half the solution, and where designing together with the client a tailor-made intervention could be much more successful than applying standard measures.[12]

Without Philosophy

Nietzsche deplored the discrediting of philosophy and the devaluation of philosophers, whose way of living could inspire others. We can add to this, psychology's neglect of Nietzsche himself, and furthermore, the dismissal of psychologists who wrote and published only a few years ago. All these are instigated by modern scientists and psychologists, full of "self-glorification and presumption," who are in fact only "specialists and nook dwellers," professionalized "industrious workers" (publish or perish), and prosaic "colorblind utility men" (*Beyond*, VI, 204).

From Religion to Medicine

While the heart of *psychologica* consists of the religious concepts of righteousness, sin, guilt, and repentance; the heart of the new *psychologica* is made up of the medical concepts of health and sickness, normalcy and pathology. The words used—patient, disease, symptom, clinic, diagnosis and therapy, imply seeing problems in living as diseases. Thus, the new *psychologica* became an uncritical subscriber to "the myth of mental illness" analyzed and brilliantly exposed by Thomas Szasz.[13] Consequently, its practitioners take charge of classifying people into normal and abnormal and, based upon it, they mandate hospitalization, drug therapy, but also release from criminal liability on the grounds of mental incapacity. Nietzsche warned about the dangers of pharmaceutical "anaesthetics and intoxication" and took it upon himself to "expose the unheard of quackery . . . The worst disease of mankind has arisen from the struggle against diseases and apparent remedies have in the long run brought about worse conditions than those which it was intended to address" (*Daybreak*, I, 52). Robert Whitaker, as if proving Nietzsche's point, described and analyzed the destructive consequences of the medicalization of mental suffering, the harmful use of psychiatric drugs, and the rise of mental illness.[14]

The main working tool of the mental health professions is the *Diagnostic and Statistical Manual* (DSM), which Nietzsche would have torn apart, as he rejected the "popular medical formulation of morality," and objected to standard measures of "health of the soul," equally applicable to all persons. He suggested instead, that people have different and unique values, and each person can only be the measure of a specific kind of health. He wanted to get rid of all notions of normalcy: normal health, normal diet, as well as a normal course of diseases. Hence, the will to exclusive health is a barbaric prejudice, because one person's health can be the opposite of another person's, and illness is necessary for gaining knowledge (*Gay*, III, 120). Moreover, health itself cannot be standardized, "for there is no health as such, and all attempts to define a thing that way have been wretched failures" (*Gay*, III, 120).

From Colportage *to Self-Help Books*

Nietzsche summed up his *Moral for Psychologists* succinctly: "Not to go in for *colportage* [book peddling] psychology" (*Twilight*, Skirmishes, 7). This French term relates to the one-time book peddlers, especially those of religious-inspirational books. Today's *colportage* books are the scores of self-help and "how to" inspirational-spiritual books, teaching how to find peace of mind, boost up self-esteem, save marriages or solve any problem in a few simple steps. The statistics are staggering: at the beginning of the twenty-first century, 92.3 million books were sold in the Body/Mind/Spirit category, representing between 8 to 9 percent of total sales of adult books (*Book Industry Study*). The self-improvement industry (including books, seminars, CDs and personal coaching) was estimated to gain $2.48 billion dollars per year in the United States alone. By 2006, a research firm (Marketdata) estimated that the self-improvement market was worth more than $9 billion, and projected revenues of over $11 billion by 2008.[15]

Such books are one of the manifestations of "losing the healthy instinct of knowing what is real and right" (*Untimely*, Strauss, 12). The "self-help" literature suggests self-sufficiency, but, in fact, is based on an assumption of inability to help oneself and encourages looking up to experts (or self-proclaimed experts) for instructions on how to live. The new *psychologica*, sometimes using "New Age" rhetoric, is oriented towards the self, evident in its use of popular terms such as self-image, self-awareness, self-fulfillment, the inner-child and its emphasis on feelings and feeling good.

In the nineteenth century, under the influence of the Protestant ethic, character, and the values of restraint, effort, authority, dignity, respect and privacy were acclaimed.[16] In the twentieth century and afterward, these values gave place to openness, feelings and sharing of feelings, which gave rise to TV confessionals, sharing of pain, using medications to ease emotional upheaval, experiences of victimhood and living under stress (which children report as well). The sharp increase in the last fifty years in the prevalence of depression, anxiety states, and attention deficit and hyperactivity disorders, is not surprising in light of the loss of nerve, deepened under the patronage of the new *psychologica* and accompanied by reduced physical activity and increased consumption of junk food.

HAILS TO THE NEW QUEEN

Psychology never had a high status in the academy. It was divorced from philosophy when liberal arts were still in their heyday, to be demoted into the then-less prestigious social sciences. Nietzsche nevertheless made a queen out of this stepdaughter:

> Never yet did a profounder world of insight reveal itself to daring travelers and adventurers, and the psychologist . . . will at least be entitled to demand in return that psychology shall once more be recognized as the queen of the sciences, for whose service and equipment the other sciences exist. For psychology is once more the path to the fundamental problems. (*Beyond*, I, 23)

Why did Nietzsche elevate psychology to such heights? Because with the death of God, the human being became the supreme value; and, therefore, psychology took the place of theology. From Nietzsche's perspective, science, truth, beauty and all other ideals, have no value by themselves, but only as a means to foster life, to make persons stronger, healthier, and more creative. The sole criterion of a science's importance is the degree to which it contributes to the quality of life, beyond mere survival. As a skeptic, Nietzsche knew that an objective knowledge is impossible, and understanding of the mind precedes the understanding of its products. Nietzsche analyzed philosophical questions psychologically. He thought it impossible to separate the thinking of philosophers from their lives, and he saw all great philosophies as involuntary and unconscious autobiographies. Often, rather than refuting an idea or doctrine, he found it enough to uncover the psychological motives and emotions behind it. He did not discuss truth philosophically, but rather looked for its psychological needs and functions (*Beyond*, I, 1).

Nietzsche, as was his wont, did not start with an abstract question of the stance of different sciences, or any other abstract question about the world, but with his own life. Not just life, in general, but more specifically with the problem of pain. He analyzed his own suffering, wishing to liberate himself from his chains and heal himself. Thus, he is foremost a psychologist and his writings are actually self-therapy, hence, psychology is queen.

I have divided the psychologically significant material, gleaned from his writings, into two parts, beginning with his general-descriptive psychology, themes usually taught at introduction to psychology courses. He, however, treated these subjects in a much more critical manner, as we saw in his treatment of *psychologica*. The second part deals with his psychotherapy and counseling and includes lessons on life wisdom and self-creating. There is something different and unique in his psychology and psychotherapy, different from what we usually encounter in these fields. Nietzsche said about himself, "he overturns what he finds concealed, spared until then by some shame; he investigates how these things look if they are overturned" (*Human*, Preface, 3). He knew and liked to perform such overturning, recognizing what is hidden to the regular human eye, and, for this reason, I will hail him "the Overturner."

THE NEW PSYCHOLOGY

Nietzsche advanced a new psychology, a physio-psychology, based on "refined immorality" (*Beyond*, I, 23). In our virtual village, fads and fashions rule the markets and the intellectual exchange must be a market as well, and thus cognitive behavioral therapy (CBT) and the bio-psycho-social model (BPS) became "best-sellers." Nietzsche's psychology, without using these exact terms, is a forerunner of their central ideas. His new psychology, "the queen of sciences," has direct implications for psychotherapy, as we will see in the second part of the book, and it can be characterized by five clusters of features.

Pragmatism, Experimentalism, and Perspectivism

Nietzsche was not satisfied with merely theorizing and he looked for practical implications of ideas, demanding that any ideal indicates how a "new circle of duties" may spring from it and that transcendental goals will be reconciled with ordinary action (*Untimely*, Schopenhauer, 5). He opened his *On the use and disadvantages of history for life* quoting Goethe, who despised "everything which merely instructs me without increasing or immediately enlivening my activity" (*Untimely*, History, Foreword), and later quoted him again:

> Man is born to a limited situation; he is able to understand simple, accessible, definite goals and he accustoms himself to employing the means that happen to lie close at hand . . . it is always misfortune when he is induced to strive after something which he cannot proceed towards through a practical activity. (Goethe, *Wilhelm Meister*, quoted in *Untimely*, Schopenhauer, 5)

Nietzsche suggested that thinkers should see their actions as an experiment, in which success and failure are primarily seen as its results (*Gay*, I, 41). He shunned idle speculations and was willing to accept only arguments that stand up to the challenge of "let us try it" (*Gay*, I, 51). At the same time, Nietzsche recognized the danger of "castrating the intellect" by disregarding emotions and by limiting oneself to one point of view or experiment. We can see things from a given perspective only, and the more emotions and observations are taken into consideration, the more complete and "objective" will be our idea (*Gay*, III, 12). My approach to Nietzsche is obviously only one possible perspective, and as I have noted before, there are many others. Many perspectives are needed, and yet all understanding is valid only for a given person. "Every soul is a world of its own; for every soul, every other soul is an afterworld" (*Thus*, III, The convalescent, 2). In the debate in psychology between the nomothetic (from the Greek *nomos* meaning "law," generalized and applicable to all) and the idiographic (from the Greek *idios*, meaning "own" or "private") approaches,[17] Nietzsche obviously sides with the second camp: "At bottom every man knows well enough that he is a unique being, only once on this earth; and by no extraordinary chance will such a marvelously picturesque piece of diversity in unity as he is ever be put together a second time" (*Untimely*, Schopenhauer, 1).

Materialism, Environmentalism, and Chance

Nietzsche opted for materialistic and environmental explanations over idealistic ones. Hence, he explained a society's typical pessimistic mood as being caused by food, alcohol, winter sickness and diminishing light hours (*Gay*, III, 134). This, he proposed, holds true in the life of individuals. Domestic peace and peace of soul are connected—the mood in which we usually exist depends upon the manner in which we maintain our environment (*Daybreak*, IV, 283). He understood human behavior in terms of the interplay between individuals and environments, and thus he posited that a genius cannot be explained by his genetics, "conditions of his origin" only. Individuals are different, the environment bears upon them selectively, and they, on their part, select and shape environments according to their needs, "The force within is infinitely superior;

much that looks like external influence is merely its adaptation from within" (*Will*, I, 70).

We cannot know all the drives and needs which constitute who we are. We are like a polyp, extending arms into its surroundings, occasionally drawing by chance nutrients which effect self-transformation (*Daybreak*, II, 119). Our drives and needs encounter the environment, seeking expression and satisfaction, and the laws of their nourishment are ruled by chance. Some of them find reinforcing nourishment; some do not, and they wither; some suffer from over-nourishment; while other unfulfilled needs find their compensation by way of a dream only.

Psychobiology, Evolution, Genetics, and Physiology

Nietzsche's position on the psycho-physical question, namely the relations between body and mind, or body and soul or spirit, was stated categorically by Zarathustra, "Behind your thoughts and feelings, my brother, there stands a mighty ruler, an unknown sage—whose name is self. In your body he dwells; he is your body" (*Thus*, I, The despisers of the body). Similarly, "Since I have known the body better . . . the spirit has been only figuratively spirit to me" (*Thus*, II, Poets). Nietzsche rebutted the common belief in the duality of body and mind and in an inner mental entity "a homunculus" that controls the body, an outlook which implies neglect of the body and inclination to all things spiritual and otherworldly. For Nietzsche, body and mind are one, and he turned the prevalent childish conception, "Body am I, and soul"[18] around: The body is sovereign, "body am I entirely, and nothing else," and the ego or mind plays a subordinate role, "soul is only a word for something about the body;" "The body is a great reason, a plurality with one sense, a war and a peace, a herd and a shepherd. An instrument of your body is also your little reason, my brother, which you call spirit—a little instrument and toy of your great reason" (*Thus*, I, The despisers of the body).

The rejection of dualism targets the body, the organism, our drives, and affects, in a word, our physiology, as the subject of psychological study, as our "starting point." The body and physiology are the coordinating, monitoring and controlling system the "regents at the head of a community" from birth to death (*Will*, III, 492). The animal functions, are "a million times more important than all our beautiful moods and heights of consciousness," whereas moods and consciousness are needed only as tools of the animal functions (*Will*, III, 674). In addition to its importance, the body is a "richer, more distinct, more graspable phenomenon" and therefore, the study of the way the body functions could be a good metaphor for our psychological processes (*Will*, III, 489).

Nietzsche explained humans' unchangeable character from an evolutionary perspective, showing that our short life span necessitates preserving the imprinted writing of many millennia, and preventing its erasure

(*Human,* II, 41). Heredity plays a crucial role in the psychological make-up of people, who carry in their bodies the characteristics and preferences of their parents and ancestors, information that education and culture can only cover up, but not change (*Beyond,* IX, 264). Our dispositions are transmitted hereditarily, although specific sickness or behaviors are the results of their interaction with the environment (*Will,* I, 47). The same hereditary perspective is used to explain exceptionally cruel and aggressive behavior. "They are backward men whose brains, because of various possible accidents of heredity, have not yet developed much delicacy or versatility." Such dreadful persons show us our origins and are not responsible for being what they are (*Human,* II, 43). Simply said, we are all in the hands of our physiology:

> Poor humanity! A single drop of blood too much or too little in the brain may render our life unspeakably miserable and difficult, and we may suffer more from this single drop of blood than Prometheus from his vulture. But the worst is when we do not know that this drop is causing our sufferings and we think it is "the devil!" Or "sin!" (*Daybreak,* I, 83)

Learning, Cognition, and Behavior

Nietzsche suggested that behind feelings there are unexamined cognitive assumptions, but also that behind cognitive assumptions there are feelings! Thus feelings are not to be accepted at face value and trusted, and because they "descent from Judgments," they must be interpreted: "Trusting in our feelings simply means obeying our grandfather and grandmother more than the gods within ourselves: our reason and experience" (*Daybreak,* I, 35).

Nietzsche formulated what would become years later the basic tenet of cognitive behavioral therapy: "We have to learn to think differently—in order at last, perhaps very late on, to attain even more: to feel differently" (*Daybreak,* II, 103). He emphasized the place of learning in creating habits and skills and saw unconsciousness as confirmation of successful learning. The rational for teaching morality was always attempting to install "the certainty of an instinct" by training persons to act almost automatically, like well-trained soldiers at war, or like mathematicians employing their combinations unconsciously. Nietzsche pointed out that "in fact, this unconsciousness belongs to any kind of perfection" (*Will,* II, 432). He concluded that "Everything is learned," and using the metaphor of acquisition of a musical taste, he differentiated between the stages of "exposure, attention, differentiation; tolerance of the new-strange, patience, missing and looking forward to another encounter" (*Gay,* IV, 334).

Morphology and Genealogy

Nietzsche defined psychology, the study of the soul, as "the morphology and doctrine of the development of the Will to Power" (*Beyond*, I, 23). Morphology is the study of structures, shapes or forms; how something looks, acts, sounds, smells and feels. In his coping psychology and psychotherapy, when actions and different behaviors were called for, he recommended a morphological, functional-descriptive approach to what are "the things themselves" and did away with questions on how they came to be. But then, in the study of morality and existing institutions (such as state and marriage), aiming at their critique, reevaluation, and change of attitude, he delved into their origins and historical roots and offered their genealogy. On a practical level, "the more we examine into origins, the less do they concern our interests." We can find knowledge when we try to get as close as possible to phenomena without preconceived notions about them; and when we explore what is close to us, and inside us at the present. We will then discover, "wealth of colors, beauties, riddles, and diversity of meaning, of which earlier humanity never dreamed" (*Daybreak*, I, 44). Nietzsche was not in love with any methodology and he did not think that the genealogical investigation was a panacea. He saw it simply as one of many uses of history for the sake of living, using a specific tool for a specific job. The same tool unsurprisingly could be wrong for another job. Not only that, a historical examination that does not serve the living can result with atrophy and degeneration (*Untimely*, History, Foreword).

NIETZSCHE *AD HOMINEM*

Nietzsche's psychology is not based on an investigation of a sample of subjects (nowadays, usually psychology undergraduate students participating in experiments for credit), but rather on the observations and experiences of one especially talented person with a developed sense of what is pertinent and humanly universal, with an ability to generalize to others, his own experiences and struggles to find meaning in life (*Human*, Preface, 7). He described himself as an observer: "A man who constantly experiences, sees, hears, suspects, hopes, and dreams extraordinary things; who is struck by his very own thoughts as if from outside, as if from above and below, as if they are experiences and lightning strikes tailor-made for him" (*Beyond*, IX, 292). From the point of view of the reigning scientific "evidence-based" psychology, which deals with statistically significant differences in a population of subjects, this exactly is Nietzsche's soft underbelly. In the best case, his psychology is no more than a case study of one atypical person. Nietzsche, we saw, had different views about science and evidence.

It was clear to him that every great philosophy, and we can add that also every great psychology, so far has been "the personal confession of its author and a kind of involuntary and unconscious memoir (*Beyond*, I, 6). His writings are full of disclosures of personal pain and suffering; their overcoming and survival. He felt that his experiences, "the history of an illness and convalescence," were not intended to remain his alone, but rather transformed into "travel books" to be sent out on a journey and be an experiment for others (*Human*, Assorted, 6). His travel books are his psychology.

This book is dedicated to Nietzsche's psychology and not to the psychology of Nietzsche the psychologist. We can only be amazed and inspired by the building of an original and innovative philosophy and psychology out of the "multifaceted torture of the psychologist" (*Beyond*, IX, 269). It will be enough to realize that he was ridden with dire flashbacks and suicidal thoughts, probably related to his upbringing and traumatic childhood experiences. He suffered from sickliness manifested in debilitating bodily pains, weakness, digestive problems, headaches, and eyestrain. In addition, he experienced extreme tearing mood swings, alternating between melancholia and euphoria. His interaction with fellow human beings was troubled: he was shy, introverted, easily hurt, and unassertive. Although he had a few friendships, most of the time he suffered from loneliness and lack of love and was ridden with feelings of contempt and disgust towards others.[19]

The Personal Factor

Nietzsche believed that one cannot not write about herself. Everything we say, says something about us, and rather than debating Kants categorical imperative, he asked, "What does such a claim tell us about the man who makes it?" (*Beyond*, IX, 187). The personal factor will always remain in the background, regardless of the amount of knowledge gained and the degree of objectivity maintained by the writer who ultimately, "reaps nothing but his own biography" (*Human*, IX, 513). Incorporating the personal in one's work is not only unavoidable, but it might as well be a condition for artistic excellence. Nietzsche who at one time admired Wagner's "great, good and perfect" musical masterpieces, explained that unlike other musicians, he suffered deeply and put himself into his music (*Contra*, 1).

He readily admitted that all significant psychological expressions, whether they were written about Zarathustra or about Wagner, were only about himself, his traits and nature (*Ecce*, Birth, 4), and that Zarathustra's task of "saying Yes to the point of justifying, of redeeming even all of the past," was actually Nietzsche's own task (*Ecce*, Thus, 8). He knew that just listing his pains and suffering would make him a "melancholy author," and not wanting to sound like one, he had to tell us "what he suffered and why he now reposes in joy" (*Human*, Wanderer, 128). Together with Schopenhauer he believed that a great philosophy is actually saying "this is the picture of all life, and learn from it the meaning of your own life." The student-reader-disciple of Nietzsche's psychology, unlike students of current psychology, enters a dialogue with the text, and through the text with the author, whose ideas and personal life holds "the hieroglyphics of universal life." One compares his life with the life of the teacher, who must give a worthwhile example. This was the way ancient Greek philosophers taught: "Through their bearing," by the way they dressed and ate, by their morals, and not by words, said or written (*Untimely*, Schopenhauer, 3), and this is also the way that Nietzsche, who declared "I am in my writings," took: "One should speak only when one may not remain silent; and then speak only of that which one has overcome—everything else is chatter, 'literature,' lack of breeding. My writings speak only of my overcomings" (*Human*, Assorted, 1).

NOTES

1. Johann Friedrich Herbart, *Textbook in Psychology*, trans. M. K. Smith (New York: Appleton & Co, 1891).
2. Herman Scheffauer, "Friedrich Nietzsche and August Strindberg," *The North American Review*, 198 (1913): 202, https://archive.org/stream/jstor-25120062/25120062_djvu.txt
3. Christopher Middleton , trans *Selected Letters of Friedrich Nietzsche* (Chicago: University of Chicago Press, 1969), 374–76.
4. Graham Parkes, *Composing the Soul* (Chicago: University of Chicago Press), 313.
5. As can be seen in the names of current graduate programs in psychology: The Behavior, Brain, & Cognition program (Washington University in St. Louis), Cognition, Brain, and Behavior (Harvard University), Cognitive & Behavioral Neuroscience (UC San Diego).
6. Jaan Valsiner, "Integrating Psychology within the Globalizing World: A Requiem to the Post-Modernist Experiment with Wissenschaft," *Integrative Psychological and Behavioral Science* 43 (2009): 11.
7. Paul C. Vitz, *Psychology as Religion: The Cult of Self-worship* (Grand Rapids, MI: Eerdmans, 1977).
8. Tom Sorell, *Scientism: Philosophy and the Infatuation with Science* (London: Routledge, 1991), 1ff .
9. Paul C. Vitz, *Psychology as Religion: The Cult of Self-worship* (Grand Rapids: Eerdmans, 1977).
10. Tom Sorell, *Scientism: Philosophy and the Infatuation with Science* (London: Routledge, 1991), 1ff .
11. APA Presidential Task Force on Evidence-Based Practice, "Evidence-based-Statement," *American Psychologist*, 61 (2006): 271–85, doi: 10.1037/0003-066X.61.4.271.
12. Serious questions about the tenability of evidence-based practice are raised by, Edward J. Mullen and David L. Streiner, "The Evidence For and Against Evidence-Based Practice," *Treatment and Crisis Intervention* 4 (2004): 111–21, doi: 10.1093/brief-treatment/mhh009.
13. Thomas Szasz, *The Myth of Mental Illness: Foundations of a Theory of Personal Conduct* (New York: Harper & Row, 1974).
14. Robert Whitaker, *Anatomy of an Epidemic: Magic Bullets, Psychiatric Drugs, and the Astonishing Rise of Mental Illness in America* (New York: Crown Publishers, 2010).

15. Hans Thomae, "The Nomothetic-Idiographic Issue: Some Roots and Recent Trends," *International Journal of Group Tensions* 28 (1999): 187–215.

16. Max Weber, *The Protestant Ethic and the Spirit of Capitalism*, ed. Stephen Kalberg (London: Routledge, 2013).

17. S. A. McLeod, "Nomothetic Idiographic Debate," *Simply Psychology*, 2007, www.simplypsychology.org/nomothetic-idiographic.html, accessed November 16, 2015.

18. Compare with Walt Whitman's poem "Song of Myself," "I am the poet of the Body and I am the poet of the Soul," in Walt Whitman, *Leaves of Grass* (Philadelphia: David McKay, 1900).

19. Uri Wernik, "Nietzsche, Trauma and Overcoming" (Unpublished Manuscript, 2015).

TWO

Cognitive Psychology

Not in vain did Nietzsche, the professor of philology, put language at the center of his psychology. Without it, conscious thinking, communication, and interpretation would not have been possible. Without the ability to understand our environment and ourselves, survival would be unimaginable; neither could society, science, art and culture have existed, not to mention Nietzsche's writing and my writing about his psychology. It is impossible to examine the origins and functions of language without taking into consideration the issues of thinking and consciousness. These three are linked and cannot be separated, and the three of them, Nietzsche will show us, are not what we thought they are. This triad is the heart of Nietzsche's cognitive psychology, and the apex of the pyramid is interpretation.

THE PSYCHOLOGY OF LANGUAGE

Language was born when our ancestors lived in a hostile and dangerous environment and had to communicate in situations of threat in fast and clear ways, in order to agree on a common line of action. The language also enabled love relations and friendships, which could not exist without communion and shared meanings. Later, language grew further through a process of making metaphors and the transformation of metaphors into concepts. With the addition of concepts, words became signs, not only for specific objects and actions, but also for ideas, which are based on frequently repeated and associated groups of experiences. Referring to these experiences by a common language results in understanding and a sense of a community (*Beyond*, IX, 268).

People became inventors of signs (*Gay*, V, 354) and their unavoidable fundamental drive to create metaphors is a central characteristic of being human (*Truth,* 2). They have a "compulsion to construct concepts, species, forms, purposes, laws," and an urge to build a "calculable, simplified, comprehensible" world that supports existence (*Will,* III, 521). The ability to incorporate personal metaphors in a schema and transform images into concepts, distinguishes humans from animals and enabled further developments which were impossible with "vivid first impressions" only (*Truth,* 1).

Language and Uncertainty

Nietzsche maintained that on one hand, we cannot know the world as it is, and must be satisfied with some slanted survival-serving approximation. On the other hand, we cannot gaze into what goes on inside us and must manage with what we consciously experience as thinking. Language stands between these two uncertainties, and it is only with language and words that we can know and understand the world and ourselves. Language, however, is metaphors-based; and metaphors, solidified into concepts hold us prisoners, as we can only see through their frames (*Truth,* 2).

Language and the World

Nietzsche started his exploration into language with the prosaic, "What is a word?" and he answered, "The image of a nerve stimulus in sounds." Beyond this fact, we stand on shaky ground, as language is not a simple copy image of "reality." Firstly, the inference of a cause outside us, based on such a nerve stimulus cannot be rationally justified. Secondly, the interpretation of sense data is made within the constraints of arbitrary assignments such as gender, and thus in Hebrew and Russian "table" is masculine while "bed" is feminine; in French or Italian, it is the other way around; while in English all nouns are neuter. Thirdly, our understanding is metaphorical, meaning that we understand things in terms of other things, and not in their own terms, and thus, for example, "language," the very topic under discussion, derives from the Latin *lingua,* which means tongue. In order to refer to one thing we transfer from another (metaphor, from the combined Latin words for "over" and "carry," that is to say, transfer) and for this reason, there is no direct one-to-one connection between words and what they are supposed to represent. Lastly, our metaphors become concepts and concepts are built on treating the similar as identical. We treat all trees as "trees," disregarding the uniqueness of a specifically given tree (*Truth,* 1). Nietzsche argued that designations are not congruent with things, and that only forgetfulness and illusions make people fancy that they hold an exact replication of the world, which they consider the "truth" (*Truth,* 1). Years later, in his *Gen-*

eral Semantics, Alfred Korzybski would pronounce, "the map is not the territory!"

Language and Thought

Nietzsche suggested that the lack of overlap between words and objects exists also between words and thoughts. "Even one's thoughts one cannot reproduce entirely in words" (*Genealogy*, III, 244), thus, the same kind of incongruence exists on both sides of our skin, and moreover, in principle, thoughts can and do take place without awareness or language (*Gay*, V, 354). Our conscious thinking is tainted by the rhetorical nature of language. "Whoever thinks in words thinks as a speaker and not as a thinker," that is to say, we do not think about objects or facts in themselves but only in relation to ourselves or our listeners (*Genealogy*, III, 8).

The World of Language

In addition to examining language and its development from the points of view of communication and communion, Nietzsche also examined it metaphorically as a world-creation. Language was developed with a specific purpose, "not 'to know' but to schematize to impose upon chaos as much regularity and form as our practical needs require" (*Will*, III, 515). Language has become a separate or parallel world and humanity, "standing upon it, it could lift the rest of the world off its hinges and make itself master of it" (*Human*, I, 11). Yet, this magnificent invented world is not as simple as it looks, as believing that concepts and names are equal to reality gives a false sense of importance, control, and understanding (*Human*, I, 11).

Utility and Beauty

Language is a perspective, reflecting not what is, even not what is registered in our sense organs, but what it seems to be to each one of us; it is, therefore, coarse and false, yet this falseness is functional and necessary, as it enables "intelligibility, comprehensibility, practicability, and beauty" (*Will*, III, 602). Language is not only a practical tool for survival and problem-solving, but also a means for creation and appreciation of beauty, as in the fields of art and myth, where unlike what usually happens elsewhere, metaphors do not turn into concepts and stay enjoyably fresh (*Truth*, 2). Furthermore, we have infused the linguistic world we created with values, which in turn help us make sense of the world. Had it been otherwise, had our language been a strictly objective recording instrument, "the deeper one looks, the more our valuations disappear—meaninglessness approaches!" (*Will*, III, 602).

Rhetoric and Politics

In his *Lecture on Ancient Rhetoric,* Nietzsche elaborated on the inherent rhetorical qualities of language. Language is an instrument, used in relation to other people (but also between parts of the self) whose task is persuasion. "Language does not desire to instruct but convey to others a subjective impulse and its acceptance. . . . Language is never objective. It cannot simply prove; it must convince." Thus, we are all rhetoricians, who use metaphors in order to persuade others to have it our way, and if we are therapists, we try to convince our clients to switch their unfruitful metaphors to others. Rhetoric has a second inherent function of establishing and defining positions of power in relationships; "whoever uses language, is invoking a set of tropes that reiterate who has power and who does not" (*Truth,* 1). Language reflects the social power structure, as those in position of power decide how to name objects and those who oppose them make up their own words, and, for this reason, deciding to call some behaviors "selfish" or "unselfish" is actually a political move (*Genealogy* I, 2). Powerful persons invent words and turn them into laws, but verbal proficiency is needed as well, "it is the greatest artists in abstraction who created the categories" (*Will,* III, 513). Language defines social class and is involved in class struggles, "the construction of a pyramidal order according to castes and degrees, the creation of a new world of laws, privileges, subordinations and clearly marked boundaries" (*Truth,* 1). Thus, by using concepts and schemata, language makes the social world possible (*Truth,* 1).

Language and Life

Language, we said, is a tool; however, the very use of this tool changes our own thoughts and understanding of ourselves and of things outside of us. Just because words and concepts exist, we are convinced that an arbitrary or a biased collection of elements is a discrete unity or essence, and by using a word we believe that we understand the "truth" of things. We are continually misguided into "imagining things as simpler than they are, separate from one another, indivisible, each existing in and for itself." Language conceals a "philosophical mythology" which continuously reinforces beliefs in freedom of will, and identity of facts and their isolation (*Human,* Wanderer, 11). A Nietzschean therapist's ears prick up the very moment notions like self-confidence, self-image, and personality are brought up. These are not things but words, and helpful they are not.

The power of words once realized, is awe-striking. "This has given me the greatest trouble and still does: to realize that *what things are called* is incomparably more important than what they are." Appearances determine significance; the cover, painted through the ages, often arbitrarily or wrongly, gradually becomes part of the thing itself and appearance turns into essence (*Gay*, I, 58). With these words, Nietzsche joined the good company of Epictetus[1] and Thomas Szasz[2] : the former posited that people are not influenced by reality, but, by the way, they understand it, obviously through the intermediary of words. The latter, criticizing *The myth of mental illness*, has shown how assigning the word "schizophrenic," for example, can doom a person to a life of stigma, harmful drugging, and hospitalization.[3]

The story of using psychiatric labels, a characteristic of the new *psychologica* (chapter 1), is a good example of Nietzsche's exclamation that "words block our path." Wherever our primitive ancestors coined a word, they considered it a discovery, which was far from being the case. Rather than solving a problem, it created an obstacle to its solution; "now, with every new piece of knowledge, we stumble over petrified words and mummified conceptions, and would rather break a leg than a word in doing so (*Daybreak*, I, 47).

Together with frustration there is hope. The power of appearances, of "what things are called," also makes change possible. Nietzsche, quite ironically, was practically commending the policy of politically correct language, as the words we use determine our attitudes. He was also implying that using reinterpretation or reframing could be a powerful tool for achieving psychological change: "We can destroy only as creators. But let us not forget this either: it is enough to create new names and estimations and probabilities in order to create in the long run new 'things'" (*Gay*, I, 58).

THE LANGUAGE OF PSYCHOLOGY

Nietzsche's psychological investigation began with an investigation of the very words used in this investigation. However, using words, and especially terms concerning the mind, is a minefield, and Nietzsche guided us in crossing over it safely. He warned us about the error of "giving a false reality to a fiction," in which we assume that events are in some way obedient to something beyond themselves, and thus, an artificial and imaginary distinction is made between actions and what supposedly activates them (*Will*, III, 521). Nietzsche, with his sharp eye, identified the faulty process of "backward inference" as the source of this error; an insight that made him feel "I am ahead of all psychologists." Such inferences take place from deeds to doers, from ideals to those who heed them, and "from every way of thinking and valuing to the *want* behind it that prompts it" (*Gay*, V, 362; *Contra*, 2). He charged Descartes for being the one who gave the faulty inference a formal approval, arguing that "there is thinking: therefore there is something that thinks." This, Nietzsche explained, is not a fact, but rather a belief and a postulate, no more than "a formulation of our grammatical custom that adds a doer to every deed" (*Will*, III, 484).

Our Inherited Concepts

Nietzsche urged us to be skeptic towards "all inherited concepts," as our concepts are, "after all, inheritance from our most remote, most foolish as well as most intelligent ancestors (*Will*, II, 409). The fact that a word exists, just like a bad check, does not mean that there is something real behind it. Thus, we use the word "forgetting" without giving it a second thought, despite the fact that "it has not been proven that forgetting exists; We only know that the act of recollection is not within our power" (*Daybreak*, II, 130).

Language was conceived "in the age of the most rudimentary form of psychology" and is plagued by fetishistic thinking, believing that objects, as well as words, have inherent values or powers, and it is this kind of thinking which lies behind religious beliefs; "I am afraid we are not rid of God because we still have faith in grammar" (*Twilight*, Reason, 5). Accepting the "presuppositions of the metaphysics of language" is a recipe for many other misconceptions: finding doers behind actions; believing in will as a cause and an effective capacity; conceiving the ego as a substance which controls being, while in fact, all these are only words (*Twilight*, Reason, 5); and he reiterated, "There exists neither 'spirit,' nor reason, nor thinking, nor consciousness, nor soul, nor will, nor truth: all are fictions that are of no use." However, in the final analysis, what matters is whether these concepts contribute to the survival and prosperity of an organism or not, and whether they promote "a certain relative rightness; above all, regularity of its perceptions, so that it can accumulate experience" (*Will*, III, 480).

Despite his warnings about "backward inference" and reservations about the "venerable old hypothesis" of soul (*Beyond*, I, 12), Nietzsche realized that in order to communicate, one must put aside reservations and use accepted language, and for this reason, he did not refrain from using fictitious terms such as soul, spirit, ego, self, "I," and body wisdom interchangeably, to describe the mind or its constituents.

The Invention of Thinking

Nietzsche, I said, tried to shake up our naive belief in our perceptions, repeatedly saying that we do not see the world as it is, but rather a distorted-edited version of it, as if our brain has some Photoshop® program running continually. Then, he went a step further, indicating that the same program is in operation whenever we try to observe the inner working of the mind itself. "Thinking" is another fiction we invented. Right now writing this sentence, thinking that I am not really thinking, or more correctly, not thinking that I am not thinking, almost makes my head spin. He jotted in his notebook, "Everything of which we become conscious is arranged, simplified, schematized, interpreted through and through."

Our perceptual and cognitive activity, "the causal connection between thoughts, feelings, desires, between subject and object," is totally hidden from us or imaginary; we construe the "apparent *inner* world" just as we construe the "outer world." We do not deal with facts, but with derived interpreted intellectual phenomena (*Will*, III, 473). Cognition does not guarantee precise knowledge about things, neither is it an instrument we control, "a thought comes when 'it' wishes, and not when 'I' wish." The statement "I think," implying that there is a specific entity "the ego" which thinks, is no more than an assumption, an unfounded assertion, and not a certainty (*Beyond*, I, 17).

The Error of Causality

Causality, a main building block of thinking, the assumption of a causal link between thoughts or events, is a fiction based on crude and clumsy observations and on filtering out other less striking features of the situation. Thinking is a simplification, which does not take many elements into account, "an artificial arrangement for the purpose of intelligibility." One false term gives birth to another, and out of "thinking" came the notions of a "pure spirit," something that thinks. Differently stated, "both the deed and the doer are fictions" (*Will*, III, 477). Behind the sentence "I think," there are only some unverifiable assertions--that we know what thinking is, where it takes place and who or what is responsible for it (*Beyond*, I, 16).

Nietzsche described four great errors, the third one being "the error of false causality," in which he struck down, in one fell swoop, all the so-called "inner facts," showing that they are no more than "phantoms." Once the phantom of the will as cause is tumbled, the ideas of consciousness ("spirit") and ego (the "subject") can be understood as no more than "a fable, a fiction, a play on words! It has altogether ceased to think, feel, or will!" Giving up false causality brings on the realization that "there are no mental causes at all" (*Twilight*, The four great errors, 3). Thoughts, pleasure and pain, feeling and willing, are not causes for behavior, but they rather co-occur with it: "epiphenomena with a quite different object than to evoke reactions; they are themselves effects within the instituted process of reaction" (*Will*, III, 478). After discussing psychotherapy in the section *Nietzsche Contra Freud* (chapter 7), I will return to his challenging of the concept of causality.

THINKING, LOGIC, AND LIES

In spite of his reservations about thinking, Nietzsche continued to use this term (as he continued to use the term "soul") and saw it, with its limitations or due to them, as a tool, fit for the task of preserving life. He saw no reason to acquire knowledge but for this purpose: "Morphology shows us how the senses and the nerves, as well as the brain, develop in proportion to the difficulty of finding nourishment" (*Will*, III, 494). Nietzsche saw knowledge as he saw the concepts of "good" or "beautiful," in a "strict and narrow anthropocentric and biological sense." A particular species can maintain itself and increase its power to the degree that it can grasp reality in a calculable and constant manner, which becomes the foundation for schemes of behavior (*Will*, III, 480).

Predictability and constancy of knowledge reduce the fear of the unknown and support survival as humans cannot live in doubt of all essential values. "Therefore, what is needed is that something must be held to be true—not that something is true" (*Will*, III, 507). The essential feature of thinking (or whatever it is we refer to as "thinking") is adjusting new material into the procrustean bed of existing schemes, "making equal what is new" (*Will*, III, 499). Thus, knowledge is "nothing more than this: Something strange is to be reduced to something familiar" (*Gay*, V, 355). It follows that the test of a concept and of all knowledge, such as the law of causality, is its usefulness rather than its truth (*Will*, III, 497).

Thinking and Logic

Logic, a kind of a user's manual for thinking, grew like language, out of the herd instinct for the purpose of "mutual agreement and dominion" (*Will*, III, 509). Logic is based on accepting, as valid, assumptions that do not correspond to real facts such as "equality of things, the identity of the same thing at different points of time," and an uncritical acceptance of such assumptions is often beneficial, and thus, the belief that straight lines, perfect circles, and absolute measurements actually exist enabled the development of mathematics (*Human*, I, 11). Logic does not guarantee a rational decision making, and thinking is not based on rational considerations, but on making decisions according to the potential of generating a mood of "cheerful action," in other words, of what "feels good" (*Daybreak*, I, 28). This lies behind much of the phenomena of seemingly irrational consumer behavior studied in behavioral economics. For this very reason, despite the low probability of winning, people fly to Las Vegas to visit their friends Black Jack and the one-armed bandits.

Logic, however, makes order out of a chaos of ideas. It invents categories and eliminates contradictions; it groups and keeps what fits together and lets what is not consistent perish (*Will*, III, 508). In addition to treating what is similar as equal, logic produces the fiction of causality by isolating two arbitrary points on a continuum (*Gay*, III, 112). Despite seeing our logical cognitive operations-distortions as necessary for survival, Nietzsche still found the "holy simplification" as something to be amazed at and nothing to be proud of: "*O sancta simplicitiatas*! In what strange simplification and falsification man lives! One can never cease wondering when once one has got eyes for beholding this marvel! How we have made everything around us clear and free and easy and simple!" (*Beyond*, II, 24).

In Praise of Lying

Nietzsche challenged our habitual ways of thinking: first he sensitized us to "backward inference," to the problematic nature of terms such as will, cause, and thinking. Next in line to be challenged were our notions of truth and lies, which was not an easy task, as all of us were trained and indoctrinated to see lies as the mother of all evil. The title of one of his first essays, *On Truth and Lies in a Nonmoral Sense*, written in 1873, is instructive, implying that "truth" is not automatically good nor are "lies" bad. Nietzsche's standard criterion of evaluation, as we already learned, was as to whether something is useful and functional for the promotion of life, and this exactly is sometimes the case with lies. The concept of causality is an advantageous lie, and so are "succession, reciprocity, relativity, compulsion, number, law, freedom, un-freedom, motive, purpose, and responsibility." Treating all these as concrete things amounts to mythological behavior (*Beyond*, I, 21).

In addition to being on occasion beneficial, lies are often unavoidable and Nietzsche proved that we cannot avoid lying. He preceded the current discussion of Machiavellian intelligence and Protean strategy as adaptive behaviors in humans and other mammals (in Greek mythology, Proteus was Poseidon's helper who eluded capture by changing his figure at will). Lies are an unavoidable part of living. We lie to ourselves, and it can be said that we treat ourselves as parents treat their two-year-old baby, who is, of course, the most beautiful, smart, never-do-wrong, and important creature on earth (*Gay*, III, 115). We lie to others, and Nietzsche made a list, of ways, with which we are all too familiar, starting with "deception, flattering, lying and cheating, talking behind the back, posing, living in borrowed splendor" (*Truth*, 1). Lying is basic and it crops up already at the very act of perception, as it is prone to biases and distortions and inherently involves disregard of details.

Nietzsche found that the same processes can also be seen in the history of science. Here too, he said in a few exhaustive sentences what philosophers of science will later describe in terms of "paradigm shift" and what will be demonstrated by many experimental psychologists in the field of perception. We have a strong tendency to stick with the familiar and the habitual, and a special effort or originality is needed to identify something novel and different. The new is mostly interpreted in terms of old ready-made schemes and our emotional states color our perceptions. In addition, we use heuristics, overlooking some bits of information and guessing others. We see a forest and not trees; trees and not branches and leaves, thus simplifying complex and detailed information to make it more manageable. Thus we are all liars, "or, to express it more politely and hypocritically, in short, more pleasantly—one is much more of an artist than one is aware of" (*Beyond*, V, 192). And again, the Overturner said that the question is not why we lie, but why the urge for truth appeared at all (*Truth*, 1).

Are we supposed now to lie through our teeth and feel good about it? Certainly not, as one can argue that Nietzsche, for the sake of the argument, included diverse and different things under one category which should be considered separately: unavoidable perceptual distortions, white lies ("Oh, you look so nice today"), self-deceit, and deliberate misleading lies. In other words, he was lying about lying.

If so, what is truth? If lies and errors are not bad, and even necessary and beneficial, the reader might wonder what, then, is truth? Nietzsche's answer will be twofold. Firstly, he described how he sees what is commonly considered and known as truth, reduced by him to an unappealing truism; secondly, he presented his own truth about truth. What is usually considered truth is basically an illusion and a metaphor, "a mobile army of metaphors, metonyms, and anthropomorphisms—in short, a sum of human relations which have been enhanced, transposed, and embellished poetically and rhetorically, and which after long use seem firm, canonical, and obligatory to a people" (*Truth*, 1).

Nietzsche had his own metaphor: "Supposing truth to be a woman" (*Beyond*, Preface). A woman must be courted and only she can decide to favor someone. The prejudices of philosophers regarding subject, ego, and soul; the temptation of language; the inventions of Plato about spirit and "good in itself" all leave her cold. The way of appearances, deception, selfishness, and appetite is closer to her heart (*Beyond*, I, 2). Lady Truth has her own preferences; "truth has never yet clang to the arm of an inflexible man" (*Thus*, Flies of the market-place); and "he who cannot lie does not know what truth is" (*Thus*, IV, The higher man, 9).

Nietzsche tried to cure us of a prejudice against laughter and gaiety in thinking. Our thinking is much too serious, its feet are heavy, and it cannot dance; "in the great majority, the intellect is a clumsy, gloomy, creaking machine that is difficult to start" (*Gay*, IV, 327). Truth is not some collection of facts, gathered in a serious painstaking manner, but an original, unconventional, and personal artistic creation. Truth is emotional, intuitive, and fluid, and Nietzsche mentioned in this context the Latin *in vino veritas*, meaning that truth is revealed when one is not overly rational (under the influence of wine) and he summed up: "It seems that here too I disagree with the rest of the world about the concept 'Truth,' with me spirit moves on the face of the waters" (*Ecce,* Clever, 1). This beautiful simile expressing the effortless flow of creative thinking, calls to mind the Biblical "And the spirit of God moved upon the face of the waters" (*Genesis,* 1, 2).

Truth, one's own truth, is not to be found in the external world, but inside us; "only dare to believe in yourselves— in yourselves and in your entrails! He who does not believe in himself always lies" (*Thus,* II, Immaculate perception). Truth is not conventional. "That which has hitherto been most stringently forbidden has always been the Truth" (*Ecce,* Preface, 3). Nietzsche saw truth as *Baubo,* the Greek goddess of hilariousness and wantonness, exposing her sex organ (*Gay,* Preface, 4), thus introducing passion and fecundity as elements of truth.

CONSCIOUSNESS AND UNAWARENESS

Nietzsche regarded psychology, not so highly appreciated by others, as a queen. Consciousness, however, usually considered as unique to humans, the apex of their intellectual development, "the genius of the species" (*Gay,* V, 354), was treated by him as born out of suffering, not a particularly admired *nouveau riche,* haughty, clumsy, and superfluous. Consciousness is the latest evolutionary development; an immature, unfinished and prone to errors product. People overestimate its importance; forget that it is not a "fixed given magnitude"; that it is a mistake to consider it as the kernel of a person; that it does not reveal the "unity of the organism"; and that instinctive behaviors (such as eating, drinking and procreating) are much more important for survival. Humanity would have been lost had consciousness alone been in charge, "by perverse judging and dreaming with open eyes, by superficiality and credulity" (*Gay,* I, 11).

In light of Nietzsche's critical views of language and thinking, we will not be surprised to learn that we should not trust consciousness too much, as our picture of reality is not sharp, and like a dream, is mixed up with our own subjective needs and feelings. We dream with open eyes and the difference between dreaming and wakefulness is only quantitative, not qualitative. "We do not live in a reality but in some appearance constructed under the influence of our animal and human past" (*Gay,* I, 54), in other words, we are "artists in love" loaded down with appraisals of reality which originated "in the passions and loves of former centuries" (*Gay,* II, 57). On occasion, he saw consciousness as hardly existing: "'Consciousness'—to what extent the idea of an idea, the idea of will, the idea of a feeling (known to ourselves alone) are totally superficial! Our inner world, too, 'appearance'! (*Will,* III, 476).

The Web of Consciousness

Consciousness is not, as we tend to believe, "the general sensorium and supreme court" and "it is not the directing agent, but an organ of the directing agent." The direction and coordination of our bodily functions go on without any conscious involvement. Our actual "supreme court" is inaccessible to consciousness and does not use words for its operation. "Pleasure" and "displeasure," acts of will or ideas are only verbal clues to what takes place in this kingdom of instincts (*Will*, III, 524).

All our sensations, being relative to our particular state of mind, are in principle wrong and we have no idea about ourselves and the real world (*Daybreak*, II, 117). Similarly, we judge others in our own terms, turning them into satellites of our own system, and we tend to attribute changes that we experienced to people with whom we interact, (*Daybreak*, II, 118). We are a spider caught in its own web; we live in the prison of our limitations and horizons. We cannot really understand our surroundings and ourselves; how can a spider know what is beyond its web? It would be, yes, idiotic to claim anything about what lies beyond it! Nietzsche is thus pulling the rug from under what is metaphysical in one swipe: God, morality, spirituality, eternity, justice, rights, what have you. The images of spiders and webs in *Thus Spoke Zarathustra* appear along with the motif of Eternal Recurrence, which must, therefore, be a poetic image, and not another metaphysical claim. Being spiders in a web, we are locked in ourselves, hence perspectivism; hence individuality; hence the philosophical and the psychological cannot be separated from the personal; hence no absolute knowledge is possible: "I would repeat it, however, a hundred times, that 'immediate certainty,' as well as 'absolute knowledge' and the 'thing in itself,' involve a *contradictio in adjecto* [contradiction in terms]" (*Beyond*, I, 16).

What we experience as feelings, thinking, and logic, is only a reconstruction or an image of what really transpires in our internal governing body. Interestingly, while, in Freud's tripartite model of id, ego, and super-ego, unconsciousness is posited as the lowest level and the more appreciated consciousness is set higher; Nietzsche sees it the other way around: consciousness is the lowest and unconsciousness is on a higher level. I will expound on this issue in my *Nietzsche Contra Freud* (chapter 7). Thus, conscious humans are not "the measure of all things," but rather their instincts are, and just as the fact of birth-giving cannot change the baby's genetics or heredity, consciousness cannot change the primacy of instincts (*Beyond*, I, 3). This implies the untenability of the project of "turning the unconscious into conscious," as the former controls the latter. The problematic nature of consciousness becomes evident once we realize that it is not necessary, and we could have managed without it. "The whole of life would be possible without, as it were, seeing itself in a mirror" (*Gay*, V, 354). It is arguable that we could give up consciousness only if we return to the Stone Age. How would we, lacking consciousness, remember our smartphones and social security numbers?

Consciousness, Bad-Conscience, and Empathy

If consciousness is superfluous and if its use involves dangerous mistakes, two questions beg to be answered. Firstly, how did it come into being and secondly, what is it good for? It was developed in the context of life in groups and humans' social-herd nature, while "a solitary human being who lived like a beast of prey would not have needed it" (*Gay*, V, 354). Consciousness is and was developed inseparably from language and neither of them would have been possible without the other, both being "only a connecting network between man and man," a means of communication necessary for survival. In time, it was developed further, based on the capacity for inventing, transmitting, receiving, and understanding signals, be they with words, gestures, or looks (*Gay*, V, 354). Consciousness began historically with suffering, with bad conscience, which was constituted by acts of violence, carried in pre-history, by rulers-invaders-oppressors against members of a nomad-tribal society. The transition to the rudimentary state involved the monopolization of aggression by the rulers and a harsh repression of the inhabitants' old independent ways (chapter 4). Up to this moment, mental life was vestigial, "thick as extended between two skins." Once the instincts were barricaded, the inner world, "has spread and unfolded, has taken on depth, breadth, height." The price of this process is unbearable, leaving humans in the position of an incarcerated animal "that beats itself raw on the bars of its cage" (*Genealogy*, II, 16).

Consciousness evolved out of terror, but also out of learning to be empathetic, which humans have brought to perfection and keep on practicing. Living in groups necessitated emotional intelligence, cooperation, mutual help, and affiliation. Empathy grew out of simulation, mediated by imitation of actions and expressions, and in the following quote we can find an early formulation of the idea of "mirror neurons":

> To understand another person, that is to imitate his feelings in ourselves, we produce the feeling in ourselves after the effects it exerts and displays on the other person by imitating with our own body the expression of his eyes, his voice, his walk, his bearing. Then a similar feeling arises in us in consequence of an ancient association between movement and sensation. (*Daybreak*, II, 142)

Consciousness, like language, became more sophisticated, as additional uses, often pleasurable, for which it was not "designed," were found and facilitated by experts, such as artists, writers, and orators, who were more skillful in observation and expression (*Gay*, V, 354).

Communication and Incorporation

Consciousness has another, less thought-of function, which turns our notions upside down. Consciousness has "the task of incorporating knowledge and making it instinctive" (*Genealogy*, I, 11), that is to say, our challenge is not to turn unconscious into conscious, which we saw is an impossible exploit, but rather the opposite, of changing what is conscious into something unconscious, by the transformation of knowledge into instincts. Thus, unconsciousness becomes a goal to strive for, while consciousness is considered to be a caricature, a form of play-acting, an expression of imperfection and sickness. "All perfect acts are unconscious and no longer subject to will" (*Will*, II, 289). Still, it must be pointed out, that the incorporation of conscious acts into instincts is also the route to maladjusted behaviors. Those of us who smoked still remember how it started as a conscious act that we controlled, and later turned into an automatic habit that eventually controlled us.

The Impossible Quest

In the discussion so far, self-knowledge was not considered as an important function of consciousness. Nietzsche contended that humans' infatuation with self-awareness, self-observation, and self-knowledge is a hopeless affair, because people can hardly observe, and especially not themselves. The maxim "know yourself" is almost a malicious one, and he offered a new dictum instead: "Everybody is farthest away—from himself" (*Gay*, IV, 335). Our quest is doomed to failure. "Why does man not see things? He himself is standing in the way: he conceals things" (*Daybreak*, V, 438).

This failure could well be the end of all searches for definite knowledge. "When we endeavor to examine the mirror in itself we discover in the end that we can detect nothing there but the things which it reflects" (*Daybreak*, IV, 243). Nietzsche, almost echoing Werner Heisenberg's Principle of Indeterminacy (1927),[4] posited that "observation is a thousand times more difficult; error is perhaps a condition of observation in general" (*Will*, III, 472). He concluded that our nature, our evolutionary heritage, and the nature of language all stand in the way to self-knowledge. Nature itself hid from us our bodily functions, the working of our organs, our brain, our neurological and hormonal activity, and "she threw away the key," leaving us only with what we perceive with our "proud, deceptive consciousness." If we will happen to glimpse into what really goes on inside us, the trauma will cure us of our need for truth: "Man rests upon the merciless, the greedy, the insatiable, the murderous, in the indifference of his ignorance—hanging in dreams, as it were, upon the back of a tiger" (*Truth*, I). This strong image is also found in Chinese, Japanese, and Indian iconography. I wonder whether Nietzsche saw in the *Museo*

Archaeologico Nazionale di Napoli the mosaic of young Dionysus riding a tiger from the House of the Faun in Pompeii, from the first century CE.

We lie and nature hides, while language is only an unskilled player in this game of hide-and-seek, making things more tangled, leading to self-delusions. Language has limited ability to describe nuances of drives and feelings, which are disregarded, with words for extremes only, resulting with a distorted picture of self and others. Given who we are, we cannot know ourselves (*Daybreak*, II, 115). Our animal consciousness is concerned only with what is useful for the herd and the species, and therefore, it can relate only to what is superficial, average, and common, and not individual (*Gay*, V, 354). Moreover, actions are unique and individualized, "but as soon as we translate them into consciousness *they no longer seem to be*" (*Gay*, V, 354). There is no point in searching for the lost key, as the door itself is imaginary. Reader, would you please read and reread the following quote? It is going to serve us well once we discuss psychotherapy: "We delude ourselves in believing that we understand the reasons for our own and others' behaviors. Action is never what is seems to be. Thus: I am not free. I do not understand what I want, why I did what I did and I am not responsible for it, neither are others" (*Daybreak*, II, 116).

INTERPRETATION AND ILLUSIONS

Narrative psychology[5] and the "narrative bend" in the social sciences are *de rigueur* now. Its main thesis is simple: We are the stories we tell ourselves (internal narratives); we are also the stories we tell others (external narratives), and these stories generate our continually evolving unique autobiographical self. According to Michael Gazzaniga,[6] a neuropsychologist, we have an internal interpreter, located in our speech and language centers of the brain's left hemisphere, which continuously makes sense of what transpires, narrating our emotions and behaviors. In other words, we are programmed to turn our life into stories.

These developments would not have surprised Nietzsche, who put an emphasis on the activity (interpretation) and not on one of its products (narrative) only. He suggested that we have to learn from the "improvising masters," the skilled and inventive musicians, how to "arrange into the structure of the score the most accidental tone and to animate the accident with a fine meaning and soul" (*Gay*, IV, 303). The difference between feeling a victim of undesired circumstances, and feeling blessed by chance occurrences, is in "our own practical and theoretical skillfulness in explaining and suitably arranging events," (*Gay*, IV, 277), in other words, our assumptions about the world and our literary skills. Interpretation produces not only life stories ("narratives"), but also art and science as well: "Ultimately, man finds in things nothing but what he himself has imported into them: the finding is called science, the importing—art, religion, love, pride" (*Will*, III, 606).

Necessary Illusions

In principle, we could make an infinite number of interpretations, however, we spiders are limited by who we are, by "the perspective character of existence." Interpretations are unavoidable but also necessary as "existence without interpretation, without 'sense' becomes 'nonsense'" (*Gay*, V, 374). Nietzsche is not denying that facts exist, but as we cannot "look around the corner," as we cannot bypass ourselves, we can only deal with how they are seen by us. In contradiction to positivists who consider phenomena only and claim that "there are only facts," he argues that "facts is precisely what there is not, only interpretations." It is impossible to establish any fact "in itself"; the world can be interpreted but not known; it has no meaning, but rather countless meanings; interpretations are not about concrete facts, but about possible ways of understanding them (*Will*, III, 481). Because untruth is a condition of life (*Beyond*, I, 4), "the falseness of an opinion is not for us any objection to it." What matters is its usefulness, "how far an opinion is life-furthering, life-preserving, species-preserving, perhaps species-rearing" (*Beyond*, I, 4).

Life as History

We are all historians of our life, and historians are storytellers who do not deal with dry facts, but rather have desired effects in mind; a historian does not study what actually happened, but only what is supposed to later have the desired effect on living (*Daybreak*, IV, 307). There are two basic ways of coping with problems in living "the twofold struggle against misfortune": one is interpretation and reinterpretation (in our head); the other is confrontation (in real life). These two are mutually exclusive, and insight and action are not bosom friends—we can either remove the cause of our difficulties or change the way a misfortune affects our feelings by seeing the advantages it offers: "The more a person tends to reinterpret and justify, the less will he confront the causes of the misfortune and eliminate them; a momentary palliation and narcotization (as used, for example, for a toothache) is also enough for him in more serious suffering" (*Human*, III, 108).

In his *On the Use and Abuse of History for Life*, Nietzsche argued that the belief that our picture of historical events or periods reflects "the empirical essence of things" is merely a myth. Our picture is an artistic one which has nothing to do with truth or justice, "thus, man spins a web over the past and tames it" (*Untimely*, History, 6); consequently interpretation made by collectives or individuals about their personal life are basically a creative activity: "Art and nothing but art! It is the great means of making life possible, the great seduction to life, the great stimulant of life. Art as the only superior counterforce to all will to denial of life" (*Will*, III, 853, 2). In the same line, Elizabeth Loftus has demonstrated in her studies that our memories and especially the earliest ones are often a constructed merger of actual memories, narratives we borrowed from others, and imaginary scenes invented by the subconscious.[7]

Lies and art are not that different in promoting life, with the distinction that art is more creative and aesthetically pleasing. The historians who study some past events and individuals who try to make sense of their life are not different either. Both of them, in different ways, have to confront their culture's pressures to conform to its standards. While the historian can retain the pretense of objectivity, an individual should better "organize the chaos in himself by recalling in himself his own real needs" and try to peel layers of imitation and cultural decoration, that cover up one's genuine character (*Untimely*, History, 10).

The World Is a Text

Nietzsche saw the world metaphorically as a text, and interpretations as a philological activity. Adopting the position of an "old philologist," he criticized faulty interpretations, such as the physicists' talk of "nature's conformity to law," as bad philology and "a naively humanitarian adjustment and perversion of meaning" (*Beyond*, I, 22). This is bad philology because the interpretation does not promote well-being and because it adds uncritically the notions of laws and obedience to laws, which do not appear in the text. Bad philology produces bad philosophy and bad psychology, and some psychotherapists are bad philologists when they suggest to their clients unconstructive textbook interpretations far removed from the "text" itself—a person's experience of life.

Necessary Illusions

Nietzsche described four necessary illusions that bias our interpretations. The first is the *activity illusion*, in which people, the prisoners of language, believe that they are in charge of their actions while in fact they are activated and acted upon (*Daybreak*, II, 120). In the *cause and effect illusion*, our intellect convinces us that regularity is the norm, that things are following others in a cause and effect connection, which excludes seeing essential connections (*Daybreak*, II, 121). Nietzsche, whom we dubbed the Overturner, described how humans confuse cause and effect—it is not that our principles and dogmas create our character, but that we choose unconsciously ideas that fit our temperament; only later after the fact, we make our thoughts and judgments to be the cause of our nature, rather than our nature dictating our thoughts (*Human*, IX, 608) — and I have thought, all these years, that I was influenced by Nietzsche…

In *the illusion of egoism*, we misjudge what is experientially closer to us as larger and more important, than what is more distant (*Gay*, III, 162). Finally, *the illusion of consistency* reminds us of the 1950s "cognitive dissonance theory" put forward by Leon Festinger.[8] In this "unconscious comedy," motivated by laziness, search for convenience, and vanity, in order to gain respect, trust, and power, people try to present themselves as consistent in character and thought (*Human*, IX, 608). We are all, to put it simply, liars and fabricators and because we are such good liars, we pull a fast one on ourselves too. All self-reflection fails, because in order to cope in life, it is useful to interpret ourselves falsely and, for this reason, we do not trust our body's messages and reject the evidence of our senses (*Will*, III, 492). Humans are often described as thinking animals; Nietzsche would have suggested that they are the self-deceiving animals: "We are like shop windows in which we are continually arranging, concealing or illuminating the supposed qualities other ascribe to us—in order to deceive ourselves" (*Daybreak*, IV, 385). It turns out that being unable to decorate our shop window might be a problem: research carried by Lauren Alloy and Lyn Yvonne Abramson supported the hypothesis of "depressive realism," that depressed persons, rather than a negative cognitive bias, have actually an accurate appraisal of the world. On the contrary, it is the non-depressed individuals who have a non-accurate positive bias. [9]

THE SPHERE OF DREAMS

Dreaming is not opposed to consciousness or thinking, as the two are interlinked with shared qualities. I have quoted Nietzsche's remark that thinking is "dreaming with open eyes," and we can equally say that dreaming is thinking with closed eyes. Dreams, like art and poetry, go hand and hand with interpretation; dreams are a window to human evolution and dreams have important survival enhancing functions.

The same processes take place in dreaming and wakefulness, and our dreams characterize us; "nothing is more your own than your dreams! Nothing more your own work! Content, form, duration, performer, spectator—in these comedies you are all of this yourself!" We have no free will and, therefore, we are not responsible for what transpires in our waking hours and in our dreams (*Daybreak*, II, 128). In dreaming we continue to respond to environmental and bodily cues, which are incorporated into the dreams: dreams of soaring and flying might be related to the changed sensation of being shoeless and not stepping on the ground. A dreamer, hearing the racket of a low flying airplane or the blare of a truck's horn, incorporates the noise, and explains it retroactively within the dream, experiencing first the circumstances (crossing the street and seeing a truck approaching) and later the effect. The error of "chronological inversion" takes place in dreams, as it does in wakefulness (*Human*, I, 13).

In wakefulness, just as we do in dreams, we invent and imagine those we interact with, and forget it immediately (*Beyond*, IV, 138); in these two states of consciousness alike, we make interpretations, which can also be value judgments of some physiological response to situations. A person walks in the market and sees someone laughing, and varied interpretations of this fact are possible, all according to the person's state of mind and emotions at that given moment. Nietzsche summed up his contention, saying that "to experience is to invent" (*Daybreak*, II, 119).

Dreams and Early Humanity

Dreams offer a window to human evolution and the impact of culture on consciousness. One culture's interpretation of wakeful experiences is not much different from another culture's interpretation of dreams (*Daybreak*, II, 119). In ancient cultures, it was accepted that the gods were talking to certain individuals while in more advanced cultures such an interpretation is confined to dreaming only. In sleep, the brain's function of memory is inhibited, which changes the quality of thinking, bringing it closer to the way it was at wakefulness in human primeval age: confused with faulty generalizations and conclusions, as can be found now in ancient mythologies (*Human*, I, 11). When we dream, we are similar to cave dwellers, where shared hallucinations, sometimes of whole communities, were the rule (*Human*, I, 12). Dreams are the source of metaphysics and spirituality since our ancestors interpreted their dreams as representing another real world. Metaphysics grew out of this division of the world into the one in wakefulness and the one beyond, at sleep. For thousands of years, humans concluded that "the dead man lives on, because he appears to the living man in dreams." This kind of thinking supported the belief in ghosts and gods as well as the belief in the separation of body and soul (*Human*, I, 5).

Dreams as Works of Art

In our dreams, we experience intensely the whole universal range of emotions, from sad to happy and from anxious to angry, "the dark aspects of life, the sudden inhibitions, the teasing of chance, the fearful expectations, in short the whole 'divine comedy' of life, including the Inferno" (*Birth*, 1). The dreamer, the producer of illusions, is the creator and interpreter of her own piece of art. A perfect dream, like a perfect work of art, is not a common occurrence. Such dreams (like good movies), in addition to a narrative, consist of "symbolic chains of scenes and images" and they are the foundation of plastic arts and poetry. Such dreams express the essence of our experiences and situation in life "with such poetic boldness and decisiveness," that we are left in a state of wonder when we wake up and remember them (*Human*, Wanderer, 194).

Our rigid regular "web of concepts" makes us feel that we are awake, and indeed when it is torn apart by art, we feel like in a dream. Production of metaphors is a basic human drive, which seeks different venues of expression in art, myth, but also in dreams "this drive continually confuses the conceptual categories and cells by bringing forward new transferences, metaphors, and metonymies." It desires to refashion the world known in the state of wakefulness, and turn it into a colorful, irregular, illogical, "charming, and eternally new . . . world of dreams" (*Truth*, II).

Dreams and Real Life

Dreams, we saw, are primarily pieces of art, and when asked to relate to client's dreams, a Nietzschean therapist becomes an art critic. Nietzsche suggested some important functions of dreaming, which could help us in their interpretation: dreams can be a compensatory measure to satisfy unfulfilled needs, which by this very fact strengthens the needs (*Daybreak*, II, 119). They clarify our values and indicate our preferences in regard to sensuality, lust for power, and selfishness. They express our basic biological needs, disregarded and denied by our "wakeful day-wisdom." They mock all "infinite worlds," the idealistic notions with which we were raised, and they inform us about our innermost feelings and attitudes about other people (*Human*, Assorted, 76). Dreams and especially ones repeated often, just like experiences in wakefulness, impact us and change who we are and therefore the constructive understanding and interpreting of them is crucial. Experiences that are possible in dreams only can be formative ones, and thus dreaming of flying gracefully and skillfully, eventually contributes to successful coping in life and happiness. Dreams are quite powerful, "and even in the brightest moments of our waking life, we are ruled to some extent by the nature of our dreams" (*Beyond*, V, 193).

Dreams about deceased close persons are usually interpreted as wish fulfillment and expression of longing, a temporary release from grief with the illusion that the dead have returned. Nietzsche suggested a less obvious interpretation, seeing such a dream as an indication that the departed person is being internalized, and, therefore, becoming mentally alive in us. The questions to ask are: What does such an image stand for? and How is it going to affect our life? This perspective offers new directions in the work of grief: "When we dream about those who are long since forgotten or dead, it is a sign that we have undergone a radical transformation and that the ground on which we live has been completely dug up: then the dead rise up, and our antiquity becomes modernity" (*Human*, Assorted, 360).

NOTES

1. Elizabeth Carter, trans. *The Enchiridion* (South Bend, IN: Infomotions, 2001).
2. Thomas Szasz, *The Myth of Mental Illness* (New York: Harper & Row, 1974).
3. Ibid.
4. Information Philosopher, "Indeterminacy," www.informationphilosopher.com/freedom/indeterminacy.html, accessed June 22, 2014.
5. Theodor R. Sarbin, ed., *Narrative Psychology: The Storied Nature of Human Conduct* (London: Praeger Press, 1986).
6. Gazzaniga, Michael, Richard B. Ivry, and George R. Mangun, *Cognitive Neuroscience: The Biology of the Mind,* 4th ed. (New York: W. W. Norton & Company, 2013).
7. Elizabeth F. Loftus and J. E. Pickrell, "The Formation of False Memories," *Psychiatric Annals* 25 (1995): 720–25.
8. Leon Festinger, *A Theory of Cognitive Dissonance* (Stanford, CA: Stanford University Press, 1957).
9. Lauren B. Alloy and Lyn Y. Abramson, "Judgment of Contingency in Depressed and Nondepressed Students: Sadder but Wiser?" *Journal of Experimental Psychology: General* (1979) 108: 441–85, doi:10.1037/0096-3445.108.4.441.

THREE

Personality Psychology

Personality, if we have learned something from Nietzsche, is first of all a fiction, a word we use to describe and explain people's behavior. Personality psychology includes such explanations, formulated as theories of factors, and explores their types, nature, development, and effects. Most people have implicit theories of personality, while psychologists usually have more complex theories (such as five or sixteen factors and different combinations of traits and types).

FROM SOUL TO PERSONALITY

Nietzsche viewed personality as an updated version of the old superstitious concept of soul and he opted to keep this "venerable old hypothesis," while giving up the old attributes of the soul being "indestructible, eternal and indivisible," and conceiving it as "mortal soul, soul of subjective multiplicity and soul as social structure of the instincts and passions" (*Beyond*, I, 12). In this delineation, the "mortal" element is unfortunately very clear: when we are gone, we are done; the other elements will be expanded later. Nietzsche's new psychology is actually a physio-psychology, the one he had crowned as "queen of science." It is based on "refined immorality," a perspective that could raise antagonism because it postulates the interdependence of "good" and "bad" impulses and the derivation of all good impulses from bad ones. Another hard to stomach assertion of the new psychology is that what are usually considered negative emotions, such as hatred, envy, greed, and domineering, are actually "life conditioning" emotions which must be present in the "general economy of life." Accepting these propositions, however, will entitle us to a "profounder world of insight" (*Beyond*, I, 23).

The Insignificance of Personality

In 1862, when he was eighteen, in his first essay *Fate and History: Thoughts,* Nietzsche had already considered questions of temperament, environments, and personality. He was wondering then whether human happiness is determined by the impact of events themselves or by our temperament, responsible for the way events are conceived. He concluded that we "encounter everything in the mirror of our personality." Our personality in turn, is colored by our temperament, which is and was influenced by the imprinting of experiences and relationships.

In later years, Nietzsche thought that what can be conceived in psychological terms has only a modest role in shaping our personality and determining our behavior. We are mainly influenced by environmental-social and physiological-constitutional factors, and only a few of us can sometimes leave their field of influence. He reasoned, "a rage, a knife thrust: what of personality is in that? (*Will,* II, 235). Consequently, we have very little of personality and most behaviors are not self-determined, but rather "acts of circumstance, merely epidermal, merely reflexes that respond to a stimulus." If this is the case, it would be an error to derive a person's personality from actions, as many other factors can play a larger role, such as socio-economic status, environment, and accidents. Seen this way, personality, the capacity for self-creation, is not a given, and "some have several, most have none." From an evolutionary point of view, having a "personality" is wasteful, as people are merely tools of the transmission of genetic codes from one generation to the next one. Most people are controlled by their life circumstances, and only a few have "a greater power of self-definition and a lower impressionability" (*Will,* IV, 886).

The cult of personality flourishes because we consistently misjudge and misattribute the reasons for our own and others' behaviors, in Zarathustra's words, "For me—how could there be an outside-of-me? There is no outside!" (*Thus,* III, The convalescent, 2). As far as others go, we tend to attribute their behaviors to psychological factors. "A person is far more likely to appear to have sound character because he persistently follows his temperament than because he persistently follows his principles" (*Human,* IX, 485).

PERSONALITY DEVELOPMENT

Personality is rooted in the interaction of nature (temperament, intelligence, talents, robustness or sickliness), upbringing (parental and cultural) and life eventualities (trauma, good or bad partners). There is no linear relation between these variables and future developments, and what is considered a damaging condition may turn out to be advantageous—"ask yourself whether a tree that is supposed to grow to a proud height can dispense with bad weather and storms." What is beneficial in one personal constellation can become injurious in another: "The poison of which weaker natures perish, strengthens the strong—nor do they call it poison" (*Gay*, I, 19).

Having the kind of personality with "a greater power of self-definition and a lower impressionability" necessitates special conditions for its formation, "early isolation, compulsion to an existence of defiance and combat" (*Will*, IV, 886). We are born into a family, and our parents continue to have a psychological presence in us. The more we suffered as children from their maltreatment, their "unresolved dissonances" in character and disposition, and the more we have unresolved issues with them, the more our suffering continues (*Human*, VII, 379). Nietzsche went beyond parental impact to expose the deeper roots of our psychological makeup in the preceding generations, including their passions, mistakes, aberrations, and crimes. It is very difficult to overcome the fact that we were derived from this past and be released from its chains (*Untimely*, History, 3). Such accumulated experiences constitute "the martial history of the individual," which can be transmitted from one generation to the next (*Human*, VII, 379).

First and Second Natures

We often experience an incompatibility between our inherited nature, our upbringing, and the way we wish to be. We then try to cultivate new habits and instincts, a second nature, in the hope that the first one will fade away, practically attempting in retrospect to invent for ourselves a new past, instead of the one we had. This is a dangerous exploit, as it is difficult to deny the past, and second natures are weaker than firsts (*Untimely*, History, 3). In addition to environmental influences and attempts at self-change, we are impacted by the consequences of our actions, which "seize us by the scruff of the neck, very indifferent to the fact that we have meanwhile 'improved'" (*Beyond*, IV, 179).

Phantom Ego

We adopt our environment's evaluations of people and behaviors as children, and out of fear pretend that these are our own, eventually believing in them. We also learn to seek from others positive evaluations of ourselves. These attitudes become fixated and are rarely changed (*Daybreak*, II, 104). Such imported evaluations lead to pseudo-egoism, an idea close in spirit to R. D. Laing's later *The Divided Self*.[1] People are liable to internalize a phantom ego, created in the minds of people around them, propagated and communicated to them by society, making them dwell in a fog of imported foreign and impersonal opinions, habits, and fictions.

Consequently, society turns people into conforming standardized products and most people fail to set up a real ego, accessible, understood, and shaped by themselves (*Daybreak*, II, 105). The other side of the coin of pseudo-egoism is the morphology of self-esteem and collective self-esteem. Collective self-esteem, which characterizes the noble class, is the best preparation for personal sovereignty: "Feelings of sympathy and communality in the family and childhood, later belonging and representing family, clan, community which is proud about itself" (*Will*, III, 763).

DIMENSIONS AND ELEMENTS OF PERSONALITY

Two contradictory trends co-exist in Nietzsche's writings: an abundance of dualities along a principled rejection of dichotomies, which he called, "the great metaphysical mistake." His first book, *The Birth of Tragedy*, is a study of the polarity of the Apollonian and the Dionysian in art, culture, and in individual life. A polarity surfaced again in his many references to strong and weak natures, types, and characters. Intellectually however, he went beyond polarities and he did not see good-evil or selfish-unselfish as different and separate opposites. Logic and unselfishness are but sublimations of the illogical and selfishness. In the eyes of natural and strong persons, who are not the typical product of their society, "love and hate, gratitude and revenge, goodness and anger, affirmative and negative action, belong to each other" (*Will*, II, 351). They realize that the abilities to be good or evil are interdependent and one is not possible without the other.

The opposite of the holistic view, an unnatural "one-sided efficiency" suffers from the disease of "hemiplegia of virtue." In this approach, the natural instincts of animosity, aggression, and revenge are amputated to produce the "good man" (*Will*, II, 351). This idealistic approach pits the wholly good with the wholly bad—God with Satan, and spirit with flesh. Accordingly, it presents a fictionalized model of a "good person" and promotes a dream of the end of all evilness (*Will*, II, 351).

Character, Nature, and Type

Nietzsche used the terms character, nature, and type interchangeably to differentiate between strong and weak, sometimes parallel to high and low personality formations. In explaining them, he considered the role of early childhood upbringing practices, together with a substantial genetic or constitutional factor, expressed also in different dietary needs and preferences: "What serves the higher type of man as food or refreshment, must to a very different and inferior type be almost poison" (*Beyond*, II, 30). The "strong good character" ("good" in the negative sense of the word) is a person of fewer motives, with fixed or almost rigid habits and principles, who therefore acts with determination and in good conscience; everything is taken as self-granted, without deliberation among options; everything is divided into right and the wrong. Such people are products of their upbringing, bound by what preceded them. Such "square" bound characters are over-socialized and manageable, useful for the state and class, exactly the way their environment wanted them to be (*Human*, V, 228). The really strong types, in contrast, are moderate, with no need for extreme beliefs, who can deal with and love accidents and nonsense and do not judge others' shortcomings. They are healthy and can cope well and fearlessly, "human beings who are sure of their power and represent the attained strength of humanity with conscious pride" (*Will*, I, 55).

Strength and Weakness

The traits and behaviors of these two types can also be viewed from the perspectives of masters and slaves (chapter 4), nobility, the Superman, and other kinds of higher persons (chapter 5). The two types differ in their threshold of reaction and restraining powers; in their relation to ambiguity and conflict; in the structure of their passions, and in the social roles they fulfill. The weaker types are intolerant of internal conflicts, seek quiet, and their happiness is "the happiness of resting, of having no interruptions, of surfeit, of the final unity, as the 'Sabbath of Sabbaths.' The opposite stronger types seek opposition, strife, temptations and victories; they represent "the real mastery and refinement in waging war with itself, and thus transmit and cultivate self-ruling and outwitting of the self" (*Beyond*, V, 200).

Strong natures are characterized by a certain *adiaphora* [indifference], they can wait and delay their reactions; weak natures respond and act immediately and sometimes foolishly in a knee-jerk fashion, not having the ability and the wisdom to refrain from doing. Such weakness and lack in self-restraint is a sign of self-harming decadence (*Will*, I, 45), causing sickness, irritability, and preoccupation with issues of pleasure and displeasure, which Nietzsche described as "hygiene of the weak" (*Will*, I, 43). Strong natures, however, are far from being phlegmatic; "happiness lies in rapidity of feeling and thinking: everything else is slow, gradual, and stupid." They know how to discover and enjoy small things; "the man who could feel the progress of a ray of light would be greatly enraptured" (*Philologists*, 181). Strong types can control desires and temptations and have one dominant passion or multiple passions coordinated in an orderly manner. Unlike them, weaker types are afraid of passions and submit easily to them; they are flooded by ill-coordinated passions, suffering from conflict and anarchy (*Will*, III, 778).

Intuition and Rationality

In an early essay Nietzsche distinguished between intuitive and rational persons. The two kinds adopt different strategies of taking control in life. The former abhor abstractions and relate mainly to the beauty of existence that lies behind words, which rational types will see as illusion. The latter, suspicious of hunches and vibes, operate by means of foresight, prudence, and regularity. The former are not rational, the latter are inartistic; the former are susceptible to disappointment and suffering, the latter lack joy and enthusiasm. Nietzsche's favorite is of course the intuitive type, and we will see that in moments of wavering, his advice would always be to trust one's intuitions over one's rational thinking. Unlike rational persons, intuitive ones are better integrated in their culture, and gain from their intuitions "a harvest of continually inflowing illumination, cheer, and redemption—in addition to obtaining a defense against misfortune" (*Truth,* 2). Fifteen years later Nietzsche will reject seeing passion and reason as independent of each other, "as if every passion did not possess its quantum of reason," and instead will describe a system of relations between various elements of passions, desires, and thoughts (*Will,* II, 387).

Plastic Force and Horizons

Nietzsche called the resiliency demonstrated by persons or cultures a "plastic force," whose main ingredient is the ability to forget the past, not letting it become "the gravedigger of the present." Additional ingredients of the plastic force are the ability to find alternative routes of behavior, reinterpreting the past and the foreign in constructive terms, self-healing, compensating for losses, and rebuilding what was destroyed. These capabilities enable fast recuperation and resiliency under crisis and misfortune (*Untimely,* History, 1).

The plastic force, symbolized by *Nike* the goddess of victory standing on a single point, makes happiness possible. It is the ability to live the moment and forget everything else, and the ability "to sense things unhistorically." Inability to do so makes it impossible to enjoy life and hampers the ability to make others happy as well. The inability to forget has far-reaching implications for all domains of life. "Forgetting belongs to all action, just as both light and darkness belong in the life of all organic things" (*Untimely,* History, 1). A diminished plastic force, an inability to let go of the past invites psychological suffering. And yet, both remembering and forgetting are needed, and a clear horizon is needed to know which of them to choose in a given situation, "for the health of a single individual, a people, and a culture the unhistorical and the historical are equally essential." A person's horizons enable a constructive use of the past, drawing from the roots, taking advantage of one's personal, familial and cultural history; absorbing and transforming the past for one's benefit (*Untimely*, History, 1).

Backward and Anticipating Persons

A backward person is an unpleasant distrustful personality who reacts with envy to the success of his competitors and neighbors and reacts violently when confronted with divergent opinions. Nietzsche considered such personalities to be relics, out of an earlier stage of civilization, when raw force was a must and such behaviors were adaptive. The opposite anticipating personalities are empathetic, make friends, and are concerned and involved with their surroundings; they look favorably at the achievements of others, realize that they do not hold the whole truth and can be skeptical enough while looking ahead and anticipating a "higher human culture" (*Human*, IX, 614). "Unpleasant" is an aesthetic judgment, not a determination of normalcy or pathology, and it is simply more pleasant to have an anticipating personality as a neighbor, rather than a backward one. In another place, Nietzsche wrote about predatory men, murderers, rapists, and robbers, as tropical monsters coming out of a primordial forest, different from temperate human beings inhabiting the "moderate zone" (*Beyond*, V, 197).

The Apollonian and the Dionysian

The idea of understanding life in terms of art appeared for the first time in *The Birth of Tragedy* and this might well be the most important contribution of the book to Nietzsche's psychology. Seen from this perspective life, like a dream, becomes an artistic creation that must be judged neither rationally nor morally, but rather as an aesthetic phenomenon; "art represents the highest task and the truly metaphysical activity of this life" (*Birth*, First preface). The idea of examining life from the perspective of art has now become much more acceptable due to the development of cinema, an art form unknown in Nietzsche's lifetime. Statements such as "his life is a movie," "she lives in a movie" are often made. The question is, of course, what kind of a movie is it, a masterpiece or just a common soap opera? *The Birth of Tragedy* is usually studied as a contribution to art, and we will now examine its main conceptualization of the Dionysian-Apollonian as a contribution to psychology. The two forces exist in a full-blown state in artists, as a need for visions and orgiastic states; it exists in daily life, in a toned-down version, as dreams and drunkenness.

The Apollonian is a force that supplies structure and forms and suggests a vision to fulfill "Apollo's deception: the eternity of beautiful forms; the aristocratic legislation, thus shall it be forever!" (*Will*, IV, 1049)

The Apollonian consists of, among other qualities, an aesthetic need, artistic talent, heroic powers of fighting hardships and restraining instinctual urges, individuality, and conceptual-analytic skills. The Dionysian is involved in gesture, passion, song and dance, pleasure, empowerment, change in the perception of time and place, bravado, and "indifference to life and death" (*Will*, III, 799). It comprises mental suffering, rage, self-destructive behaviors, powerful sexual drive, affiliation need, empathy, excitation, and acceptance of all facets of life. In Nietzsche's words:

> The word "Dionysian" means unity, reaching out beyond personality, darker, fuller floating states, pantheistic sharing of joy and sorrow, will to procreation, fruitfulness, and recurrence, creation and destruction. The word "Apollonian" means perfect self-sufficiency, individualism, simplification, clarity, strength, unambiguous, rules and concept. (*Will*, IV, 1050)

Between Madness and Creativity

The true hero of Nietzsche's book is the Dionysian, as the conception of the Apollonian is less detailed and without any novel insights. Nietzsche's description of the Dionysian is not that different from reports of hippomanic states, in which persons prone to them quite often decline to take their medications, not wanting to lose such an "I can do everything" and "no limits" elated feeling. The Dionysian state of being is experienced as fullness and joy, and it incorporates the elements of "sexuality, intoxication, cruelty—all belonging to the oldest festal joys of mankind" (*Will*, III, 801). This can be conceived as sheer animality, in which a person is driven by instincts, without regard to social conventions and prohibitions, reaching a feeling of perfection "that is the extraordinary expansion of its feeling of power, riches, necessary overflowing of all limits." Nietzsche touched on the physiological aspects of this state, and in doing so, described the brain's pleasure center, which was later discovered in the 1950's:

> When we encounter things that display this transfiguration and fullness, the animal responds with an excitement of those spheres in which all those pleasurable states are situated—and blending of these very delicate nuances of animal well-being and desires constitutes the *aesthetic state*. The latter appears only in natures capable of that bestowing and overflowing fullness of bodily vigor; it is this that is always the *primum mobile* [prime mover]. (*Will*, III, 801)

Being in love is the prototype of creativity: in both conditions, there is a search for perfection and beauty, and in the two of them our "cerebral system is bursting with sexual energy" in a state of "aphrodisiac bliss" (*Will*, III, 805). Nietzsche described "Dionysian histrionicism," portraying the Dionysian type as uninhibited, manic, and hysteric. What was normal in early civilizations became abnormal in later periods; what is usually considered abnormal becomes an essential component in the creation of art. Writing about the physiological state of the Dionysian madness, out of which the comic and tragic arts were developed, Nietzsche pondered: "Is it possible that madness is not necessarily a symptom of degeneration, of decline, of a decadent culture? Perhaps this is a question for alienists—there are neuroses of health? [. . .] What if it was madness itself, to use a word of Plato's, which conferred the greatest blessings upon Hellas?" (*Ecce*, Criticism, 4).

Considered as a contribution to personality psychology, this polarity suffers from some problems: the moment one postulates two major wide-scope forces, one also invites a question: why these particular two, why not three or more? Each arm of this pair holds many variables that keep on changing in different references and are not necessarily connected. Besides, it is not clear whether the two are discrete or poles in a continuum. Nietzsche posited that the two forces are natural instincts, built-in structures that are needed together for life and creation, a necessary antagonism for the development of art, in the same way that the antagonism between the sexes is needed for the development of humans (*Birth*, 1). These terms can explain creativity after the fact, but it is not clear whether they can be enhanced or modified at all. The Apollonian-Dionysian is usually thought to be an important variable of personality, but we found that it is not useful as such. It does, however, offer an important insight into the role of manic states, characterized by "the ease of metamorphosis, the inability not to react" (*Twilight*, Skirmishes, 10), in the life of creators and the creative act.

PERSONALITY, BODY, AND POLITICS

Nietzsche used two metaphors in his conceptualization of personality, one biological, the other sociological; one suggests a division into organs and functions, the other proposes maneuvering in order to gain control and power. Nietzsche combined the two metaphors in his discussion of the "basic will of the spirit," what would be called today our executive function. He was careful not to treat an abstract idea in concrete terms, and thus he alternated between words such as will, control, ego, spirit and "the something which commands," a fact that can also be construed, by way of criticism, as an inconsistent use of terms. This "something" seeks mastery over other parts, "out of multiplicity it has the will to simplicity, a will which binds together and tames, desires to dominate and rule" (*Beyond*, VII, 230).

This "something" operates like an organism with a "digesting stomach" that selects, simplifies, and organizes incoming stimuli. It uses protean strategy to deceive itself and others and is willing to pretend and manipulate to achieve its goals (*Beyond*, VII, 230). Human evolution is a result of struggles between such parts, certain parts gaining control, "victory or predominance of individual parts"—others losing it, and becoming atrophied (*Will*, III, 647). In another similar analogy, he compared the ego to a cell: "The 'ego' subdues and kills: it operates like an organic cell: it is a violent robber; it wants to give birth to its god and see all mankind at his feet" (*Will*, III, 768). The last poetic sentence can be understood as suggesting that the macro of the Superman and the Will to Power already exists in the micro of the cellular level. Nietzsche went on and penned another brilliant sentence which summed up the central idea of Marvin Minsky's influential *The Society of Mind,*[2] "Indeed, our body is but a social structure composed of many souls" (*Beyond*, I, 19).

The body and physiology attest to the "nature of our subject-unity, namely as regents at the head of a communality" (*Will*, III, 492). Nietzsche wrote similarly about "the body as a political structure," seeing the mind as an agent of the body, but at the same time the body as a metaphor of mind. In the body, struggles between cells and tissues and division of labor in the form of specialized tasks are a matter of routine; in the body, a ruling class—aristocracy, gives instructions to subservient classes, which carry them out; this commanding and obeying mutually define and perpetuate the power relations (*Will*, III, 660).

Nietzsche described self-management in terms suitable for managing large bodies as businesses or armies, in which the chief executive officer is advised to deal with policy-making, delegate authority, and not be involved in minute details. He talked in praise of not knowing, simplifying matters, and seeing the large picture from different perspectives. Our internal ruler and subjects have their feeling, willing, and thinking, and an internal politics of wheeling and dealing between them, which goes on unobserved behind the scenes (*Will*, III, 492). Thus, the common experiences of competition between drives or emotions, and the state of one drive overpowering the intellect can be understood in terms of political power struggles (*Will*, III, 613).

Nietzsche's claim that a strong central authority is needed for the sake of proper functioning of body and mind is in agreement with his belief that aristocracy is the most appropriate system of government of the state (*Will*, III, 660), and the two beliefs were probably mutually reinforcing. However, power for its own sake is not enough; it must be used for the purpose of increasing the well-being of the whole system. The governing class of the mind, like a happy well-run commonwealth, identifies itself with the success of the whole community (*Beyond*, I, 19). No form of organization is free from changes brought about by natural forces such as drought, floods, or personal disasters. This introduces uncertainty into our life and the potential for abrupt changes, not knowing in advance which part in us will take control: "All of us harbor concealed gardens and plantings; and, to use another metaphor, we are all of us, growing volcanoes that approach the hour of eruption; but how near or distant that is, nobody knows—not even God" (*Gay*, I, 10). Nietzsche could not know, when he wrote these words in 1882, that his volcano would erupt seven years later. In 1889, he suffered a mental breakdown and was eventually committed to an asylum—we, however, still do not know our own hour.

Struggles of the Mind

A person's personality is the outcome of internal struggles between different elements, drives, motives, instincts, and affects. Most of them go on unconsciously, with chance events influencing the process, presenting the challenge of reaching a creative integration of the fighting parties. What we identify as knowing and thinking is the end result of struggles and agreements between different rivaling instincts, and for this reason, most philosophical thinking about knowledge might be totally wrong (*Gay*, IV, 333). Internal struggles are inherent features of humans, and consequently their interpretations of the world, tinted by the strife of drives, are not objective: "Every drive is a kind of lust to rule; each one has its perspective that it would like to compel all the other drives to accept as a norm" (*Will*, III, 481).

The struggle for control between different parts is not a moral war between good and evil, but a natural competition between parts that do their best to win control. "The will to overcome an emotion, is ultimately only the will of another, or of several other, emotions" (*Beyond*, IV, 117). An ascetic moral socialization delegitimizes some parts and makes people try to uproot them; "man prays to one part of himself as God, and to do so he finds it necessary to demonize the remaining part" (*Human*, III, 137). The question is not whether some parts in us are good or evil, but whether they are quick and resourceful, "seize the word, give the order—that decides about the whole rank ordering of its values" (*Beyond*, IX, 268). It is not that we are strong or weak and, therefore, act in a certain way, but rather that some drive is stronger than another one and gains the upper hand, putting an end to conflict and hesitation; it is the drive that decides and not us (*Human*, II, 107). Although we lack direct control over the internal struggles, we are still faced with the challenge of finding working integrated solutions: "The greatest souls are those that combine the most contradictory elements, desires, cravings, and aspirations all into a unitary whole by yoking them together in a rigorously controlled, artistic way, just as in a well-constructed and happy commonwealth" (*Beyond*, I, 19).

One must be ready and equipped to withstand and wage internal struggles, despite the fact that the result depends to some degree on external circumstances. In periods of dissolution and transition, weaker types will strive for happiness and rest by ending and avoiding inner conflicts. Unlike them, stronger and more creative types like Caesar or

Leonardo da Vinci, "those enigmatic men predestined for victory and temptation," will turn conflicts into creation, cultivating "self-ruling and outwitting of the self" (*Beyond*, V, 200). I will later show (chapter 7) that outwitting implies not brute force, but lightness, shrewdness, humor, and paradox as means of self-control.

Multiplicity and Unity

We like to believe that we make decisions in a rational systematic manner, choosing an option after considering the available alternatives and their possible consequences. This is not the case: our actions are determined by many factors such as chance, other people's influence, environmental contingencies, habitual patterns, and caprice. We are not aware of these factors and we exclude them in accounting for our actions, creating an illusion of resolve (*Daybreak*, II, 130). Nietzsche went one step further concluding that "Everything that enters consciousness as 'unity' is already tremendously complex: we always have only a semblance of unity" (*Will*, III, 489). Unity is an illusion, and it is doubtful whether the assumption of one single subject is necessary; "perhaps it is just as permissible to assume a multiplicity of subjects, whose interaction and struggle is the basis of our thought and our consciousness in general." At this point, Nietzsche put forward the main thesis of his personality theory: "*My hypotheses:* The subject as multiplicity" (*Will*, III, 490).

Our Many Faces

In addition to biological and evolutionary reasons for our multiplicity, Nietzsche took into consideration psychological factors: the fact that we are usually born into a family with two parents exposes us to a "double series of experiences [and] means of access to two worlds that seem so far asunder"; this exposure is reflected in our nature. "I have an alter ego: I have a "second" sight, as well as a first; Perhaps I even have a third sight" (*Ecce*, Wise, 3).

Nietzsche was predisposed to the idea of multiplicity, studying early in his life Plato's metaphor of the soul as a polis. In addition, he was not an admirer of monotheism and felt an affinity with ancient Greece's polytheism, with "many gods, different varieties of heroes, overmen, near-men and undermen—dwarfs, fairies, centaurs, satyrs, demons and devils" (*Gay*, III, 143). More importantly, he found multiplicity in his own life experience; "the only thing I have always suffered from is 'multitude,' the infinite variety of my own soul" (*Ecce*, Clever, 10). His multiplicity came to the open after he lost his mind, when the different parts of his soul came to the open, as was clearly evident in his letter to Cosima

Wagner, whom he addressed as "Ariadne, My Beloved" (Turin, January 3, 1889):

> Among the Hindus I was Buddha, in Greece Dionysus—Alexander and Caesar were incarnations of me, as well as the poet of Shakespeare, Lord Bacon. Most recently I was Voltaire and Napoleon, perhaps also Richard Wagner. . . . However, I now come as Dionysus victorious, who will prepare a great festival on Earth. . . . Not as though I had much time. . . . The heavens rejoice to see me here. . . . I also hung on the cross.[3]

WILL, DRIVES, AND EMOTION

A theory of personality is a tool used to understand why people behave as they do and if possible predict how they will behave in the future. Such a theory invites looking at motivation, drives, instincts, impulses, passions, and wills. Nietzsche did not offer a systematic list of drives and he used all these terms interchangeably, readily baptizing new items, such as the impulse to doubt, to deny, and to wait, which he termed the "ephectic impulse" (*Genealogy*, III, 9). At least in my reading, Nietzsche's forte was not in presenting a taxonomy of drives and emotions but rather in turning our assumptions and conventions about them upside down.

The Perspectives of Will

Nietzsche looked at motivation from two different perspectives. The first, in his descriptive, empirical psychology, put survival in the center; the second, in his meta-psychology disposed of it, in favor of the Will to Power. In the first perspective, survival of the species is a basic instinct of the herd and preservation is the purpose of existence and of all behaviors, even those that at first sight seem to be detrimental. He named this basic fact "the eternal comedy of existence," in which whatever we do, there is always something bigger than us that calls the shots. "One can only laugh at the fact that whatever we do, right or wrong we will always act within this frame 'the species is everything, one is always none'" (*Gay*, I, 1).

From this perspective, we are puppets on a string, and this knowledge offers us liberation and relief from the burden of responsibility. All actions, good and supposedly evil, are innocent, being motivated by the drive for survival, experienced by individuals as a wish to increase pleasure and avoid displeasure. We do not intend to harm, pity, or please others, as these actions are only by-products of taking care of our own interests (*Human*, II, 99) and whatever humans do, they do for their own good, as they happen to understand it (*Human*, II, 102), a view that will be later adopted and popularized by Ayn Rand.[4] Under the influence of morality and religion, which supply reasons and purposes to what really lacks reasons and purposes, this comedy is experienced as a tragedy. This, in a way, is another comedy, as such fictions promote faith in reason and in life and ultimately support survival. Human beings must believe and know why they exist, a need which turns them into "fantastic animals" (*Gay*, I, 1).

All this being said, Nietzsche asked us in his meta-psychology to drop the premise that self-preservation is the most basic instinct of organisms, and accept that "a living thing seeks above all to discharge its strength—life itself is Will to Power; self-preservation is only one of the indirect and most frequent results thereof" (*Beyond*, I, 13). On one hand we saw that Nietzsche was moving from psychology (the soul), to physiology (the body); on the other hand he was propelling from biology (survival) to psychology (Will to Power), although for him the psychological and the physiological are one. Nietzsche emphasized the difference between the two wills, between the "will of psychology," which he proposed is an unjustified generalization, and the "Will to Power," which is not a kind of "will" nor identical to it, and has nothing to do with desiring or commanding (*Will*, III, 692). I will return to the Will to Power towards the end of the book (and I will explain then why I do not treat it extensively) and I will discuss here the "will of psychology."

The Trickiness of the Will

In a high-school composition, Nietzsche had already conceived free will as an abstraction and not a concrete thing—an abstraction that denotes conscious action, while in reality things are more complicated, as many factors conscious as well as unconscious, together with environmental cues and chance events are involved in acting (*Freedom of Will and Fate*, 1862). Later he continued this line of critique with succinct observations and reservations: Firstly, willing, just like the idea of the "ego," is an illusionary by-product of language (*Daybreak*, II, 115). Secondly, the notion of will is the fruit of faulty thinking, which makes us reason like "a man who, stepping out of his room at the very minute when the sun is rising, says, 'It is my will that the sun shall rise.'" In other words, the will is "A retroactive explanation of our behavior" (*Daybreak*, II, 124). Thirdly, willing is not an activity, but rather an experience and a perception "in our intellect and experience we are free and can will anything, even impossible things while in reality it is only a superficiality, surface, and self-satisfaction" (*Daybreak*, II, 125). Lastly, willing is an appearance, while other forces are the real movers and shakers: "Our intellect is rather merely the blind instrument of another rival craving, whether it be the impulse to repose, or the fear of disgrace and other evil consequences, or love" (*Daybreak*, II, 109).

A Blindfolded Monkey

Had they known about Nietzsche, economic psychologists could have adopted him as their forefather. Burton Malkiel suggested in his *A Ran-*

dom Walk down Wall Street that "a blindfolded monkey throwing darts at a newspaper's financial pages could select a portfolio that would do just as well as one carefully selected by experts"[5] and Nassim Taleb in his *Fooled by Randomness* demonstrated how such experts, like the rest of us, attribute successes to their intelligence and skills, and impute failures to uncontrollable circumstances and chance.[6] Nietzsche described these phenomena as adopting a selective view of the world; "we have learned to believe in will and purpose, and to disregard chance and accidents" (*Daybreak*, II, 130). If the will is reduced to meager proportions, its companion, "the hundred-times-refuted theory of a 'free will'" (*Beyond*, I, 18), must be given up as well. Nietzsche exposed its psychological motivations: "The doctrine of freedom of will has human pride and feeling of power for its mother and father" (*Daybreak*, II, 128), and thus "extravagant pride" has led humans to believe that they are autonomous creatures with an entirely free will, fully in control of their actions, absolving God, society, and chance of any responsibility. They wish to become "*causa sui* " [its own cause] and thus to pull themselves "up into existence by the hair, out of a swamp of nothingness" (*Beyond*, I, 21).

Humans take it as self-evident that their actions are the result of willing them. They assume a cause-and-effect relation between the two, without pondering its mechanics (*Gay*, III, 127). David Wegner, who often quoted Nietzsche in his various publications, demonstrated the illusion of control, in which people are convinced that their will shapes events that were actually determined by someone else. The will, he claimed, is an illusion or a construction while unconscious processes are actually responsible for intentions as well as behaviors.[7]

Nietzsche disassembled this term, showing that it is a unity only by name, a popular and stubborn prejudice, while in practice it is a complicated conglomerate consisting of different constellations of physical sensations and feelings associated with approach and avoidance behaviors; cognitive operations such as commanding and obeying, self-statements, attention, concentration, and evaluations; and a variety of emotions, among them feelings of superiority, independence of the commanding unit, compulsions and inhibitions, resistance and pressure to comply (*Beyond*, I, 19). Willing is also composed of memories and consequences of prior successful actions that reinforce the belief in "freedom of will," the development of effective "under-wills" or under-souls, and the pleasure derived from the success of one's "executive agents." Finally on top of these, there is an element of self-deception, in which the duality of commanding and obeying components is denied, in favor of using the synthetic concept "I."' This reinforces the belief that simply willing leads to action, and action is the result of will (*Beyond*, I, 19). In short, beyond trivial actions, like raising our left hand now, Nietzsche argued that willing is not a simple matter of command and performance, and he even went further and rejected the prevalent truism that we know or should be conscious of what we want. In so doing, he turned his back to the "know yourself" dictum carved on a stone above the doors of Apollo's temple at Delphi. He suggested that it is an impossible feat, nor a desirable one:

> But how do we recognize ourselves? How can man know himself? He is a dark and hidden thing; whereas the hare is said to have seven skins, man can take off seven times seventy skins and still not be able to say: "That is you as you really are, that is no longer mere appearance." Besides, it is a painful and dangerous undertaking to dig down into oneself in this way and to descend violently and directly into the shaft of one's being. How easily he could injure himself doing this, so that no doctor could cure him. (*Untimely*, Schopenhauer, 1)

The Paradox of Will

If the will is weak and self-knowledge is limited, how could Nietzsche write "Willing sets you free: that is the true doctrine of will and freedom—thus Zarathustra instructs you" (*Thus*, II, Upon the Blessed Isles)? How could he advise, "Do whatever you will, but first be such as are able to will" (*Thus*, III, Virtue that makes small)? If we do not know ourselves, how could he call us to become who we are, to design ourselves, and even strive to go beyond ourselves? This question becomes more urgent as we realize that in addition to discrediting will and self-knowledge, Nietzsche, unlike most psychologists, recognized the large role that our biological makeup and chance play in our life.

Thus, it seems that Nietzsche's theory of motivation suffers from a self-contradiction or a paradox. How can a paralyzed and blind person move when the earth is shaking and strong winds are blowing? I will address the call to act when action is seemingly impossible, as the paradox of action, and I intend to delve into the problem and suggest ways out of it, when I deal with Nietzsche's teachings on chance and action (chapter 6).

Drives and Needs

Nietzsche the Overturner pointed out that "need is considered the cause why something came to be; but in truth it is often merely an effect of what has come to be" (*Gay*, III, 205). Needs are one element in a cycle of feedback, in which our needs prompt actions, and our actions reinforce the needs behind them. He differentiated between two aspects of drives, between reasons for activity and reasons for a specific action; the former is the result of pent-up tension in need of discharge; the latter, an upshot of exposure to a given random, trivial trigger. Nietzsche dispensed with the notions of purpose and vocation, seeing them as only *post hoc* rationalizations of our behaviors. Similarly, he saw goals as only directing and not pushing forces, and he considered this insight as "one of my most essential steps and advances." Humans, out of vanity and self-deception, cannot acknowledge that they are not the captains of their life, but rather drifting boats: "The ship is following the current into which it has entered accidentally. It 'wills' to go that way because it . . . must . . . it has a direction, to be sure, but . . . no steersman at all" (*Gay*, V, 360).

The Value of Instincts

Nietzsche considered biologically and physiologically ingrained drives and instincts (terms he used interchangeably), shaped to a large extent by learning and influenced by environmental cues, to be more important than psychological factors. Instincts are necessary for survival, and in comparison to them, as every psychologist knows, psychological variables such as states of consciousness, beliefs, and attitudes, are fifth-rank matters of complete indifference (*Antichrist*, 39). All drives alike want to be masters, and thus each philosophizes and maneuvers by using words to represent just *itself* as the ultimate purpose of existence and the legitimate *master* of all the other drives (*Beyond*, I, 6; *Will*, III, 481). The drives' lust to rule is innocent and blind, and they can equally act for and against the self. Drives lack intelligence, cannot see the general picture, and do not recognize the best interests of the whole individual. They sacrifice differing drives easily and, if they were not checked by other drives, they could lead to excess and destruction. However, as often happens in state politics, had other drives been in power, they would have behaved exactly the same (*Will*, II, 372). The blindness is bi-directional and just as the drives are blind to our best interests, we are blind to them. Even if we gain some self-knowledge, we will not be able to recognize our most prominent drives; neither can we know their fluctuations, number, and strength, not to mention the totality of our drives or the laws of their strengthening and weakening (*Daybreak*, II, 119).

Our drives, "sovereign instincts striving for mastery," meet us Little Red Riding Hoods as a wolf in Grandma's clothes, and thus carnal desires or desires for power, for example, might masquerade as Christian values. The most trivial fabrication would be a particular drive using the "I" pronoun, making us understand "I want a cigarette now" as a wish of the whole self, and not merely of a particular sub-part in a multiplicity. We can, however, detect such maneuvers and distinguish between a drive and its misleading expression only after the need had been satisfied. Nietzsche concluded that "falsity is common and necessary; the will is opposed to direct self-knowledge, the will to truth itself is a disguise" (*Will*, II, 377).

Passions go through stages of ebb and flow. In the flow phase they are dangerous, when they drag down their victim with the weight of stupidity; ebbing, in a much later phase, they wed the spirit, when they "spiritualize" themselves. Desires should be spiritualized or sublimated, but not uprooted aggressively, as weaker degenerated persons who cannot resist an urge attempt to do an attack on the roots of passion means an attack on the roots of life (*Twilight*, Morality, 1). The result of spiritualization of drives is the creation of demons, that is to say, a richer inner world, humankind's growing inwardness. Thus, aggression becomes striving for knowledge; the ability to lie and dissimulate turns to art (*Will*, II, 376); the spiritualization of sensuality becomes the demon of love; and hostility becomes creativity. The spiritualization of hostility sets up inner struggles and internal enemies, which make us multicolored and more fruitful. Persons who can contain inner tensions and struggles without escaping to peace of mind remain young and active. The opposite, of a cow-like, moralistic self-satisfaction and good-conscience, is actually a renunciation of the "great life" (*Twilight*, Morality, 3). Nietzsche, we saw, argued that the believers in willpower do not bother to inquire about its mechanics and do not wonder how an intention turns into action. This criticism can be turned against him, as it is not clear how aggression turns into knowledge. Is it a conscious decision? Can every aggressive person become a sage? Or perhaps, it is the other way around, and persons with artistic ability have also a talent for lying, and when they succeed with its help, they do not have to lie anymore.

The passions change us and the way we experience ourselves by sharpening our sensations and focusing our attention. Motivational arousal is like the state of falling in love, when attention is focused on one object. Such an arousal activates and changes the significance given to what captivates us, often giving it a higher importance than what it deserves, disregarding caution, conscience, and knowledge. It also fosters forgetting in order to concentrate on what is at hand, turning us into "a small living vortex in a dead sea of night and forgetting." In this state, perceptions change, everything else dims, while the object of desires is perceived with all the senses, more than ever as true, close, "colored, resounding and illuminated" (*Untimely*, History, 1). All momentous achievements and failures, fair and unfair, creative and destructive alike, are born in such motivational states of arousal. "And no artist would achieve his picture, no field marshal his victory, and no people its freedom, without previously having desired and striven for them in that sort of unhistorical condition" (*Untimely*, History, 1).

THE REALM OF EMOTIONS

I hope that I do not have to remind you, my dear readers, that "emotion," like "personality," is but a word, coined in order to understand better something about human behavior. Falling in love or being hungry or thirsty can be conceived as drives or as emotions (in the following emotions and feelings will be used interchangeably). Usually, emotions are distinguished from cognitions, or metaphorically, the head and heart speak differently, raising the question of how to relate to their often conflicting messages.

Riding Our Emotions

Emotions can be conceived as an ancient activation system, engraved in our mammal brain, that we must learn to read carefully and delay responding until we decide on a line of action. This delay of automatic dispositions is the sign of a strong, far from hysteric, character. We should control emotions and not let them control us: "To have and not have one's affects [emotions], one's for and against, at will, to condescend to have them for a few hours; to seat oneself on them as on horses, often as on asses—for one has to know how to employ their stupidity as well as their fire" (*Beyond*, VII, 214).

It would be a grave mistake to buy into the notion of "an order of rank among the passions," according to which one should be guided by reason only, taking care not to be misguided by passions which are "abnormal, dangerous, semi-animal" (*Will*, II, 387). On the contrary, we must listen and take our feelings into account, as not doing so will hinder our thinking; "one should hold fast to one's heart; for if one lets it go, how soon one loses one's head, too!" (*Thus*, II, The compassionate). When we find it befitting, we should entrust ourselves gracefully to instincts, adhering to Nietzsche's advice, "Do not fear the 'evil character' of nature. Be a freedom bird. Fly where you feel" (*Gay*, IV, 294).

In managing our emotions, we have two routes open to us: One would be translation to action, "All feeling suffers in me and is my prison: but my willing always comes to me as my liberator and bringer of joy" (*Thus*, II, The blissful island), and, if action is not possible or desirable, the other would be resorting to indirect means of expression. What we do with an emotion changes the emotion itself, which gets weakened or modified by suppression, or strengthened by actions and verbal and bodily expressions. Emotions follow the trail of behavior, and the very expression of emotions is a behavior too (*Gay*, I, 47). Nietzsche was far from commending an "express your feelings" policy, and certainly not in the case of anger.

Emotion and Cognition

After tackling the belief that actions are a matter of free will, Nietzsche took on the common belief that feelings are arbitrary as if they arise out of us isolated, unconnected to our history of learning, reasons, and purposes. We only feel that we are hungry, and not that the organism aims to stay alive or that it is our habitual lunchtime (*Human*, I, 18). In fact, all intense moods are easily conditioned, "they seem to stir up memory," arousing related feelings and moods through repeated and rapid repetitions, connecting feelings and thoughts and feelings with other feelings. Thus, our feelings are actually compounded, though we tend to disregard that idea and experience integrities rather than composites. Feelings named moral or religious are far from being a unity but "in truth they are rivers with a hundred sources and tributaries. As is so often the case, the unity of the word does not guarantee the unity of the thing" (*Human*, I, 14).

The Construction of Emotions

Against the belief in emotions as an independent entity, Nietzsche put forward his version of a two-factors theory of emotion (remindful of the 1880s James-Lange[8] and the 1960s Schachter-Singer[9] theories): "Emotions are a construction of the intellect, an invention of causes that do not exist. All general bodily feelings that we do not understand are interpreted intellectually." Humans seek reasons to account for their feelings, be they personal, inter-personal, or circumstantial. Later, in the service of comprehension, the feeling and its explanation are merged and chronologically reversed, resulting in constructions such as "I have a stomachache because I ate something bad." Emotions are thus a product of learning by association, a combination of repetition and interpretation, "Frequent rushes of blood to the brain accompanied by choking sensation are interpreted as 'anger'" (*Will*, III, 670). This interpretation, after many trials, is reinforced (by relief of tension) and habituated, making us believe that some stimuli aroused the emotion.

Because the language of images or bodily sensations is foreign to us, emotions, just like dreams, invite interpretation; suffering or happy-go-lucky persons are convinced that the reasons for their specific feelings are easily accessible, but in fact, the reasons are hidden from them and cannot be found. Nietzsche expounded on the maneuver of chronological inversion, where an illusion of understanding is created by taking the consequences of such conditions for causes. Thus when a task, carried out under a good mood, turns out to be successful, people tend to see the success as the reason for the good mood, while in fact, both the success and the good mood were determined by fortunate physiological factors, enhanced by the good mood (*Will*, II, 229).

Head and Heart

The question as to which one, emotion or cognition, is a more reliable guide for action, was historically discussed in theology in terms of "faith" versus "knowledge" or, simply put, in terms of instinct and reason. Nietzsche, however, rejected an "either-or" approach and suggested that we integrate the two elements—that is, follow our instincts and concurrently rely on reason by raising arguments in "a kind of self-outwitting," keeping in mind that reason is only a tool and its products are no more than options (*Beyond*, V, 191). Passion (a strong emotion) and reason are not two independent entities, but rather "a system of relations between various passions and desires," and every passion "possesses its quantum, of reason" (*Will*, II, 387).

Our emotions, desires, and passions are the basic given reality, the rest are just constructions on top of them, "for thinking is only the relationship of these drives to one another" (*Beyond*, II, 36). Thoughts impact emotions and emotions bear on thoughts, in a bi-directional process, "Thoughts are the shadows of our feelings" (*Gay*, III, 179) and "From passions grow opinions; intellectual laziness lets these harden into convictions" (*Human*, IX, 637).

Life Conditioning Emotions

Nietzsche differentiated between two sorts of emotions, "life conditioning emotions" and "the absurd animal's emotions." In *Homer's Contest,* one of his early essays (1872), he rejected the natural versus human dichotomy on the grounds that human beings are part of nature and are at their best when they live accordingly. The very capacities that are considered as terrible and inhuman could as well be "the fertile soil from which alone all humanity, in feelings, deeds and works, can grow forth." Accordingly, he regarded the emotions of hatred, envy, avarice, and domination as life-conditioning emotions, "as factors which must be present, fundamentally and essentially, in the general economy of life" (*Beyond*, I, 23).

Cruelty

The first emotion Nietzsche described and "rehabilitated" was cruelty. In the early essay mentioned above, he had already pointed out that ancient Greek law was derived from murder and its atonement. "Finer culture, too, takes its first victor's wreath from the altar of atonement for murder" (*Homer's Contest*). Nietzsche reminded us that cruelty is a basic fact of life, found at the hearts of cultures and religions; it is the essence and nature of power in general, "which is always evil." Nietzsche, who wanted us to see cruelty realistically as a feature of life, wrote poetically: "Every moment devours the preceding one, every birth is the death of countless beings, procreating, and living and murdering are all one. Therefore, we have the right to compare the magnificent culture to a victor dripping with blood who, in his triumphal procession, drags the vanquished along chained to his carriage as slaves" (*Greek*).

Envy and Vanity

Nietzsche differentiated between two Eris (Envy) goddesses, each one with a different disposition. The cruel one promotes war and feuding; the beneficial one drives people to work and try harder and compete with others for riches and achievement (*Homer's Contest*). Another pair of emotions is vanity and arrogance. The former is a dependent and deceitful expression of slave morality—"vanity is atavism"—in which one is trying to create a positive impression in the eyes of others in order to later internalize their evaluation. The latter, involves active impression management, exporting one's own self-evaluation, be it out of arrogance or modesty, without letting others decide on one's value (*Beyond*, IX, 261).

Arrogance, not tolerated by the conformity demanding society, is closely related to self-respect. "I wish men would begin by *respecting* themselves: everything else follows from that." Self-respect is different from common, indulging, blind self-love, "fatalism of love," a needy love, which can also exist in relation to a lover and connotes contempt for what one loves (*Will*, IV, 919).

Love and Possession

A reader might think that Nietzsche turned the seven deadly sins upside-down and made them a lively bunch, and this is in fact the case with avarice. Love of people, knowledge, and objects is actually a wish for possessions, experienced as love, mostly before we have them, and as possession after a period of getting used to them. People usually get tired of their last possession after a three-month period and start looking for new ones—"possessions are generally diminished by possession." What is called love, and the need for exclusion of others, is thus the ultimate form of egoism (*Gay*, I, 14). If the mother-infant bond, according to attachment theory, is the prototype of love, the parental words of endearment, "I want to eat you up" actually illustrate Nietzsche's point. I will return to intimate love as part of Nietzsche's social psychology (chapter 5).

The Absurd Animal's Emotions

We move now from "life conditioning emotions" and a "proper physio-psychology," to the opposite of the sentimental hypocrisy of "immaculate perception" and the emotions of "the absurd animal." Here, "pure knowledge" is proclaimed, the earthly is despised, and the fact that our entrails are the stronger part of us, is proscribed. The denial of life conditioning emotions and desires, their suppression and defaming lead to "shame and bad conscience, desires losing their innocence" (*Thus*, II, Immaculate perception). Divorce from nature turned us into pathetic beings, which Nietzsche described from the perspective of animals: "I fear the animals regard man as a being like themselves, seriously endangered by the loss of sound animal common sense; they regard him perhaps as the absurd animal, the laughing animal, the crying animal, the miserable animal" (*Gay*, III, 224).

We are divorced from nature not only due to the "immaculate perception" inherent in moralistic ideology, but also because of pampering life conditions. The less pain, dangers, and suffering in life, the more they are feared and hated; and the easier life conditions are, the greater the misery experienced. Conditions of abundance and security are the breeding ground for pessimistic philosophy. "The answer? Some real suffering" (*Gay*, I, 48). It is easy to guess which emotions will be considered by Nietzsche as unwanted, negative, and acquired, as they are all feelings not found in the animal world. Hence suffering is acceptable, but misery is not. Misery's bedfellows are sin, shame, guilt, pity, resentment, nihilism, as well as self-love, vanity, and destructive envy. These emotions share the quality ascribed to pity which "fixes itself firmly, eats into him, spreads out, and grows like a polyp in every breadth and depth" (*Gay* II, 21).

Nietzsche teaches the absurd animal—that is, you and me—to identify these feelings, understand their background, and hopefully oppose and overcome them. We will meet these feelings again, in the discussion of mental suffering (chapter 7), and we will understand free spirits as persons who got rid of them (chapter 8).

NOTES

1. Ronald David Laing, *The Divided Self: An Existential Study in Sanity and Madness* (Harmondsworth, UK: Penguin, 1960).
2. Marvin Minsky, *The Society of Mind* (New York: Simon & Schuster, 1986).
3. The Nietzsche Channel, "Nietzsche's Letters of Insanity, 1889," www.thenietzschechannel.com/correspondence/eng/nlett-1889.htm, accessed June 22, 2014.
4. Ayn Rand, *The Virtue of Selfishness* (New York: Penguin, 1964).
5. Burton Malkiel, *A Random Walk down Wall Street: The Time-Tested Strategy for Successful Investing*, 11th ed. (New York: W. W. Norton & Company, 2015).
6. Nassim Nicholas Taleb, *Fooled by Randomness: The Hidden Role of Chance in Life and in the Markets*, 2nd updated ed. (New York: Random House Trade Paperbacks, 2005).
7. David M. Wegner, *The Illusion of Conscious Will* (Cambridge, MA: MIT Press, 2002).
8. The two namesakes of the James–Lange theory of emotion were William James and Carl Lange. See Dunlap Knight, ed., *The Emotions: Carl Lange and William James* (Baltimore: Williams and Wilkins Company, 1922), archive.org/stream/emotionsvolumei007644mbp/emotionsvolumei007644mbp_djvu.txt, accessed June 22, 2014.
9. Stanley Schachter and Jerome Singer, "Cognitive, Social, and Physiological Determinants of Emotional State," *Psychological Review* 69 (1962): 379–99.

FOUR

Psychology of Morality

Nietzsche is popularly known as the one who proclaimed the death of God. Atheistic ideas were already well known in Nietzsche's time as many thinkers before him, since the eighteenth century, wrote and identified themselves as atheists, among them Baron d'Holbach who in 1770 in his *Système de la Nature,*[1] made the idea of God superfluous, and Marquis de Sade, who is known more for being a libertine rather than an atheistic libertarian, as manifested in his 1782 *Dialogue Between a Priest and a Dying Man.*[2]

Nietzsche knew the writings of some of his contemporaries, who held similar ideas; his wording, however, must have hit a raw nerve. Atheists, poor souls, are usually excused for "not knowing the truth," while Nietzsche's shocking formulation was seen as sacrilege. In fact, some half-wits still keep spraying on walls the two-line graffiti "God is dead! Nietzsche" and next to it "Nietzsche is dead! God." Little do they know that Nietzsche sought to wipe out something much sneakier, something that most people take for granted without any questions asked, something which descended on us like fog and penetrated the way we feel, think, and behave. This something, called morality, operates hidden from us, obstructs our vision, and makes us blind to ourselves and the world (*Will*, II, 275).

ON STUDYING MORALITY

The graffiti sprayers (and, of course, many others) probably reckon that if God is dead, they are left alone in the world without his or her benign supervision. Even so, human beings have the talent for believing in dead gods too, and they can comfort themselves that morality is still around to hold their hand on the crooked paths of life; "those who have abandoned

God cling that much more firmly to the faith in morality" (*Will*, I, 18). The demise of morality is terrifying: if morality is gone too, how will they be able to decide between right and wrong? If morality is also a dead non-entity, they ask immediately, "What will prevent people from murdering each other?" This is too much to take, and possibly, for this reason, Nietzsche's stance and the declaration, "I am the first Immoralist" (*Ecce*, Untimely, 2), are simply glossed over. He was not against all kinds of morality, but against the mandatory "entire old morality," which he depreciated and rejected. "We have outlived it, we are no longer coarse and naive enough to have to let ourselves be deceived in this fashion (*Will*, II, 459).

He investigated morality as a psychologist and in his eyes, and justifiably so, he was a pioneer, taking on a task not performed before: "Thus nobody up to now has examined the value of that most famous of all medicines which is called morality." He took the first step to remedy the situation, by questioning it (*Gay*, V, 345) and he saw himself as Odysseus outsmarting Circe, the goddess of magic, who wished to distract him. As an explorer of hidden caves and an astronomer discovering uncharted celestial bodies, Nietzsche pointed out, "it is to be *inferred* that there are countless dark bodies near the sun—such as we shall never see. Among ourselves, this is an allegory; and the psychologist of morals reads the whole star-writing merely as an allegorical and symbolic language in which much may be unexpressed" (*Beyond*, V, 196).

Contra Idealism

Nietzsche was an atypical psychologist, who did not treat moral development as if it was an equivalent of verbal ability or motor eye-hand co-ordination, genetically predetermined and not socially constructed. His conclusions were not concocted sitting on an armchair, nor in a psychology lab testing under which conditions children are willing to share their candies, but reached through his experiences and observations of the ways and causes of human idealizing and moralizing "in a manner very different from that which may seem ordinarily desirable" (*Ecce*, Preface, 4). He was a different psychologist, but also different from the philosophers before him, who served Christian morality and did not examine what hides behind it. "What one of the philosophers preceding me was a real psychologist, and not its very reverse, a 'superior swindler,' an 'Idealist?'" (*Ecce*, Wagner, 4).

Let us zoom in on the last word in this quote, as it says it all. Whenever Nietzsche heard the word "idealism" he reached for his revolver. Are not "Idealists" the nice guys, the ones who are honest, unselfish good-doers? Does Nietzsche recommend dishonesty, stinginess, and evil-doing? What is wrong with morality, equality, democracy, and human rights for example? Nothing at all! The problem is not with specific behaviors, but with the way they are justified. "Idealists" are ones who demand from others, and less often from themselves, to act not according to their own feelings, but in the name of some catchwords, abstract ideas turned into obligatory guiding values. Such abstractions are swindlers; looking harmless they hide unsuspected implications swallowed hook, line, and sinker.

Nietzsche considered idealism as a mystifying "superfluous and stupid element," a real curse on life. Idealism, the parent of morality, is the opposite of the tangible, the body and physiology, the natural and the concrete. He could not forget the poisonous atmosphere of his upbringing, saturated with "Christian" ideals and admonitions, which taught him that nothing good can come out of idealism and nothing can mend its damages. It gave birth to embarrassing mistakes, distortions of instincts and compensations, which diverted him from his life mission, and pushed him to become a philologist rather than a physician as he really wished. Idealism precluded a healthy egoism and strong instincts: "I was in a condition for which I can never forgive myself. When I had almost reached the end, simply because I had almost reached it, I began to reflect upon the basic absurdity of my life 'Idealism.' It was an illness that first brought me to reason" (*Ecce*, Clever, 2).

The Attack on Morality

Nietzsche, as a thirteen year old boy, was already preoccupied with the question of the origin of the terms good and evil, subsequently writing his first philosophical essay on this issue. His skepticism and curiosity were so unexpected, unavoidable, and not in accord with his environment and family traditions that he saw it as a fateful turning point (*Genealogy*, Prologue, 3). Later, he started his examination of morality with a survey of his own life experience. Then, he asked some critical questions: How is morality to be studied? What is the value of values? What is the origin of the basic values of good and bad, good and evil? What are the different kinds and stages of morality ("morality as consequence, as symptom, as mask, as *Tartufferie* [hypocrisy], as illness, as misunderstanding, but also morality as cause, as means of healing, as stimulant, as scruple, as poison")? What is the function of morality? How was it developed and changed through the ages? How is it instilled in individuals? What are morality's effects on people's life? What would be the consequences of giving up morality? What could serve as alternatives to morality, in the life of individuals and societies? (*Genealogy*, Prologue, 6).

The subtitle of *On the Genealogy of Morality*, Nietzsche's major treatise on morality, is *A polemic*. A polemic, a declaration of a war of ideas, calls for a battle strategy, which can be reconstructed as follows: first, he aimed to bring attention to the problematic nature of morality, for "in every 'Science of Morals' hitherto, strange as it may sound, the problem of morality itself has been omitted: there has been no suspicion that there was anything problematic there!" (*Beyond*, V, 186). Second, in order to evaluate morality, and in order to avoid having "prejudice about prejudices" he needed a point of view, higher and outside of morality; "some point beyond good and evil to which one has to rise, climb or fly" (*Gay*, V, 380). Stemming from the point of view of the Dionysian philosophy of celebrating life, he could examine morality and evaluations as to whether they have "hindered or fostered human well-being up to now . . . Are they a sign of some emergency, of impoverishment, of an atrophying life? Or is it the other way around? Do they indicate fullness, power, a will for living, courage, confidence, his future?" (*Genealogy*, Prologue, 3).

Third, he had to carry a "find and destroy" mission against contrary positions, among them, those held by psychologists of the "English" school, including his friend Paul Rée (*Genealogy*, Prologue, 7); those held by philosophers and primarily Kant, the champion of imperatives (*Antichrist*, 11), and his great teacher Schopenhauer, the sponsor of the "un egoistic" and the accompanying values of self-denial and pity (*Genealogy*, Prologue, 5); and most important of all, the source of these all, the anti-life values constituted by Judaism and Christianity. These are the religions which brought into the world the idea of sin and self-sacrifice, the ethic of "love your neighbor" and ascetic practices.

The investigation had to be performed simultaneously on three levels, conceptual, social, and individual: he set out to analyze the very act of evaluation and distinction between good and bad, describe the development of norms and mores and their enforcement, and explore bad conscience and guilt feelings. In other words, he intended to study evaluation, morality, and conscience. Accomplishing all these, he would achieve his primary aim of dethroning moral judgments and evaluations. Still, he had to suggest alternative non-moralistic ways of self-management and living with others.

Genealogy, History, and Stories

Nietzsche contended in his *On the Uses and Disadvantages of History for Life* that history is our interpretation of the past to suit our goals now. Being more stories than history, with more or less a hold on reality, it would be better to treat his reconstructions as metaphors. However, the very decision to undertake a genealogical study is a decision not to accept moral judgments as absolute truths, but rather as fluid signs to be interpreted. When he set out to investigate "under what conditions did man devise these value judgments good and evil" (*Genealogy*, Prologue, 3), he was aware of the problem of reconstructing historical developments: "For, indeed, it's obvious which color must be a hundred times more important for a genealogist of morality than this blue: namely, gray, in other words, what has been documented, what can be established as the truth, what really took place, in short, the long and difficult-to-decipher hieroglyphic writing of the past in human morality" (*Genealogy*, Prologue, 7).

VALUES, CONSCIENCE, AND MORALITY

Nietzsche had Zarathustra say, "Many lands saw Zarathustra, and many peoples: thus he discovered the good and bad of many peoples. No greater power did Zarathustra find on earth than good and bad" (*Thus*, I, The thousand and one goals). Evaluations are the utmost act of human creation, the essence of being human. This "greatest power," the opposition of good and bad, is the means of classifying others, the world around us, and subsequently ourselves. There are also other classifications, categories and adjectives, such as truth and lies, strong and weak, and beautiful and ugly; which are sometimes collapsed into the good-bad one.

The Value of Evaluations

Zarathustra taught that evaluations are necessary for physical survival, enabling distinctions between friend and foe, rainy and dry seasons, beasts of prey and harmless animals, and so on. Furthermore, values unite herds as unique and dissimilar to others; "no people could live without first valuing; if a people will maintain itself, however, it must not value as its neighbor values." He also pointed out that values are culturally relative, as each group establishes its own "table of excellencies" which represents "whatever makes them rule and conquer and shine, to the dismay and envy of their neighbors." Such values, like loyalty to comrades, bravery at war, and respect for one's elders, are regarded then as supreme and the meaning of everything else (*Thus*, I, The thousand and one goals).

Morality as Constraint

Evaluations are crucial in the life of individuals: our life, in addition to genes, environment, and chance, is the result of many evaluations followed by decisions, such as where to live, what to study, whom to date, and what to read. Nietzsche suggested a positive understanding of morality as a principle, as a rule of "protracted constraint," narrowing down the number of viable options, therefore being "a sort of tyranny against 'nature' and also against 'reason.'" Morality in this regard is a heuristic for evaluation and narrowing of options, a second-hand booklet with the right answers already penciled in, telling us, even instructing us, which option is "good" and which one is "bad." Thinking, ruling, and acting would not be possible without the discipline of constraint, which is necessary for the trivial reason that it is impossible to do everything together at the same time. This holds true for learning, discovery, and the creation of art, in which choices must be made and priorities set. In this respect, the approach of *laisser-aller*, "everything goes," the hallmark of freedom, is inappropriate and can lead only to mediocre achievements; while the "narrowing of perspectives," the limiting of horizons which incidentally is also an attribute of stupidity, enables life and development. The creative discipline must be learned, and Nietzsche thought that the moral imperative of nature is, "Thou must obey someone, and for a long time; otherwise thou wilt come to grief, and lose all respect for thyself" (*Beyond*, V, 188).

Perspectives of Morality

Evaluations are not absolute; "all evaluation is made from a definite perspective: that of preservation of the individual, a community, a race, a state, a church, a faith, a culture." Unlike animals, whose instinctual behaviors are controlled by circumstances only, people first evaluate a potential action. However, not realizing that evaluations are perspective-bound and not neutral, they tend to experience their evaluations as their own internal states, opening themselves to conflicts between evaluations and drives. The positive side of this "diseased condition" is that it permits examination of the many sides of issues before reaching decisions (*Will*, II, 259).

The Herd and the Individual

In order to comprehend evaluations, morality, and conscience, we must take a look at our origins: humans are animals and they are all members of a herd; from a herd we came and the herd is still in us. Zarathustra made it clear that the creation of values started with the herd, and only later did individuals become creators of values. Individuality is a creation of the herd; "joy in the herd is older than joy in the Ego: and as long as the good conscience is called herd, only the bad conscience says: I" (*Thus*, I, The thousand and one goals), and given this, it is not surprising that guilt feelings will arise when we act against the ancient herd mores.

References to the herd appeared in most of Nietzsche's writings, among them, "morality is herd instinct in the individual" (*Gay*, III, 116) and "morality today in Europe is the morality of the herd animal" (*Beyond*, V, 202). The motif of the birth of morality out of the herd was especially elaborated in two of Nietzsche books, *On the Genealogy of Morality* (1887) and *Beyond Good and Evil* (1886): the first one asked, "Where did we morally come from?" and the second, "Where do we want to go from here?" Expounding on the herd morality, Nietzsche suggested that what was considered moral or extra-moral kept changing and that what supported the survival of the group was considered good; what endangered it was seen as bad. In peaceful times, consideration, fairness, and kindness were considered virtuous; when war broke, daring shiftiness and desire for mastery were more esteemed (*Beyond*, IX, 262).

Fear and Obedience

Morality is built not on love but rather on fear of one's neighbor; "fear is once again the mother of morality." Thus, individuality, independence of mind, what is above and beyond the herd's mediocrity, is treated as dangerous and evil; while conformity, belief in equality and "the happy medium", is glorified as moral and honorable. Fear creates a "morality of timidity," in which everything deemed punishable is avoided, consequently leading to passivity, decay, and decadence (*Beyond*, V, 201). We still carry the herd instinct of obeying authorities under a shallow skin of humanness, and are therefore prone to accept unconditional commands of the "thou shall" or "thou shall not" kind, and most of us still feel guilty to take responsibility and hold positions of command, and prefer to pretend that we only carry out orders (*Beyond*, V, 199).

The Different Shades of Good

Evaluations, we saw, boil down to good or bad, right or wrong marks, and after analyzing the nature of evaluations and exposing their roots in the herd, Nietzsche went on to ask questions about the meaning of "good," in regard to things, persons, and deeds. He did not have to examine any further evaluation in terms of truth or lie, as they were already analyzed and debunked in his *On Truth and Lies in a Nonmoral Sense*, written thirteen years before his *Beyond Good and Evil*.

Good for Whom?

Initially someone was considered "good" if he or she, as if through self-initiative, without external compulsion, was good for something. This something, according to the community mores, could have been practicing revenge, protecting the family's honor, or just being a helpful neighbor. In a gradual and protracted process, such mores became traditions, and traditions became laws. At this point, in order to serve the ultimate "purpose of maintaining a community," any behavior which contradicted the old traditions, from eating prohibited foods to harming one's fellows, was defined as immoral (*Human*, III, 96).

The trick of designating a person as "good," is used by moralizing agents, "the teachers of unselfishness," not because some virtues are good for the person, but because they are desired by society. Thus, the individual becomes a victim of virtues, a function, and an instrument of others. Moral education aims to convince individuals to adopt social values "for their own good." Nietzsche exposed the self-contradiction in such practices, arguing that if altruism is a value, then its reinforcement by society is a show of egoism (*Gay*, I, 21).

The Good of the Good

Unlike the "English psychologists" who claimed that what is considered "good," was historically associated with praise, which served as a reinforcement of altruistic behaviors, Nietzsche suggested that the "good" originated by people who saw themselves as good. They were noble, powerful, higher-ranking, and higher-thinking people who felt and set themselves and their actions up as good, in opposition to everything low, low-minded, common, and vulgar. From this pathos of distance, they felt entitled to define and create their own values as an act of nobility and not from a consideration of utility (*Genealogy*, I, 2). He supported this hypothesis with an etymological argument that in many languages "good" refers to noble persons and "bad" to common lowly ones (*Genealogy*, I, 4).

Stages and Shades of Morality

Nietzsche described the development of morality from historical and sociological points of view. He started his review with pre-history, with "the morality of utility" (*Human*, III, 94), also called "the pre-historical pre-moral period" (*Beyond*, II, 32), an age when the human characteristics of delay of satisfaction, reasoning, and problem-solving skills emerged. Actions were judged then according to their consequences--what served survival was good, what hampered it was not. Next came the "moral period," which began about ten thousand years ago and continues up to the present day. He also envisioned a future development, a post-moral period which will be described when we will deal with moralities rather than a morality.

Conscience and bad conscience are the reflection, the internalization of a society's morality, turned into self-judgment and guiding principle for the behavior of individuals. People are not aware that such a device was implanted in them; by exposing it, Nietzsche helped us cope better with our scourge, the pangs of conscience. He stated his position outright: "The bite of conscience, like a dog biting a stone, is a stupidity" (*Human*, Wanderer, 38). He identified three stages-transitions-revolutions in human civilization, accompanied by much violence and pain, which resulted with the moralities of fear and custom, legal morality, and theistic morality (*Beyond*, II, 32). Each one of them led to typical forms of conscience, which changed human nature and psychology and, combined, constituted conscience as we know now.

Morality of Fear and Custom

The morality of custom established the character of humanity and became a turning point in its history (*Genealogy*, III, 9). The "moral period" commenced with the transition to living in communities, which necessitated agreements and regulation. In this stage, people followed the "principle of honor," making efforts to maintain their peers' respect, by adhering to common mores (*Human*, III, 94). Economic transactions necessitated the development of memory, the basis of making and keeping promises. Humans started living within a time frame, committing themselves to pay in the future for something given in the past. This installing of memory and responsibility was a far cry from a peaceful revolution, and without brutal means, blood, torture, martyrs, sacrifices and mutilations, we would not have "modern psychology," and humans as we know them today:

> Indeed, there is perhaps nothing more fearful and more terrible in the entire prehistory of human beings than the *technique for developing his memory*. "We burn something in so that it remains in the memory. Only something which never ceases to cause pain remains in the memory"—that is a leading principle of the most ancient (unfortunately also the longest) psychology on earth. (*Genealogy*, II, 3)

The emergence of bad conscience, feelings of guilt (in German *Schuld*) was based on the mechanism of debt (*Schulden*): unpaid debts entitled the creditor to inflict physical punishment on the debtor, as a satisfactory, and in those times openly enjoyable expression of anger and getting back an equivalent of what was owed (*Genealogy*, III, 6). This was an act for an act, or a transactional rule of behavior, an association of an act with a memory of pain, without designating the person as bad or a carrier of evil intentions (*Genealogy*, III, 4).

The State and Morality of Law

Laws are tools of ruling legislated by the state. The rudimentary state started as a cruel machine of tyranny and oppression, shaping half-animals into submissive and governable humans. The characteristics of states and humans are therefore an outgrowth of cruelty, inflicted by persons who could command, masters by nature, unscrupulous in the threat and use of violence. While the first type of conscience, with no less cruelty, emerged from voluntary contractual arrangements between members of a community, the second type of conscience emerged out of an external forceful invasion:

> What has he to do with making contracts! We do not negotiate with such beings. They come like fate, without cause, reason, consideration, or pretext. They are present as lightning is present, too fearsome, too sudden, too convincing, too "different" even to become merely hated. Their work is the instinctive creation of forms, the imposition of forms. (*Genealogy*, II, 17)

In order to maintain their position of power, the invaders-rulers used an additional wave of violence. The "subjugation under the law," namely the transition from custom to law morality, was a critical watershed in the evolution of conscience. It was achieved with coercion, pain, and loss of dignity, which took place when the "noble races" were forced by the power of the law to renounce their honor, vendetta, and other forms of revenge. They submitted to this power only under pressure and with feelings of shame (*Genealogy*, III, 9). Nietzsche compared this tremendous change to the transformation of sea animals into land animals: all the instincts that served well the half-beast, such as roaming the wilderness, hunting and killing, enmity, cruelty, the joy of pursuit, attack, and destruction—suddenly became null, and they had to adopt new, more calculated, ways of coping (*Genealogy*, II, 16).

Nietzsche speculated that when their "old instincts for freedom" were crushed and blocked, humans had to turn their violent instincts against themselves. The obstruction of pent-up violence, "the *internalization* of man," brought with it a crucial change, giving birth to the soul, the psychological, and the bad conscience (*Genealogy*, II, 16). This hypothesis can be criticized for disregarding his own theories about the earlier development of language and thinking as tools for survival and living in groups (chapter 2) and for being a claim that cannot be replicated and proven or disproven. In addition, humans did not have to turn cruelty inwards, as they must have already learned how to regulate their instincts. After all, animals and humans are usually prone to violence only when they can get away with it; and even before the state, those who tried to attack stronger foes were obviously killed.

Religion and Sin-Based Conscience

Nietzsche accredited the priests, in the third essay of *On the Genealogy of Morality*, with the development of the latest, ingenious sin-based type of bad conscience. This development took place, at the convergence of two processes: on one hand, the ever-present bifurcation of communities and societies into upper-dogs and underdogs, aristocracy and plebeians, rich and poor, and the natural animosity between these camps; on the other hand, the ascendance of monotheism, the rise of institutionalized religion, and the strengthening of the clerical cast and its use of cunning and psychological manipulation to gain and maintain power.

The clerical cast resorted to scheming and maneuvering between the two sectors to keep its hold on people. Its members, presuming to be God's agent on earth, invented the notions of sin and redemption, and heavenly reward and punishment, which became in their hands weapons of power (*Antichrist*, 26). These notions fell on a fertile ground of the weak, economically and politically underprivileged, who wallowed in feelings of hate and resentment towards the upper-classes and needed to maintain a sense of self-worth and protect themselves from despair. The marriage of priests and plebs gave birth to a morality that, in "the revolt in the morality of the slaves," upturned the existing values, seeing the masters-aristocrats and everything they stood for as a bad and evil enemy, while seeing themselves as just and good victims. This morality subsequently taught to hate and despise not only the perpetrators but also the basic trait of rulers, their Will to Power (*Will*, I, 55).

The theistic morality is a reactive one: if nobility, assertiveness, and happiness are condemned as immoral, then timidity, submissiveness, and piousness are held as moral. Such morals are internalized under the influence of the Church, which has people reckon that if they suffer it must be because they are sinners, and in order to avoid God's punishment they must repent (*Genealogy*, III, 20), which in practice means suffer some more. While the former kind of bad conscience shaped us as human beings, the sin-based bad-conscience added the burden of ascetism and took away our joy of life.

Masters and Slaves

Out of the discussion of the "revolt in morality of the slaves" emerged one of Nietzsche's main themes—the dichotomy of the moralities of masters and slaves. Many threads are woven into this conception—the herd and the last man; nobility, higher persons and the Superman; the fierce and fearless fighting societies, the blond beasts, and the disgusting, weak, poisoned, and domesticated humans, "a teeming mass of worms" (*Genealogy*, I, 11). Nietzsche used this dichotomy to criticize what he considered the slavish mentality of his times' society and culture and to offer instead an illustrious alternative. He is also addressing individuals, who are requested to study the two moralities, re-evaluate their way of life, and choose between two modes of experiencing and directing their life.

The Morality of Masters

Masters are concerned with quality of life, nobility, prestige, and honor. They feel vigorous and proud, not needing anyone's pity. They entertain feelings of gratitude and revenge within the circle of their peers for a long time. They are impulsive, willing to take risks, explosive, readily expressing anger as well as love and appreciation. They evaluate persons, situations, and actions in relation to themselves and their own values of good-bad and noble-base. They despise slaves, seeing them as cowards, suspicious, anxious, narrow-minded, inhibited, and self-abasing, "the species of human dogs who allow themselves to be mistreated, the begging flatterer, above all, the liar." They are hostile and have contempt for "selflessness," feelings of pity, and the "warm heart." They have a profound reverence for the past and ancestral traditions and they reject newcomers, hopes for the future, and "progress." Masters honor duties only with respect to equals and treat others of lower rank at their own discretion. These aristocrats are moved by "pathos of distance," have a hard heart, and are hard on themselves; they are happy in doing and acting, passionate in love, enthusiastic about art.

The Morality of Slaves

Slaves, in an almost a mirror image of the prior morality, are concerned with issues of surviving and making a living. Their life is hard and they do not have the luxury of self-contemplation. Most of the time, they feel oppressed, depressed, suffering, and worn out. They are pessimistic, condemning, cynical, and suspicious towards the entire human situation; they mistrust what appears as free, good, happy, and honored. They evaluate actions and persons in terms of metaphysical-religious ideals of good-evil and in light of defensive criteria of safe-dangerous and loss-gain. They are generally "other-oriented" and need an external antagonist world against which to define themselves—"They are evil, therefore we are good." Slaves experience resentment, avoid action in favor of reaction, and reject everything different from them. They see the masters as selfish, aggressive, dangerous, pitiless, and proud—they, therefore, hate, wish the masters ill, and have fantasies of taking revenge. Slaves have a proclivity for secretiveness, darkness, waiting, cleverness, and retaining long-term poisonous feelings. Their idea of the good person is the harmless one: good-natured, easy to deceive, perhaps a bit stupid, a *bonhomme* (good fellow) blessed with pity, selflessness, warmness, patience, diligence, and helpfulness. The slaves' duty in life is "Love thy neighbor"; their love is a pity; and their happiness is rest (Sabbath), intoxication, and passivity.

Questions and Qualifications

We can expect an enchanting and enticing tune the minute Nietzsche starts playing polarity songs with his Pan flutes, such as Apollonian and Dionysian, masters and slaves, nobility and herd. When the music comes to its end, though, we should not forget to reconsider it, remembering Nietzsche's own admonishment against a one-sided view, "hemiplegia of virtue" (*Will*, II, 351). The criticism of the Apollonian-Dionysian dichotomy (chapter 3) is pertinent here too: Do masters and slaves have essential integral discrete traits or a situation-dependent constellation of many variables on a continuum? Are slaves and masters homogeneous groups, without sub-classes and internal power struggles? Besides, is not the nobility of masters motivated by self-interest as any other group, and does not the law of effect hold true in their case? Don't masters care about utility and survival, and do they not feel depressed after defeat? Did not the nobility demand conformity to its norms? Are their concerns about status, reputation, extravaganza, and caring only about their own kind really so enticing? Moreover, is it not a case of mutual interactive definition, where one group would not have existed without the other?

THE ILLS OF MORALITY

Now that we have a better idea about the origins of morality, its functions, and kinds, we are prepared to face the massive psychological damages of the prevailing morality and its internalization as conscience. Nietzsche's conclusion is trenchant: "The human being has imprisoned itself thanks to his 'formal conscience.'" (*Beyond*, 188) And his verdict was clear-cut: "Morality itself, in the form of honesty, compels us to deny morality (*Will*, II, 404). We must understand the sneakiness, the psychological distortions, and ill consequences of morality, "the Circe of mankind," in order to avoid its punishment; "it has demoralized everything, even to the terrible nonsense of making love 'altruistic'" (*Ecce*, Books, 5).

Morality was needed in the early stages of human development; many chains were shackled on persons to distinguish them from animals, and indeed they became "gentler, more spiritual, more joyful, more reflective than any animal." As far as enlightened people are concerned, the chains are not useful anymore and their burden painfully restricts the freedom of movement. Some people should better remain chained, because breaking the chains is not suitable for all; "only the ennobled may be given freedom of the spirit." They alone are capable of "living for the sake of joy and no other goal" (*Human*, Wanderer, 350). Did I hear right, "Joy and no other goal"? What about life's mission (chapter 8), the Superman, and the Will to Power? And how does it agree with Nietzsche's dismissal of happiness? Well, as he said, "One is fruitful only at the cost of being rich in contradictions" (*Twilight*, Morality, 2) and being fruitful ourselves, we will have to make up our mind on how to lead our life.

The Medicine of Morality

Nietzsche called morality "that most famous of all medicines" (*Gay*, V, 345) and he showed us how this medicine was dispensed, in the darker ages of pre-history and history, by means of terror, pain, and suffering. He has also shown how it continued to be maintained daily from birth on, by means of moral socialization. Nietzsche recalled his own childhood to describe how children are made to swallow this bitter pill in their family environment, where the all-powerful parents convince a loving, dependent child that it is all done for her or his own good and happiness. Allegedly for this purpose, they castrate the will to mastery and power, and repress emotions, inclinations, and passions, portraying them all as dangerous and bad. The means used in this indoctrination are not always physically violent, not necessarily sophisticated or scientific: "Small and great clever sayings and affectations, afflicted with the musty enclosed smell of ancient household remedies or old women's wisdom, all baroque and unreasonable in form—because they direct themselves to 'all,' because they generalize where we should not generalize" (*Beyond*, V, 198).

As an adult recollecting his upbringing memories, he still had to exclaim repeatedly: "Prudence, prudence, prudence, mixed in with stupidity, stupidity, stupidity," making the reader feel his pain and revulsion. The regular demands made in childhood, without any reason, by admired or feared parents and other adults, constitute the content of our conscience, giving it the nature of compulsion to obey unconditionally in acting or refraining from acting. Conscience precludes asking, "*Why* must I?"; while giving up on conscience entails acting with "because" and "why." Nietzsche concluded, "The belief in authorities is the source of the conscience: it is therefore not the voice of God in the heart of man but the voice of some men in man" (*Will*, I, 52).

Mores are born out of the combined effect of two values cultivated in children by their parents: one is "society is worth more than the individual"; the other is "an enduring advantage is to be preferred to ephemeral advantage." Consequently, individuals feel that they have to sacrifice their interests in favor of the group. We have been brought up "not as an individual but as a member of a whole, as a digit of a majority." After a job so well done, there is no more need for external coercion, because "an individual brings to bear upon himself, by means of his morality, the tyranny of the majority" (*Human*, Assorted, 89). Moral socialization is further cemented by adding to these two values the errors of free will and responsibility, which are perpetuated through child-rearing practices. People are made first responsible for their actions and the consequences of their actions, and later for their feelings and nature, which is often translated by parents into "bad child" admonitions, "shame on you" exclamations, and "you should not have done it" rebukes. Nietzsche concluded, "and thus we come to understand that the history of moral feelings is the history of an error, an error called 'responsibility,' which in turn rests on an error called 'freedom of the will'" (*Human*, II, 39).

The Dangers of Fictions

A distinction must be made between objects and their evaluations; "the world is not good or evil" neither is it "the best or the worst"—it is what it is. Moral evaluations can be made only in regard to persons, and even then it is not always justified. In any case, we must give up "both the reviling and the glorifying view of the world" (*Human*, I, 28) and more generally, "there are altogether no moral facts." Moral evaluations, like religions, take for granted a belief in "realities which are no realities." Morality is just an interpretation, or actually misinterpretation of facts, typical of ignorant ages, lacking the concept of truth, in which the real and the imaginary are not yet distinguished (*Twilight*, Mankind, 1). Nietzsche reiterated, saying it as loud as he could, "There is no such thing as moral phenomena, but only a moral interpretation of phenomena" (*Beyond*, IV, 108), and if this was not enough, he added, "My chief proposition: there are no moral phenomena, there is only a moral interpretation of these phenomena. This interpretation itself is of extra-moral origin" (*Will*, II, 258). If there are no moral phenomena, values and concepts of "good" and "evil" must be all delusions, providing us with the illusion of permanence, which is hard to get rid of. Zarathustra taught us that "unchanging good and evil does not exist! From out of themselves they must overcome themselves again and again" (*Thus*, II, Self-overcoming).

Morality against Life

Nietzsche proclaimed that "Morality is vampirism," because it teaches contempt of the primary life instincts. It invented soul and spirit in order to overpass the body, to find impurity in sex, to see as evil the need to expand and love the self. It rejects nature altogether and sanctifies the unnatural, making persons subservient to the law of the Categorical Imperative. The anti-life moral values in themselves, lauding selflessness, objectivity, and neighbor love, are signs of decay and loss of direction, making Nietzsche wonder, "What! Is humanity itself in a state of decadence? Has it always been so?" (*Ecce*, Destiny, 7). Adopting such a morality implies giving up the instinct for privileges, the feeling of entitlement, and the freedom of creative natures, consequently placing such persons and minds in a low order of rank (*Will*, IV, 879).

The self-righteousness of the "good and just" is dangerous to other people and to humanity at large. They feel and say, "we already know what is good and just, we possess it too; woe to those who are still searching for it!" These bearers of the "truth" are the enemies of all creation and innovation, calling anyone daring to think and act differently a law-breaker (*Thus*, Old and new law-tables, 26). The distance between calling a person a law breaker, imprisonment, and execution, can be very short. Reader, please think about nowadays' "good and just" and remember their murdered victims.

Morality Kept Alive

If morality is a dangerous fiction, why do persons subscribe to it? Why do they not give it up? The decision to stick to morality is not a moral decision, and neither are these persons moral. In addition to supplying a *post hoc* rationalization for decisions, Nietzsche suggested additional psychological reasons, among them subservience to authorities, pride, egoism, despair, and lack of critical thinking (*Daybreak,* II, 97). Morality is kept alive as a decision-making rule, which for practical purposes limits one's viable options, leading in some cases to achievements that make life worth living (*Beyond,* V, 188). This, however, is totally different from the religion-flavored morality of imperatives, "Do this and that, refrain from this and that—and then you will be happy! And if you don't . . ." This kind of morality is "the original sin of reason, the immortal unreason." Happy and admirable human beings, in contradistinction, rely on their instincts and impulses to act or avoid action, to manage their relations with the world and other people. Their morality is not above them but rather something internal (*Twilight,* Errors, 2). Modern scholastic ethicists toil with what is known as the "trolley problem,"[3] debating which of two actions is more ethical: do nothing and let five people die, or intervene and save them by actively leading to the death of a fat bystander. Nietzsche would have told them to wait patiently until they encounter this imaginary situation and then let their instincts take over.

In his notes, Nietzsche asked "to what extent morality has been detrimental to life," and we already know some of the answers. He then moved to "counter-reckoning," pointing out its "usefulness for life": it serves as a principle, an instrument that preserves the general whole by putting limitations on its members; it protects humans from the inner peril of their passions, albeit by keeping them "mediocre"; it comforts humans exposed to the life-destroying effects of profound misery and sorrow, by a promise of a better afterworld; finally, it is a principle that opposes the fearful outbursts of the powerful against "the lowly" (*Will,* II, 266).

Skepticism regarding morality is commendable; yet, giving it up completely risks falling into nihilism (*Will,* I, 3). Nietzsche's audience was not the majority, "the herd," but rather a select group of higher individuals. Having them in mind, his complicated challenge was to destroy the old morality, avoid nihilism, and still have pride left, "Morality as the only scheme of interpretation by which man can endure himself—a kind of pride" (*Will,* II, 270).

From Morality to Moralities

If morality is indeed a dangerous fiction and if we are brave enough to forgo it, what then? Are we doomed to be clueless? What northern star will give us direction in life? How are we going to answer the question, "Then is no man accountable?" (*Human*, Assorted, 33). Nietzsche rejected the one and only morality and suggested, instead, moving from a ready-made morality to many varied moralities made to order. "The will to a single morality is thereby proved to be a tyranny over other types" (*Will*, II, 315). He envisioned an "extra-moral stage" (*Beyond*, II, 32) and "self-determined morality" (*Human*, III, 94), in which morality is transcended and becomes irrelevant to the evaluation of human deeds; in which people, who know that morality is an illusion, live and behave as "a collective of individuals," following their inclinations and using their insight about the origins and functions of morality in their considerations (*Human*, Wanderer, 44). The one-morality claim of the "herding animal" must be rejected. And instead of the Christo-European morality, "many other moralities, and above all higher moralities, are or should be possible" (*Beyond*, V, 203).

In addition to ruling out a "one and only" exclusive morality, Nietzsche rejected a "*goal* that stands above mankind and above the individual" and called for an experimental morality, for giving oneself a goal—not permanent, not determined by others, nor above the person but rather from within, self-determined and tentative (*Will*, II, 260). A plethora of individualized moralities is called for because there are many individual wills, affects, and temperaments. Nietzsche the Overturner concluded, "in short, systems of morals are only *a sign-language of the emotions*" (*Beyond*, V, 187). The same idea was also phrased in terms of the Will to Power: "Aim of moral evaluations is life: life is Will to Power, its meaning is exegesis, interpretation carried by our affects, our physiological conditions" (*Will*, II, 255). This perspective will help us read existing systems of morality by backtracking from abstract principles to the feelings and personalities of the persons who postulated or subscribed to them. More importantly, it will help us write our own morality. Thus Nietzsche annulled Christian morality by showing that it is an expression of its slavish founders' feeling of resentment, and he contested Kant's categorical imperative by arguing that it proves only that Kant himself was prone to obedience.

Morality-Free Judgments

Persons who judge themselves in moral terms might feel and see it as a supreme achievement. Zarathustra saw them as people who relapsed into a lowly suffering-inducing condition that can only be redeemed by a quick death. Nietzsche advocated life without moralistic judgments, self-righteousness, and guilt-feelings; in other words, to live as the title of his book taught, "Beyond good and evil." Abandoning moralistic judgments, we should appraise things differently. "You should say 'enemy' but not 'miscreant'; you should say 'invalid' but not 'scoundrel'; you should say 'fool' but not 'sinner'" (*Thus*, I, The pale criminal). He wished to end moral dichotomies altogether by showing that what is praised as moral is in principle identical to what is seen as immoral, and that the very designation "moral" is made with immoral means for immoral ends: "My purpose: to demonstrate the absolute homogeneity of all events and the application of moral distinctions as conditioned by perspective" (*Will*, II, 272).

A High Spirituality

Morality is superfluous because higher life-supporting values exist; "a high spirituality is beyond comparison with any sort of good behavior or worthiness of a merely moral man" (*Beyond*, VII, 219). Against the limiting and prohibiting Christian morality, which he unmasked, Nietzsche put forward the ancient Greek Dionysian-tragic ideal. He sharpened and emphasized the differences between these two worlds: "Have you understood me? Dionysus versus Christ" (*Ecce*, Zarathustra, 7). His preference of Dionysus over Christ already appeared in an early publication, where he maintained that the Greeks were more ethical than modern humanity: "The whole visibility of their soul in action shows that they were without shame. They did not know the bad conscience. They were more open, more passionate, as artists are; they carried with them a kind of childlike naivety, and so all the bad things they did carry with them a kind of purity, something approaching the holy" (*Philologists*).

Emergent Morality

Could the examination of one's emotions be all it takes to build a personal system of morality? It is not as simple as that, because the language of emotions, like the language of dreams, needs interpretation. Interpretations are not obvious as we are multiplicities, and different parts in us might feel unlike the others. Our drives struggle to gain control over other drives without taking into account our general good, and with little room for our conscious intervention. Whatever we decide will represent something in us, and for this reason "selflessness does not exist." Each decision is a decision to prefer one thought or wish over another. Thus we divide ourselves and sacrifice one part for another: "In morality, man treats himself not as an '*individuum*,' but as a '*dividuum*'" (*Human*, II, 57).

Creating our own values is not necessarily a somber act of inscribing on stone with hammer and chisel; it is sometimes not so different from developing an individual taste, in which persons determine their own preferences and check whether they like something or not (*Thus*, II, The sublime ones). Nietzsche acclaims a new self-reinforcing private virtue, not based on the ideas of a heavenly paymaster. To be virtuous, we must purge ourselves of all remnants of the ingrained good-bad evaluations. "You are too pure for the dirt of the words: revenge, punishment, reward, retribution" (*Thus*, II, The virtuous). We create our values by action, which should be therefore chosen well; "the light of your virtue is still traveling even when its task is done." We should aspire for higher values, not dictated by external forces, neither conditioned by weak drives or strong inhibitions ("tick-tock-virtue") nor drawn by one's devil (*Thus*, II, The virtuous). Nietzsche offered us virtuous virtues instead: "Ah, my friends! That *your* Self be in the action, as the mother is in the child: let that be *your* maxim of virtue!" (*Thus*, II, The virtuous).

The Gospel of Innocence and Irresponsibility

The critique of morality was reinforced by Nietzsche's affirmation of life, deriving from his notion of Eternal Recurrence, in which life events are seen as a necessity and fatality: everything is the way it is, because it had to be so, and could not have been otherwise; the direct implication being that humans are innocent and irresponsible and cannot be held accountable for their actions and decisions. Nietzsche saw this position as his new gospel, new knowledge, and new habit. Unlike the old opposite gospel of sin and guilt, there is no place here, for blaming or praising nature and necessity—all evaluations, distinctions, condemnations, and appreciations are worthless. Human behavior is the result of "chemical processes, and the clash of elements"; humans are torn between different motives, and it is one of them—not us—that wins and decides for us. We are in the hands of our abilities and drives; "man may act as he can, that is, as he must." Nevertheless, our intelligence (if we are not stupid) has some role in deciding how far to let the wish for pleasure carry us (*Human*, II, 107).

Nietzsche anticipated adamant resistance to these ideas, as they go against the customary ways of thinking and seeing the world. However, "the sun of the new gospel," can offer consolation, affirmation, and wisdom, and he tried to help us swallow the bitter pill arguing that pleasure, egoism, and vanity, as well as errors and illusions, often grant "a sense for true and just knowledge" and some degree of "self-illumination and self-redemption." Besides, everything in the field of morality has evolved, is mutable and vacillating, "everything is fluid" and hence, rather than judging, Nietzsche called for a different kind of knowledge, "that of understanding, non-loving, non-hating, surveying," in other words, he was condoning mindfulness, a habit with which we can hopefully become wise and innocent ourselves (*Human*, II, 107). Ten years later, Nietzsche's "new gospel," appeared as the answer to the question, "What alone can be our doctrine?" and the principles of irresponsibility, innocence, and necessity were put forward in forceful words:

> That no one gives a man his qualities—neither God, nor society, nor his parents and ancestors, nor he himself . . . No one is responsible for man's being there at all, for his being such-and-such, or for his being in these circumstances or in this environment. The fatality of his essence is not to be disentangled from the fatality of all that has been and will be. (*Twilight*, The four great errors, 8)

The doctrine reaffirmed that humans do not exist for some purpose, or because of some will, and are not intended to attain any ideals of happiness and morality. "We have invented the concept of 'end': in reality there is no end." We cannot be held responsible, as there is no *causa prima*, an independent primary cause for actions; "one is necessary, one is a piece of fatefulness, one belongs to the whole, one is in the whole." It follows that there is nothing that could judge, measure, or compare our actions, as they are an integral part of everything there is. This perspective is the "great liberation; with this alone is the innocence of becoming restored" (*Twilight*, The four great errors, 8). The new doctors of the soul understand that it is their role to help people regain their innocence; the problem-difficulty they have to deal with is burdensome enough. We are the result of our traits, dispositions, and past failures, and not their cause, and yet, we are also a cause of what comes after us, a link or bridge into the future. We are thus a fatality in two senses: "You yourself, poor fearful man, are the implacable *Moira* [fate] enthroned even above the gods that govern all that happens; you are the blessing and the curse and in any event the fetters in which the strongest lies captive; in you the whole future of man is redetermined: it is of no use for you to shudder when you look at yourself" (*Will*, I, 61).

No Room for Alarm

To those of us who are alarmed by such blame-free attitudes, Nietzsche promised casually that immoralists cannot harm virtue, any more than anarchists can harm princes—on the contrary, "it is only because they have been shot at that they once again sit securely on their thrones. Moral: we must shoot at morals" (*Twilight*, Maxims, 36). He reassured further, that giving up morality is not a license to commit hideous crimes: "It goes without saying that I do not deny— unless I am a fool— that many actions called immoral ought to be avoided and resisted or that many called moral ought to be done and encouraged—but I think the one should be encouraged and the other avoided for other reasons than hitherto" (*Daybreak*, II, 103).

Nietzsche shunned the exclusive and obligatory morality, but he did not call for revolutions and certainly had his notions of decency. He made fiery declarations indeed—"everything is false, nothing is forbidden"—but they were declared as a matter of principle, while in practice Nietzsche advised "to do one's duty according to a definite rough scheme within which a community [exists]." Moreover, it is fine to use the expressions "right" and "wrong" in a narrow "bourgeois" sense (*Will*, II, 267). Paradoxically, now that we understand how conventional morality is made of lies and appearance, and have exposed virtue as a form of immorality, Nietzsche lets them reenter through the back door, permitting us to employ virtue, the "fairest of falsehoods." Morality is part of "fundamental immorality of all existence," a form of dear and rare vice, made more acceptable by Nietzsche's saving it from the despotism of the majority, and from its rigidity, emptiness, fraudulence, and coercion (*Will*, II, 328).

We thus find ourselves in an interesting situation, where not behaviors but motivations are evaluated, resulting in identical behaviors being judged differently. Suppose a person helps a stranger: if it was motivated by a "love thy neighbor" religion-inspired upbringing, it is seen negatively. If the person is helpful by nature or enjoys helping, it will be viewed positively. The problem is that determining motivations is not a clear-cut matter and we are liable to commit the error of "the excluded middle," not allowing for a certain upbringing combined with a helpful disposition.

APPLIED MORALITY

To recapitulate, we went *Beyond Good and Evil*, meaning that we had a meta-morality discussion of morality's origins and function and that we learned to see ourselves and the world in non-moralistic terms. We then considered switching from one standard morality to a variety of moralities. Most of the discussion centered on individuals' choice-making. However, morality is also used in the political and public domains, in the relations between citizens and states, either out of an honest wish to do the right thing or as a maneuver serving self-interests. It is in this realm that the terms rights, duties, and justice are often heard. Morality is a cornerstone of criminology, where criminals are seen as evil and therefore duly punished. How did Nietzsche relate to these terms and uses?

Rights, Justice, and the State

Nietzsche provides a down-to-earth transactional or symmetrical way of understanding justice, one based on contract ethics. Justice or fairness, it is presumed, began with processes of negotiation and bartering between claims of persons with equal power. "Thus, justice is requital and exchange on the assumption of approximately equal positions of strength" (*Human*, III, 92). Justice supports survival, as two parties decided each on his or her part, out of egoistic reasons, that it is safer to give in a little than risk getting hurt and losing everything. Justice is the feeling that, after a process of voluntary negotiation, a fair deal was reached, and in this respect, gratitude as well as revenge are in the realm of justice, giving the feeling of a fair response corresponding to the actions of others.

Rights are gained whenever we are given something of value (support, education, or goods), by persons considered as equals, competent to negotiate, with enough resources to give in return. Everything determined without the two elements of equal force and voluntary negotiation has nothing to do with justice. This is also the case with duties, which are based on mutuality of give-and-take, and thus we owe nothing to those with whom we made no contract or did not carry any exchange of services. However, when these conditions are met, it would be an act of nobility to recognize and fulfill our duties while in all other cases, when these conditions are not met, "one acts as one thinks best: that justice can be hoped for (unfortunately not counted on) only *inter pares* [among equals]" (*Will*, IV, 943). Pay attention to "as one thinks best": Nietzsche did not object to personal acts of generosity, such as giving away or sharing one's fortune with others if one feels like doing so. He only decried religious and political indoctrination and enforcement, which make such acts mandatory. The very fulfilling of duties is self-reinforcing, as it bolsters the perception and recognition of the self and others as powerful enough to give back in proportion to what was received. "That is how rights originate: recognized and guaranteed degrees of power" (*Daybreak*, II, 112).

Equality and Human Rights

Nowadays, the idea of the equality of all human beings is considered to be an essential feature of morality, and Nietzsche's reluctance to agree with this assumption is seen by some moralists as sacrilege. How could they expect an immoralist to see any political interest as a matter of morality? Nietzsche, of course, would have seen marching with the banners of "social justice" and "affirmative action" under the flag of equality as a modern version of the slave morality and the utmost indications of decadence and pessimism. I am not sure as to whether, had he lived later, he would have mentioned John Rawls by name, but for sure he would have rejected the distinction between "genuine" equality of opportunity, and "formal" equality of opportunity,[4] as another version of the Christian anti-life "true world." He would have reminded us that equality, genuine and formal alike, is no more than any other ideal, a "swindler" abstract term.

Human rights are conceived as inalienable, fundamental, universal (applicable everywhere), and egalitarian (the same for everyone). As a political development, such doctrines, declarations, and beliefs are welcome, especially if they diminish killings, persecutions, and undue imprisonments. Nevertheless, Nietzsche would have obviously questioned the terms natural, egalitarian, and universal. As far as he was concerned, no one is born with inherent rights—"one has no right to existence or to work, to say nothing of a right to 'happiness': the individual human being is in precisely the same case as the lowest worm" (*Will*, III, 759). Yet, Nietzsche did recognize modest rights of weaker parties. He gave as an example a city under siege by a greater power, which can establish some form of equalization by threatening to burn itself down, thus inflicting damages on the stronger party. Likewise, a conceived potential of vehement demonstration of dissatisfaction by the masses is behind the recognition of some rights: "The right originally extends as far as the one appears to the other to be valuable, essential, permanent, invincible, and the like. In this regard, even the weaker of the two has rights though they are more modest" (*Human*, III, 93).

In countries where an extreme gap in income exists between the top and bottom echelons, the lower ones receive some form of monetary compensation, described in democracies as their right, or in autocracies as the ruler's benevolent gifts. In both cases, this is actually done in order to avoid a threat to the regime in the form of economic collapse, political unrest, strikes, demonstrations, and riots. Nietzsche would have said that behind the current discourse about rights lies a political agenda and that in principle, nobody has a right for free education or free medical care, and even "freedom of speech" is not a right, as in these cases nothing is exchanged and nothing is contracted. He would not have denied that the rhetoric of rights and justice can be an effective political tool. We disillusioned witnesses of the political game, who understand the falsity of justice and rights, will simply have to consider the demands for benefits and privileges on their own merit, asking ourselves whether we prefer the practical consequences of supporting or opposing them.

Allegiance to the State

Nietzsche remained silent about a more crucial question, mandatory in any comprehensive discussion of morality, namely, whether obeying the laws is a moral issue at all. This, of course, is what the state claims, often with the backing of religion, which gives a heavenly approval to the dictates of the ruling party. Differently put, in addition to the fear of punishment, do we have any duties towards the state? The state tries to convince us that we do and that we contracted with it by means of the democratic process. Nietzsche saw the state as a necessary evil, certainly better than anarchy, and he maintained that humans cannot exist safely and peacefully without it. Similarly, despite serious reservations about democracy, he granted that it might well be better than other systems of governing. Thus, not out of love, but out of responsibility, not wanting to undermine these institutions, he kept silent about the question of duties towards them.

In any case, immoralists are not impressed by the claim that the laws have something to do with (the non-existing) morality, and nothing can change the basic fact that the state can put each one of us in jail if we do not do obey its ordinances; while we, on our side, can in the best case write a letter of complaint to the local newspaper. Finding the remote roots of the state in a violent act of invasion, Nietzsche commented, "What has he to do with making contracts! We do not negotiate with such beings" (*Genealogy*, II, 17). Thus, we did not contract with the state and equal we are certainly not. Although, Nietzsche did not say so explicitly, it can be concluded that no justice, no duties, and no rights are relevant to a person's relation with the state. I will return to the state in the next chapter, this time from the perspective of Nietzsche's social psychology.

The Penal System

Nietzsche the Overturner applied his personality and morality psychologies to the issues of crime, criminals, and punishment, to arrive at a new approach to criminology. The standard common-sense line of reasoning is that persons who committed an evil act are not different from others with the exception of having an evil side to them. Being responsible for their actions, such persons deserve to be punished and shamed. The punishment will rehabilitate the criminal and deter him or her, as well as others, from committing crimes in the future. Nietzsche held that all these conjectures are wrong.

Zarathustra taught that criminals are predators by nature, simple-minded or mad persons whose constitution and faulty interpretation of murder wishes (that others probably control successfully) lead them to actual crimes. They are not evil, neither is society good, and they cannot be rehabilitated. Criminals do not feel and are not influenced by remorse and atonement. We must recognize their need for murder and restrain them "for the love of life," to prevent more casualties, but not as punishment (*Thus*, I, The pale Criminal).

Crime is natural in the sense of having past evolutionary advantages. Aggressive behaviors express the drive for preserving life and the need to gain pleasure and avoid displeasure. "Giving pain in and of itself does not exist. Criminal actions are not based on free will or free choice, just as is the case with a dog killing a kitten" (*Human*, III, 99). We misunderstand predatory animals and are afraid of them, forgetting that predatory humans, such as Cesar Borgia, exist too. This misunderstanding of nature, and the need to maintain "moderate zones" led to looking for pathology or evilness in these "healthiest of all tropical monsters," resulting with discrediting the "tropical man" as sick or sinful (*Beyond*, V, 197).

Nietzsche's dictum of human innocence and complete irresponsibility disputes the customary association between behaviors and punishment or reward. A person who is punished does not deserve it, as the person did nothing intentionally, and is only used by society to frighten and deter others from doing the same. Similarly, a person rewarded did not do anything intentionally and again she is used to as an example to others. Society needs such means and, therefore, needs to maintain these fictions; "the wise man punishes not because men have acted badly, but so they will not act badly" and thus, punishment and reward, blame and praise, built upon people's vanity, became an effective means of socialization (*Human*, IV, 105).

Punishment, like other social institutions, underwent many changes and served a variety of purposes (*Genealogy*, II, 13). Yet, its effect on those punished, remained basically the same: "On the whole, punishment makes men harder and colder, it concentrates, it sharpens the feeling of alienation; it strengthens the power to resist" (*Genealogy*, II, 14). Punishment, even more than the crime performed, only isolates persons from their society, leaving them with injuries and incurable hurt. "One emerges from punishment as an enemy of society. From then on, it has one more enemy" (*Will*, III, 742). Nietzsche agreed that in many cases criminals must be incarcerated for long periods, if necessary, with a small but significant difference—not as punishment against them, but as a safety measure for the sake of society. We should not judge them morally, but with understanding, as if they were Neanderthals suddenly caught in a high-tech world, or alternatively, as rebels holding a grudge against the social order. Their actions are not necessarily admirable, but can often be understood and they should not be punished, but rather suppressed. The security measure is needed, but contempt and punishment are not called for; "punishment does not purify, for crime does not sully." Criminals should be considered as persons of courage, who risk their lives, honor, and freedom, and, therefore, they can be somewhat amended only if treated respectfully: "moral contempt causes greater indignity and harm than any crime" (*Will*, III, 740).

NOTES

1. Paul Henri Thiry Holbach and Denis Diderot, *The System of Nature or, Laws of the Moral and Physical World* (Kitchener, Ont.: Batoche, 2001).

2. Richard Seaver, *The Marquis De Sade: The Complete Justine, Philosophy in the Bedroom, and Other Writings* (New York: Grove Press, 1965).
http://www.sade-ecrivain.com/Dialogue-Between-a-Priest-and-a-Dying-Man.html

3. The problem was first introduced by Philippa Foot in her "The Problem of Abortion and the Doctrine of the Double Effect in Virtues and Vices," *Oxford Review* 5 (1967): 1–7. It was debated in many additional papers and a later discussion can be

found in David Edmonds, *Would You Kill the Fat Man? The Trolley Problem and What Your Answer Tells Us about Right and Wrong* (Princeton, NJ: Princeton University Press, 2013).

4. John Rawls, *A Theory of Justice*, Revised ed. (Cambridge, MA: Harvard University Press, 1999).

FIVE

Social Psychology

The word "society" is derived from the Latin *Socius* (companion) and *Socialis* (united, living with others). Historically, as we saw in the last chapter, the herd preceded individuality and humans could not have survived living by themselves. Yet living with others is not a simple matter at all. We all share, in different degrees, Nietzsche's dilemma: "In solitude the solitary man consumes himself, in the crowd the crowd consumes him, Now choose" (*Human*, Assorted, 348).

OUT OF THE HERD

Nietzsche's material collated here to make up his social psychology, deals with the interrelations between individuals, and between individuals and human-made social institutions. Unlike most social psychologists, Nietzsche was open about his social difficulties and about his guiding values, and he confessed "that every association of human beings makes us shudder slightly . . . we cannot persuade our nose to give up its prejudice against the proximity of a human being" (*Gay*, V, 379). His goal was the advancement of humans, at least, those who are up to it, from herd creatures to individuality and personhood. Self-improvement does not stop here, and he challenged persons to grow further, ascending on a ladder of ranks, climbing up the pyramid, through intertwined routes: from slaves to masters; from commons to nobility; from the last man to the Superman; from small people to higher persons. Nietzsche's social psychology is about individuals in societies, and he certainly did not commit what he saw as a basic error, "to place the goal in the herd and not in single individuals! The herd is a means, no more!" (*Will*, III, 766).

Nietzsche describe the social realm, but also criticized it, and seeing himself as an "architect of the future" (*Untimely*, History, 6), he studied and compared the weak world of the moderns, "with our anxious self-solicitude and neighbor-love, with our virtues of work, modesty, legality, and scientism—accumulating, economic, machinelike," with the "gold standard" of the great ages of the Renaissance and the ancient Greek world (*Twilight*, Skirmishes, 37). He studied individuals, friendships, and couple relations in the context of their immediate environment, class, culture, and state. While psychotherapists are very careful to avoid such "value-laden" issues, Nietzsche believed that self-transformation would be impossible without a keen understanding of the impact, often detrimental, of politics and culture on the life of persons. Individuality must be guarded against external influences as people are in danger of internalizing "a phantom ego," created and transmitted by their society. People live in "a fog of habits, opinions, and fictions." Consequently, society turns people into conforming standardized products and most people fail to set up a real ego, accessible and understood by them (*Daybreak*, II, 105).

Know Your Environment

Nietzsche rejected the "know yourself" Socratic dictum because he preferred life and action over contemplation, and because it is inherently an impossible project to accomplish. His social psychology, in effect, replaced it with a new pronouncement, that we can deem "know your environment!" His advice would be to examine our social institutions and culture carefully and know what of them to adopt and what to avoid or counteract. He criticized the sociology of his times for promoting decadence and weakness, by virtue of its denial of differences among people, and its unconditional acceptance and support of their culture's values. It is arguable that the current social psychology is not that much different.

As an alternative, Nietzsche put forward his "fundamental innovations," which included "In place of 'sociology,' a theory of the forms of domination and in place of 'society,' the culture complex as my chief interest" (*Will*, II, 462). My understanding of Nietzsche's innovation is that "the system" (society and state combined) controls and shapes individuals by means of sheer power ("domination") and by means of transmission of values and attitudes, ingrained in the innocent looking ingredients of culture ("complex").

An Indifferent Observer

Nietzsche's views on society and individuals clashed with his times' notions of morality, and his criticism of the "morality of sympathy" can be easily directed at the various promoters of the "social justice" agenda today. He did not delude himself, knowing that once such notions were absorbed into culture, nothing much could be done about them. "To be indifferent—that too is a form of strength" (*Twilight*, Skirmishes, 37).

Knowing that politics will not promote the values he believed in, Nietzsche had very low expectations from it. Therefore, philosophers (lovers of wisdom) have to resort to observing their culture with enough irony and detachment; draw their conclusions and go about their own business:

> Every philosophy which believes that the problem of existence is touched on, not to say solved, by a political event is a joke and pseudo-philosophy. Many states have been founded since the world began; that is an old story. How should a political innovation suffice to turn men once and for all into contented inhabitants of the earth? (*Untimely*, Schopenhauer, 4)

All of us live in two kinds of relationships—with others and with ourselves, and Nietzsche presented two basic orientations to them, vertical and horizontal, which we will explore. This will be followed by reviewing his notions of individuality and personhood, the conditions of being differentiated from the masses and being above them. From here we will go to examine nobility and the gallery of higher persons and move to Nietzsche's observations about intimate relations—friendship, love, marriage, and sexuality. Lastly, we will examine individuals in the larger contexts of "forms of domination" of state, economy, military and the "culture complex."

THE PYRAMID AND THE LEVEL PLAYING FIELD

The metaphor of a pyramid connotes a vertical orientation, with different levels in a hierarchy, such as from childhood to maturity and from the practical and the mundane to the spiritual and sublime. It describes different levels from low to high, in social class, income, or any other attribute. The level playing field metaphor, in contradistinction, implies a horizontal orientation of relations between equals; it describes a range of variables, on a common denominator, all of similar value. Nietzsche did not use this metaphor explicitly, although he mentioned "leveling down" (*Gay*, V, 377). The image is taken from the world of sport, where competing teams or individuals must have an equal chance of winning and it is the root of social justice or 'leveling' philosophies and politics. One orientation, seen by him as an "ascending form of life," calls for climbing up, striving for goals, self-improvement, being better than others, joining the few, becoming differentiated from and disdainful of what is considered base. The other orientation invites reaching out, pity and compassion, being equal to others, and staying together with the many, which Nietzsche considered to be a descending mode.

After some exposure to Nietzsche's stance on this polarity, we realize that with a clever use of rhetoric, proponents of each orientation can describe themselves in glowing terms, and portray their antagonists with depreciating adjectives. Could any arguments change our initial disposition towards one of the orientations? We can only suspect that it was not only theoretical considerations, but also his temperament and experiences that led Nietzsche to support one orientation against the other. He presented us with an either-or situation, confronting two unbridgeable opposites, identifying totally with one of them and bashing the other mercilessly. It can be said that he was only mirroring or reacting to society's stance of praising one orientation and nullifying the other, and that by this overturning he made us reevaluate our own position. Only towards the end of his discourse on *What Is Noble?* did he raise the possibility that a person with high aspirations who used others in his ascent "either as a means or as a delay and an obstacle—or as a temporary place to rest" can, upon reaching his goals, show his fellow human beings "high-quality goodness" (*Beyond*, IX, 273).

Hierarchy and Order of Rank

Nietzsche discussed ranking frequently, declaring, "my philosophy aims at an ordering of rank" (*Will*, II, 287) and, "One believes in an order of rank and not in equality and equal rights" (*Beyond*, II, 30). Supporters of equality, equate it with justice, and he clarified that justice is not theirs only. "For justice speaks thus to me: 'Men are not equal'" (*Thus*, II, The Tarantulas). The high ranks in a pyramid are necessarily narrow. "All great, all beautiful things can never be common property: beauty is for the few" (*Twilight*, Germans, 5). He repeated this saying in reference to the superior caste, "only the most intellectual of men have any right to beauty, to the beautiful; only in them can goodness escape being weakness" (*Antichrist*, 57). Social hierarchies are an essential human characteristic, inherent in language itself. The unique human achievement of transforming perceptual metaphors into concepts enabled something impossible until then, "the construction of a pyramidal order according to castes and degrees, the creation of a new world of laws, privileges, subordinations, and clearly marked boundaries" (*Truth*, 1).

Pyramids appeared in Nietzsche's writing whenever he discussed the highest rank of achievement in knowledge (*Birth*, 15), science, and philosophy (*Human*, Preface, 6). Following Plato, he claimed that "high culture is a pyramid: it can stand only on a broad base; its first presupposition is a strong and soundly consolidated mediocrity." He also believed that low-level workers with a service mentality are needed as "a public utility, a wheel, a function," persons who are happy to serve, happy to be mediocre, adept at narrow specializations by nature (*Antichrist*, 57). He insisted that human enhancement and culture building can only take place in a "society which believes in a long scale of rank ordering and differences in worth between man and man, and which, in some sense or other, requires slavery" (*Beyond*, IX, 257). In an early essay he determined that "slavery belongs to the essence of a culture." Culture, which is most of all a hunger for art, can only grow on a deep and fertile soil where the overworked deprived majority release the indulgent minority from "the struggle for existence," in favor of "a new world of necessities" (*Greek*).

Taken on face value, Nietzsche's tolerance and justification of slavery, alongside his admiration of aristocracy, are offensive to modern ears. In his defense, he did not advocate weekend slave markets in the town's shopping malls. We must also realize that irrespective of all the democratic and liberal rhetoric, most countries nowadays exploit foreign workers and do not mind outsourcing jobs to sweatshops using child labor in poor countries. In an aphorism on *Slaves and Workers,* Nietzsche asked whether the conditions of modern workers are not even worse than those of slaves (*Human*, IX, 457), actually saying that only the words change, but not the realities. Nietzsche, "the last anti-political German" (*Ecce*, Wise, 3), was not calling for counter-revolution, the rebirth of oligarchy and return to slavery, but was seeking ways to revive the "most vigorous and exuberant vitality of Greek culture" (*Untimely*, Schopenhauer, 3).

Resentment, Idealism, and Mediocrity

The best defense is a good offense and, in order to vindicate his idea of order of rank, Nietzsche attacked the opposite views of socialism and the social justice agenda. As he often did, he started by examining the motivation of their proponents, seeing them as theories born out of resentment, a sickness typical of "underprivileged" human beings who hate and blame others for their difficulties, who lack real power and confidence (*Twilight*, Skirmishes, 34). In Zarathustra's words, they are Tarantulas, who speak about justice but actually want to punish (*Thus*, II, The Tarantulas). They enjoy the feeling of revenge, which is typical of the "least and dumbest" members of society (*Will*, I, 125), or differently put, the most self-righteous and manipulative ones, who do not care about others and have only their own interests in mind (*Will*, II, 373).

The next line of attack was genealogical, identifying the origin of leveling ideas in eighteenth-century romantic idealism. Idealism, in Nietzsche's eyes, was not ideal at all; "this is my pessimism, to have recognized how the 'higher feelings' are a source of misfortune and man's loss of value" (*Will*, I, 80). Such ideas, taken from Rousseau, idealize humans, deify nature, and deny what is known about human nature, to fit it into an artful superficial unrealistic utopia, used as a means of propaganda for social-political reforms (*Will*, I, 97). The levelers, with their absurd optimism concerning the "good man" and natural drives, promise a heaven on earth, the moment the old order is abolished (*Will*, III, 755). Against romantic idealism, Nietzsche posited his realistic naturalism, "anti-idealistic, more concrete, more fearless, industrious, moderate, suspicious against sudden changes, *antirevolutionary*" (*Will*, I, 117). In this worldview, the desire to possess is an old healthy instinct, an expression of life and "the morality of development" (*Will*, I, 125). Nietzsche's naturalism is in line with his Dionysian pessimism of accepting the less pleasant aspects of life—"waste, decay, elimination need not be condemned: they are necessary consequences of life, of the growth of life" (*Will*, I, 40).

Finally, Nietzsche argued that the practical implications of leveling theories are harmful to political organizations and individuals alike. They lower the value of humans, making them small, weak, and governable: "Perfect herd animal[s]" (*Beyond*, V, 203). The vision of "justice and concord" will only lead to decay, mediocrity, and uniformity of persons (*Gay*, V, 377). In strong ages, in contradistinction, individuals dare to stand out and be themselves, and are able to tolerate tensions and maintain division between people, statuses, and plurality of types (*Twilight*, Skirmishes, 37).

The Last Man and Superfluous People

Nietzsche summed up his message saying, "I teach that there are higher and lower men" (*Will*, IV, 997). The Superman, as the very word indicates, is obviously above the low, regular, and average; he is something at the tip of a hierarchy. Hence, self-overcoming and getting over obstacles on the way becomes the act of a continuous climbing up along the different ranks from bottom to top: beginning with the last man and lower small people, together with invalids, ascetics, and apostates, all those who make up life in the big city; continuing with average and mediocre, nihilists and Christians, good people (in the negative sense of the word); ultimately ascending to the realm of higher persons, which together or separately bring us closer to the goal of the Superman.

To begin the climb, one must want to join the few higher persons and reject in theory and practice the common "market-place" assumption of equality of people and notions of "happiness for the greatest number" (*Thus*, IV, The higher man, 1). One must accept life without authoritative guidelines and the resulting uncertainty, as well as surpass the petty virtues, policy, and "ant-hill trumpery," and give up triviality and the search for comfort (*Thus*, IV, The higher man, 3). The "enhancement in the type 'man,'" must be based on "pathos of distance" between classes and persons, generalized or internalized into pathos of distance in the soul itself. Nietzsche challenged his readers to transcend the herd part in them and distance themselves from those who are of lower rank, still herd creatures, those with the mentality of slaves, the rabble, and the variety of sheep who follow leaders, conventions, and fashions (*Beyond*, IX, 257).

Small People

In his treatment of low-ranking persons, Zarathustra-Nietzsche appears as a prophet of wrath, despising and hateful, over-generalizing and lacking in empathy. We, however, must try to be patient, understanding that people with a cause are not necessarily easygoing and pleasant. In his defense, we can notice that Nietzsche tried hard to curb such feelings, and in his notes he reminded himself that "hatred of mediocrity is unworthy of a philosopher . . . he has to keep the mediocre in good heart" (*Will*, IV, 893).

Zarathustra targeted "the last man" (the latest version of man, the one who precedes the Superman, or the one he hopes will disappear?) as the epitome of the majority of normal people searching for convenient life and happiness (*Thus*, Prologue, 5). He described them in terms of herd and mob, uniformity and mediocrity, conventionality, conservatism, and conformity. Nietzsche-Zarathustra dedicated a whole sermon to describe a world of multitudes, nuisance and insignificance, dealing and wheeling in a market economy (*Thus*, I, Flies of the market place). The last man is a small man—"for small people small virtues are necessary"—and they become even smaller because of their virtues and their "doctrine of happiness." The list of shortcomings of average human beings is long and includes ingenuity, hypocrisy, and service mentality; harm avoidance and tepid virtues—"they are clever, their virtue have clever fingers. But they lack fists." Zarathustra detested these modest and tame submissive domesticated animals, wolves that were turned into dogs: "wherever there is anything small and sick and scabby, there they crawl like lice; and only my disgust stops me from cracking them" (*Thus*, III, Virtues that makes small, 2). The "superfluous people," also designated as "impotent," are addicted to the media, money, and power: "they vomit their bile and call it a newspaper . . . they acquire wealth and make themselves poorer with it; and to power, for the sake of power . . . they desire power and especially the lever of power" (*Thus*, I, The tree on the mountainside). In short they are a rabble, "the power-rabble, the scribbling-rabble, and the pleasure-rabble" (*Thus*, II, The rabble). There is no need to go into more detail here, as we know very well how most of us try to "make a living," consume brand names, are brainwashed by the media, and all the rest.

Individuality and Personhood

Nietzsche saw society as a beehive with a queen bee and worker bees. Among his depictions of this partition were "general run of mankind" versus "man's lucky hits" (*Genealogy*, III, 1); "human lowlands" versus the "higher brighter humanity" (*Will*, IV, 993); "domestic animal" or "animal herd" versus "exceptions" or "fortunate accidents of great success"

(*Antichrist*, 3 and 4). This division, in which few are special and most are regular is, according to him, both unavoidable and desirable. However it must be said that those who set their mind to it can hopefully, with Nietzsche's help, switch sides.

Individuality is a late development: "Verily, the individual himself is still the most recent invention" (*Thus*, Prologue, 3). Humans started as herd animals and in many ways we are still part of a herd, equipped with all the appropriate instincts ready to take over control, "For many generations, being separated from the herd was a punishment and guilt was acting not in accord with its interests." Becoming a self, evaluating oneself according to self-determined values, was a crucial turn in human development (*Gay*, I, 14). Individuality, practically being extraordinary and seeing things in different new ways, is a prerequisite for creativity, for becoming one's own lawmaker, and for being a free spirit: "Ultimately, the individual derives the values of his acts from himself; because he has to interpret in a quite individual way even the words he has inherited" (*Will*, III, 767).

Individuality and Community

Individuality presents a dilemma, as it is impossible without separation from the herd, and it is also impossible to survive without belonging to it. In his first book, Nietzsche wrote about "the contrariety at the center of the universe," consisting of two basic principles or human themes found in life, art, and mythology, which call for a creative integration: one pole is the *Principium Individuationis*, the principle of individuation, represented by Apollo, which implies rational cognition and boundaries, separating us from others and from the world as a whole. The other pole is universality, in which we transcend the differences between individuals, acting and experiencing ourselves as a community and in unity with the world, driven by emotions under the spell of the ecstatic Dionysian joy. Moreover, going beyond appearances, we then experience ourselves as in tune with a cosmic oneness (*Birth*, 9). The problem, though, is that Nietzsche did not clarify the difference between taking part in a Dionysian bacchanalia and participating in a mob's riot.

The Challenge of Independence

Individuality is not self-evident and is not for everyone; it is possible only at the top of the pyramid, and for its proper functioning the majority must stay loyal to norms, shared worldviews and customs. Besides, not everyone is courageous enough for the challenge of independence: "It is the business of the very few to be independent; it is a privilege of the strong" (*Beyond*, II, 29). Aristocracy and nobility is based on the realization that throughout history, including the present time, the majority of people were dependent on what the masters, those in position of power, thought of them; they were unable and not used to set their own values; and instinctively submitted to the evaluations of others (*Beyond*, IX, 261). We still carry this historical heritage within us, and when we are suddenly confronted with a question or problem, the first response that occurs to us "is usually not our own but only the current one pertaining to our class, position, or parentage; our own opinions seldom swim on the surface" (*Human*, IX, 571).

Entering the labyrinth of independence is dangerous with a high price to pay: isolation from others and the loss of their empathy; and an inner precariousness, the "Minotaur's tearing pangs of conscience" and finding no way back (*Beyond*, II, 29). Being an extraordinary person and living in "a society that worships the ordinary" may become fatal. "Such uncommon characters are first cowed, then become sick and melancholy, and then die" (*Untimely*, Schopenhauer, 3). People know in their hearts that they are unique, that they will live only once and will not have a second chance to express their many sides as a unity; but still they hide this knowledge out of fear of their conformity demanding neighbors (*Untimely*, Schopenhauer, 1). Why cannot the herd tolerate individuality and not be hostile to it? Because those who live by their own unconventional standards make the herd "feel degraded, like ordinary beings" (*Human*, IX, 495). For this reason, it is dangerous to show openly one's loathing and rejection of the "Herd-humanity," as one who is not careful with them, "will no doubt be overtaken by them and impaled on their horns" (*Human*, Assorted, 233). A possible implication is that we must be able to pretend that "we are loyal members of the herd" and keep our contempt well hidden.

Given the high price of individuality, it is no wonder that some dependent persons, out of vanity, fake independence; while wise persons do the exact opposite, they appear to be dependent, while in reality they are not (*Philologists*, 136). This suggests that individuality is not necessarily a matter of behavior or appearance, but rather a frame of mind and intellectual honesty. Whatever choice is made, the consequences are not rosy: "He who strays from tradition becomes a sacrifice to the extraordinary; he who remains in tradition is its slave. Demise follows in any case (*Human*, IX, 552). At this point, we are offered a taste of Nietzsche's rare elixir of pessimism blended with optimism, of the "don't worry, you are going to die anyhow" kind.

Roles and Identities

The separation from the herd begins with overcoming ingrained dispositions, fears, and pressures, but it must continue with additional steps. The first is the refusal to be a cog in a machine and relinquishing attachments to roles, which Nietzsche saw as a principal deficiency of those he called "active men," ones who neglect their individuality and continue mechanically, out of obedience and stupidity, to perform their tasks as if it was a package deal. In current terms they are the executives, organization people, in business, bureaucracy, or the academy, "generic creatures" and not unique beings (*Human*, I, 283). The next step towards a separation from the herd mentality will be casting aside our habitual self-identity. We are raised in a family and culture that socialize and indoctrinate us to feel as parts of a whole, be it country, race, nation, class, tribe, or faith. Nietzsche opens our eyes to the realization that "All that is not you":

> Orient and Occident are chalk lines drawn before us to fool our timidity. I want to make an attempt to reach freedom, the youthful soul says to itself; and it will be prevented by the fact that, coincidentally, two nations hate and fight one another, or that two continents are separated by an ocean, or that all around it a religion is taught which, nevertheless, did not exist a few thousand years ago. All that is not you, it says to itself. (*Untimely*, Schopenhauer, 3)

From Individuality to Personhood

Persons who reached individuality live an ascending and not descending life; one which has some original contribution, rather than being a parasite on those doing better (*Twilight*, Skirmishes, 33). In his notes, Nietzsche differentiated between being an individual, which is an unconscious and modest stage of the Will to Power, and being a person. Individuals freed themselves from the domination of society and from being one of many similar individuals; persons, more advanced and conscious, are individuals who express and fulfill their uniqueness (*Will*, III, 784). He saw Schopenhauer as both an individual and a person, a valuable model of disengagement from the herd who cultivated independence from the "learned tribe," state and society, and advanced his ideal of escaping "the chains of circumstance" (*Untimely*, Schopenhauer, 3).

Individuality, conceived as differentiation from the herd, difficult as it may be to achieve, is merely a negative definition, while a positive definition would entail asking what we intend to do with our individuality. This is something that most people find very difficult to accomplish, but the moment it is realized, "there appears around him a strange penumbra which is the mark of his singularity (*Untimely*, Schopenhauer, 3). Personhood must further be protected and maintained, as taking part in the herd's popular culture can suck us in, causing us to give up our "language, taste, choice and courage" to be part of the crowd (*Gay*, V, 369).

Higher and Higher

In our discussion so far, we climbed up the ladder, from the herd to individuality, and from individuality to personhood. Nietzsche envisioned additional higher ranks that we can opt to achieve, bringing us closer to the apex of the pyramid, farther away from the herd. This transition is facilitated or hindered by environmental and biological factors, such as the political reality, religion, economic conditions, states of war or peace, and individual dispositions (*Will*, III, 752). I mentioned before several routes, perspectives of self-advancement. One route from slaves to masters was described in Nietzsche's psychology of morality (chapter 4). The routes of free spirits, Schopenhauerian, and Dionysian persons, will be reviewed in the context of self-design (chapter 8). I will now follow the route of nobility, higher persons, and the Superman. It is possible to see the first as a historical antecedent, the second as possible approximations and variations, and the third as an ideal to strive for.

Nobility

Nietzsche's conception of nobility expressed his longing for the endangered aristocratic values of the past, values that will be also heralded under the banners of the Will to Power, the Superman, and free spirits. Nobility is not a matter of symbols and privileges, but rather of behaviors and attitudes. Nietzsche did not talk about the old inherited nobility, but rather about the "new nobility," one that has no price, cannot be bought and involves responsibility—"you shall become procreators and breeders and sowers of the future"—and also demands longing and the willingness "to get beyond yourselves" (*Thus*, Old and new law-tables, 12). Therefore, there is nothing to prevent us from becoming nobles ourselves. But before we knight ourselves noble, let us remember our reservations about Nietzsche's tunes of polarity, and take in consideration our qualifications about the dichotomy of masters and slaves morality, which is interwoven with the idea of nobility. I also suggest treating Nietzsche's characterization of nobility as a list of options, which we do not have to accept as a whole and are entitled to adapt to our own needs.

The ninth part of *Beyond Good and Evil* is dedicated to answering the question "What Is Noble?" The answer consists of a list of qualities. First among them is a feeling of entitlement: that "nobles" are better than others; that society exists for their sake (*Beyond*, IX, 258). They are self-centered, egoistic, and expect common people to sacrifice themselves for their betters (*Beyond*, IX, 265). Noble persons are their own law-makers; they live by their own evaluations, not carrying about what other people believe or say (*Beyond*, IX, 261). The other side of the coin of entitlement is willing to pay its stiff price of giving up the need for affiliation and compassion. Seeing society naked as "a comedy with concealed ends" brings with it poisonous loneliness (*Beyond*, IX, 273). Things do not get easier for such persons; "life always becomes harder towards the *summit*,—the cold increases, responsibility increases" (*Antichrist*, 57).

Nobility is the opposite of aimless existence; it is life with a calling and a mission, a topic I will expand on later (chapter 8); it is the opposite of conventional, average, ordinary, herd-like, standard existence. Noble persons resist the push to advance into similarity, *"progressus in simile"*, and by being extraordinary they can become society's "significance and highest justification" (*Beyond*, IX, 268). Life with a mission necessitates passion, not a search for peace and happiness but rather "morals as art and enthusiasm in reverence and in devotion." In love as in all endeavors, it seeks experiences of emotional intensity, not caring too much about utility and safety (*Beyond*, IX, 260).

Nobility is a far cry from neurotic shyness and inhibition; it is a mark of robustness, assertiveness, health, and psychological well-being. For the noble ones, "vanity is an atavism" (*Beyond*, IX, 261) and they can easily declare, "That pleases me. I take that for my own and will protect it and defend it against everyone." They can execute tasks, implement decisions, be loyal to their principles, keep up relationships (my translation of "hold onto a woman"), deter and punish attacks, and be authoritative with their "anger and sword." With such masterly qualities, others are willing to obey and oblige, and accept their pity as something of value (*Beyond*, IX, 293). Noble persons are "hard hearts," self-demanding, appreciative of powerfulness, esteeming bravery and honor; the opposite of warm hearts prone to pity and selflessness (*Beyond*, IX, 260).

Noble persons are conservative, who ward the morality and handed-down privileges of the powerful and reject new values. They have a "profound reverence for age and for ancestral tradition" and ,unlike persons with "modern ideas," they do not believe in "progress" and the "future" (*Beyond*, IX, 260). They have "an instinct for rank," which is by itself an indication of a high rank. Noble persons also have an "instinct of reverence," which enables delight in finding and identifying high grades of quality unmarked and undiscovered until then (*Beyond*, IX, 263).

What is the advantage for life in the resurrected, somewhat nostalgic, concept of nobility? It can serve as a useful empowering tool for people who wish to advance themselves, seekers of self-help and psychotherapy clients, who find it difficult to take the necessary steps towards change. Many of them feel that they do not deserve any better; that they are missing a goal or project in life; are apathetic, unassertive, inhibited, lack resiliency, and worry too much over "what will others say." Release from slavery and becoming a noble free person are enticing and mobilizing goals—metaphors, open to individual interpretations and suggesting defined steps to take and attitudes to adopt.

The Way to the Superman

Masters, aristocrats, and noble persons existed already in the past; the Superman is a hope for the "masters of the future" (*Thus*, Prologue, 3).

The former are the opposite and a reaction to slaves and small people; the latter is antithetical to the state and modern persons: "There, where the state ceases—there only commences the man who is not superfluous." Where the state ceases, there commences the "the rainbow and the bridges of the Superman" (*Thus*, I, The new idol). The Superman is an ideal, and as such it cannot be materialized, although some people get closer to it than others: "Never yet has there been a Superman. I have seen them both naked, the greatest and the smallest men—and they are still all-too-similar to one another. Verily, even the greatest I found to be—all-too-human" (*Thus*, II, The Priests).

The select few who advanced in the way of the Superman are "nature's most excellent human products" and Nietzsche introduced Zarathustra as an admired exemplar of them, "carved from a single block, which is hard, sweet, and fragrant." He is "more Caesar Borgia then Parsifal, a type opposed to 'modern' men, 'good' men, Christians, nihilists, not an 'ideal type'" (*Ecce*, Books). A person strong enough to make everything turn to his own advantage, in other words, a survivor who overcomes; in other words Dionysus, in other words, Nietzsche as he saw himself, or perhaps wished to be. This person is self-directing and sets limits and horizons; has an ability to affect self-healing; turns bad accidents into advantages; exhibits self-respect and rejects "bad luck" and guilt; processes and, when necessary, forgets experiences.

The Superman and other closely related higher persons are described from many perspectives: they sense themselves as noble, are dedicated to their goals, willing to stand alone and be different (*Gay*, III, 143). They are "synthetic, summarizing, justifying" persons, committed and focused, whose goal is the Superman and not humanity (*Will*, IV, 1001). These synthetic persons and rulers, each a "Roman Caesar with Christ's soul" (*Will*, IV, 983), enjoy the "eternal contradiction, begetter of all things" (*Birth*, 4), and can endure, control, and coordinate conflicting drives (*Will*, IV, 966). They possess physical, mental, and creative "overflowing power" (*Will*, IV, 966) and the higher the power, the higher their rank (*Will*, IV, 898). Power itself is not enough, and they know how to control and use it (*Will*, IV, 933) to create some meaning of life in a meaningless world (*Will*, III, 585).

The Superman aspirants, who wish to transcend the lowly "human all too human" (*Will*, IV, 999), are enlightened "as to the character of existence" and strive to go beyond basic existence to become, "philosophers, artists, and saints" (*Untimely*, Schopenhauer, 5). They must be self-sufficient (*Gay*, VI, 212), and their own self-legislators (*Untimely*, Schopenhauer, 1). They are creators, a special type of Prometheus-like barbarians, conquerors "in search of material to mold" (*Will*, IV, 900) and as such, they abide by the Nietzschean command, "create beyond itself" (*Thus*, I, On the despisers of the body), to become who they are—"the new, the unique, the incomparable, the self-legislators, the self-creators" (*Gay*, IV,

336). In other words, they become metaphorically creating Gods (*Gay*, III, 143).

The Higher Persons

Higher human beings are not merely role-playing cogs in the machine. Their inner world is filled with more pleasures and interests; they are better at perceiving and observing. They are "spectators in the spectacle, of life" and poets of their life; creators of their own evaluations, perspectives, scales, affirmations, and negations (*Gay*, IV, 301). By virtue of their creativity, and not necessarily in being useful, they have a strong and lasting impact on their human environment (*Will*, IV, 877; *Will*, IV, 999). Caesar, Homer, Aristophanes, Leonardo, and Goethe are examples of such persons, great creators, skeptic immoralists, who could will and did not need faith (*Will*, II, 380).

In addition to describing their qualities, Nietzsche presented a gallery of types of higher persons, and their standing in Nietzsche's order of rank is not always clear. Some of them are of the present; some are paving the way for future higher persons; few are almost there, close to the Superman and they all represent the promise of a "higher form of being," the Superman being an apt metaphor for them (*Will*, IV, 866). Higher persons are the *children of the future,* homeless in the culture of their times, who refuse to "compromise, to be captured, reconciled and castrated." They live "untimely on mountains' top in the past or in the future" (*Gay*, V, 377), and "have different and varied moralities, tolerate ambiguities and change easily" (*Gay*, VII, 215). The *Good Europeans* stand in opposition to "the men of fatherlands," being atheists and immoralists at heart who pretend to support their societies' norms and institutions, but in truth hope to topple off the existing culture, preparing themselves to become "legislators of the future, the masters of the earth" (*Will*, I, 132). The *Europeans of the day-after-tomorrow* are highly individualistic, looking for their virtues in the depth of their soul, in their private labyrinth (*Gay*, VII, 214). The senses of the *sensualists in the best faith* surpass those using mainly their analytic and rational apparatus. Nietzsche, "the teacher of the Superman," added to the list the *sublime man* (*Will*, IV, 996) and the *great human being*, persons, who like him, fulfill the roles of philosophers, educators, and sages (*Will*, IV, 987).

From this point on, the ranks leading to the top of the pyramid, to the Superman, become narrower and slipperier, and the higher persons are turned into forbidding warriors. The *redeeming man*, also called the *man of the future*, is a powerful, fierce warrior of great health, with "sublime maliciousness, an ultimate self-conscious willfulness of knowledge"; a creative spirit, a Caesar and Jesus combined, full of love and contempt, an anti-Christ and anti-nihilist, a "conqueror of God and of nothingness" (*Genealogy*, II, 24). *Preparatory human beings* are courageous heroes—warriors who will fight and destroy "the sand and slime of present day civilization and metropolitanism" (*Human*, IV, 283). Nietzsche hoped for the coming of the "new barbarians," who are cynics, experimenters, conquerors who achieve "union of spiritual superiority with well-being and an excess of strength" (*Will*, IV, 899).

When I met Nietzsche's contemptuous attitude towards the majority of common people, who are just trying to survive, I felt trepidation which I tried to overcome. Now, witnessing Nietzsche moving to the opposite end of uncurbed adoration and hero worship of higher persons and their depiction as posters and not as real persons, I start to have misgivings again. Nietzsche himself admitted that his enthusiasm got out of hand, describing "a world so over-rich in the beautiful, the strange, the questionable, the frightful, and the divine" (*Gay*, V, 382; *Ecce*, Zarathustra, 2). Yet it got much worse, continuing with plans to breed the Superman (*Untimely*, Schopenhauer, 6; *Antichrist*, 3; *Will*, IV, 877) and a "stronger race" (*Will*, IV, 898), culminating in his call to annihilate inferior races in favor of a master domineering one (*Will*, IV, 862).

FRIENDSHIP, LOVE, SEXUALITY, AND MARRIAGE

All roads lead to Rome, and with Nietzsche all roads lead to the same goal, to the affirmation and ascendance of life, its "fullness, power, confidence" (*Genealogy*, Prologue, 3) and beyond, to the improvement of humankind and to the Superman. All intimate relations are primarily examined from these perspectives, taking in consideration that all social relations, friendly, sexual, and intimate, are based on pleasure and instinct, that is to say, biological and psychological needs. Nietzsche raised some interesting hypotheses about the sources of such pleasures: that they are extensions or generalizations of pleasure derived from self-touch; and that they are inherited from our animal past, as animals enjoy playing with each other and with their young offspring. The pleasure derived from shared joy in human interaction improves the nature of humans, making them more trusting, less envious, able to have a positive view of themselves and their peers, able to feel strongly, and, most importantly, learn empathy: "Analogous expressions of pleasure awaken the fantasy of empathy, the feeling of being alike. Shared sorrows do it, too: the same storms, dangers, enemies" (*Human*, II, 98).

At this point in the book, we should already be used to Nietzsche's custom of using the same words to denote different meanings: the noun "friend," for example, is used by him to describe an intimate acquaintance but also to describe a more specific type of friendship. When he said, "Not all men can be friends, but women can't be ones at all" (*Thus*, I, The Friend), we must not reach immediately for the political correctness gun. We should rather understand it as if he was saying that women are better at being friends in the general sense, characterized by affection and dedication, while men are better at friendship in the specific sense of detached objectivity and mutual criticism (and yet the two sexes are actually capable of both). This statement, and others too, exemplify Nietzsche's belief in gender-specific traits and behaviors.

Friendship

Nowadays, when many have at least three hundred friends on their Facebook page, a common saying is "if you want a friend, get a dog!" Nietzsche wrote *In Honor of Friendship*, comparing his times with antiquity when friendship was glorified and considered the highest feeling, more important and holier than the self-sufficiency of a sage (*Gay*, I, 61). They had experiences of strong bonds, "meditated upon it, and almost took it to the grave with it." We, on the other hand, "can point to our idealization of sexual love." He lamented the decline of friendship, and the demise of male bonding, of man "standing side by side with man," as in antiquity (*Daybreak*, V, 503). Nowadays, the idealization of sex has only become more extreme, but we can comfort ourselves, if we so wish, with the current celebration of female sisterhood and the friendships between males and females ("my wife is my best friend").

Between One and None

Discussing Schopenhauer, Nietzsche described loneliness in moving terms, and he revealed later that the description was true for him too. A philosopher, who has independent views and lives in a conformist society, must keep his thoughts undercover. This is a situation that invites suffering, isolation, and loneliness, that can only be helped by love and friends with whom it is possible to be open, sincere and have a break from silence and hypocrisy: "He was absolutely alone, with no single friend of his own kind to comfort him; and between one and none there lies infinity—as ever between something and nothing" (*Untimely*, Schopenhauer, 3).

The way we relate to friends tells who we are; "our faith in others betrays wherein we would dearly love to have faith in ourselves. Our longing for a friend is our betrayer" (*Thus*, I, The Friend). And our longing can betray envy and vulnerability; "a want of friends points to envy or arrogance" (*Human*, IX, 559). We can also betray an inability to reciprocate—"the most offensive beast of man I ever found I baptized Parasite: it would not love, yet wanted to live by love" (*Thus*, III, The Spirit of Gravity). Friendship demands self-respect and respect of the other. "Are you a slave? Then you cannot be a friend. Are you a tyrant? Then you cannot have friends" (*Thus*, I, The Friend). However, we sometimes betray the undesirable tendency of overconsideration: "Always love your neighbor as yourselves—but first be such as love themselves" (*Thus*, III, Virtue that makes small). In addition, we often forget the fact that friendship is a matter of chemistry, not always a fully rational choice. "When we cannot stand certain people, we try to have suspicions about them" (*Human*, IX, 557).

In order to enjoy friendships we must be tolerant and realize that differences of opinion, character, occupation, and environment are unavoidable. Modesty, self-irony, and knowing when to keep silent are necessary too. We can easily find faults in friends, but we can just as easily despise ourselves; therefore, we should bear with the other as we bear with ourselves (*Human*, VI, 376).

The Map of Friendship

Two types of persons, ladders and circles, have a talent for friendship. "Ladders" are people who are continually developing, who find in each stage of their life friends appropriate to their needs. Their friends, different from each other, are usually not interconnected. "Circles" attract a variety of friends with different talents and temperaments, who gradually, through the "circle," get to be friends with each other too, creating a circle of friends. Nietzsche added that "on many people, incidentally, the gift of having good friends is much greater than the gift of being a good friend" (*Human*, VI, 368). Zarathustra distinguished between friends, comrades, and neighbors: "I do not teach you the neighbor but the friend" (*Thus*, I, Love of the neighbor) and "there is comradeship: may there be friendship!" (*Thus*, I, The friend). A comrade is a "buddy" we can go out with to have a beer or jog together; neighbors are other sheep in the human herd.

Zarathustra explained that "the 'you' is older than the 'I'; the 'you' has been canonized, but not yet the 'I.'" Thus, people seek their neighbors, whose proximity enables escape from individuality, the comforts of community, familiarity, and clear expectations. Zarathustra described the psychological mechanism of self-deception and deception of others operating in such relations: "Your neighborly love is your bad love of yourselves." Those who lack self-love, self-respect, and self-sufficiency manipulate impressions, aiming to find favor with their neighbors turned witnesses. Afterward, such persons incorporate the positive view that others supposedly have, in order to inflate their own self-image (*Thus*, I, Love of one's neighbor). Such interactions are destructive; "the one goes to his neighbor because he seeks himself and the other because he wants to lose himself." Whenever comrades and neighbors associate together, pretense and acting are the rules, and the authentic and different few ones are persecuted. "It is those further away who must pay for your love of neighbor; and as soon as there are five of you together, a sixth one must always die" (*Thus*, I, Love of one's neighbor). As long as what determines humans' happiness is what others think and know about them, and not what they themselves do, impression management will remain necessary. This holds true for us too; "who has not for the sake of his reputation—sacrificed himself?" (*Beyond*, IV, 92), and in fact, it is still more difficult for us to deal with bad reputation than with bad conscience (*Gay*, I, 52).

Doctors of the Soul and Friends

Zarathustra used the word "friend" to describe a complementary relationship, unlike the symmetrical relationship of camaraderie. Among a pair of friends, one is practically a spiritual teacher or a mentor; the other is a disciple or protégé. A friend is not supposed to make us feel good about ourselves, give us support, or share our secrets, but only helps us get closer to becoming a higher person—"may the friend be the feast of the earth for you and an anticipation of the Superman." The creative friend, "who always has a complete world to bestow," helps us advance by means of objective criticism and personal example (*Thus*, I, The Friend). Mentioning fullness and ripeness as qualities of the friend, the very same adjectives used to describe Zarathustra, it seems that the friend is Zarathustra, who is Nietzsche, who wishes to befriend us disciples and readers.

Zarathustra's description of proper attitudes and behaviors in a productive friendship can be easily applied to the psychotherapeutic relationship. Therapy is a special kind of friendship. Nietzsche-Zarathustra suggested that the need for a friend begins with a person's relation to oneself; "I and me are always too wrapped up in conversation: how could that be endured unless there was a friend?" The friend is thus a third person, who interferes and prevents the other internal figures from "sinking into the depths" (*Thus*, I, The Friend). Likewise, a psychotherapist can be conceived as a friend who takes a role in a person's internal drama of parts in strife.

The receiving friend in such relationships must be mature enough, open, motivated, and goal-directed; "one must be a sponge if one would be loved by hearts that are overfull." While seeing the mentor-friend as a model, it is important to maintain one's individuality and separateness, and when it is called for, oppose, resist, and confront the friend. "If one wants to have a friend, then one must also be willing to wage war for him: and in order to wage war, one must be capable of being an enemy." The soul doctor on her part should welcome such confrontations. A dignified degree of reserve is another condition for such friendship—"you cannot dress finely enough for your friend"—and the two must accept their human imperfections, and avoid searching for what is private and hidden while remaining perceptive and intuitive about the needs of their friend (*Thus*, I, The Friend).

The Problem of Man and Woman

Nietzsche built his psychology of the relations between the sexes on an assumption of differentiation of roles and natures and the desirability of the "most profound antagonism here and the necessity of an eternally hostile tension." Thus, the relationship is conceived as "the problem of man and woman," and only superficial thinkers, he said, will approach this problem in terms of "equal rights, equal education, equal entitlements and duties" (*Beyond*, VII, 238). However, only a superficial thinker will not realize how much has changed since Nietzsche's times: man and woman, at least in Western societies, are similar to each other in education and work, and their relationship is more of a partnership of peers, not to mention same-sex marriages and parenthoods. Nietzsche's ideas of antagonism and hostility between the two sexes could serve as a testimony to his times and his issues with women and life.

Female and Male Mothers

If Freud asked, "What does a woman want?"[1] for Nietzsche the answer was perfectly clear—everything about her is related to pregnancy. "A man is for woman a means: the end is always the child." The question of what the man wants remained quite baffling. He seeks danger and play, and a woman for him is a "dangerous plaything" (*Thus*, I, Old and young women). Nietzsche's solution of the riddle is not convincing—all human relationships are a means to some end; in this respect, women and men are not different. While pregnancy is self-evident from an evolutionary point of view, play and danger-seeking are not; a man indeed is needed for impregnation, but men can certainly play dangerously with each other (which they do). In any case, in Nietzsche's eyes, pregnancy and motherhood are always present in the picture; "in every kind of female love, something of maternal love appears also" (*Human*, VII, 392). Artists and contemplative types are close in spirit to the "feminine character," and Nietzsche saw himself as a "male mother" who gave birth to his books—his children (*Gay*, II, 72).

Interdependence

Aside from the supposedly inherent differences between females and males (*Gay*, I, 24; *Thus*, III, Old and new law-tables, 23), which we will not review here, Nietzsche believed that they can still transcend their differences through sexuality, love, and marriage, ultimately giving birth to the shining "ray of star," the Superman (*Thus*, I, Old and young women). The two sexes influence and shape each other's behaviors and attitudes, "for only he who is sufficiently a man will redeem the woman in woman" (*Thus*, III, Virtue that makes small), and their perceptions of each other tend to fulfill themselves. "It is man who creates for himself the image of woman, and woman forms herself according to this image" (*Gay*, II, 68). Women and men alike deceive themselves and each other, in displaying features that, though contrary to their natures, they believe are desired by the other sex, "the reason being that at bottom they honor and love only themselves (or their own ideal, to express it more agreeably)" (*Beyond*, IV, 131).

The two sexes have an idealized, wishful image of the other sex, and in the case of women, "the best elements of man apart from his sex have become an incarnate ideal" (*Gay*, II, 70), and their awakening can be quite appalling. Women in the nineteenth century grew up uninformed about sex, with internalized notions of shame and honor, and then, once they get married, they were exposed to male sexuality, introduced by their own husbands' "unexpected neighborhood of god and beast!" Nietzsche was empathic to the rough transition women underwent, exclaiming, "In sum, one cannot be too kind about women" (*Gay*, II, 71).

Kinds of Love

We hear that "love makes the world go round" and that "love heals all wounds," and of course, the Beatles' "all you need is love, love, love" still reverberates in our ears. We talk about love of friends, ideas, and self; love of God, country, and life. Personally, Nietzsche divulged that "indeed my foolishness and modesty in love is laughable" (*Thus*, III, Wanderer); intellectually, however, he gave it much thought. He examined the different ways in which the two sexes experience and conceive love, probed the emotional reality behind the idealized and romanticized notion of love, and explored the conditions which facilitate loving relationship.

Love and Egoism

Almost all of Nietzsche's ideas about love must be updated and adapted to the new reality of similarity between the sexes, at least in those societies where women are not suppressed and controlled in the name of God. I am therefore going to skip his observations about the differences in love between the sexes, and bring only his insight into the nature of love itself. Nietzsche the Overturner showed that love, unlike the stereotype of ultimate selflessness, is actually based on selfishness, possessiveness, and self-deception. Probing love and sympathy as manifested by women, he asked, "And if they sacrifice themselves, their honor, their reputation, to whom do they sacrifice themselves? To the man? Or is it not rather to an unbridled urge?" We should add that similar "unbridled urges" obviously operate in men too. Ultimately, what we desire, even if it pleases others and gains their gratitude, is no more than our own egoistic selfish desire (*Will*, III, 777). When in love, we simply deceive ourselves by editing our picture of the past to suit our vanity, believing that such "self-oblivion in love," and "absorption of the ego in the other person" never happened before (*Human*, Assorted, 37).

Possession and Suspicion

Intimate relations with partners and children are based on the need of having and possessing. People have secure or insecure connections, based on the strength of this need and on the degree of their suspiciousness, and when they seek reassurance, they are liable to control the sexuality of their partners, demand sacrifices, and put the others to tests of loyalty and acceptance (*Beyond*, V, 194). The transactions of love between the sexes involve "severe, frightful, enigmatical, and unmoral elements" (*Gay*, V, 363). The combination of these elements with difficulties in intimacy and extreme possessiveness is dangerous. In extreme cases, the discovery that the lover intends to leave or has found a new love could lead to abominable murders. In his aphorism "love's cruel notion," Nietzsche exposed the psychological root of the murder wish and its terrible fulfillment: "Every great love brings with it the cruel idea of killing the object of its love so that it may be removed once and for all from the wicked game of change: for love dreads change even more than annihilation" (*Human*, Assorted, 280).

Conditions for Love

Love is made possible when the following preconditions are fulfilled: an ability to love and show kindness, which, like hating, is learned in childhood; "if education or chance give us no opportunity to practice these feelings, our soul becomes dry and unsuited even to understanding the tender inventions of loving people" (*Human*, IX, 601). One cannot love others without loving one's own inner "irreconcilable duality" (or multiplicity). Loving demands an attitude of tolerance, acceptance, and even celebration of differences between the self and the other (*Human*, Assorted, 75). Lastly, in order to love one must overcome fears, and especially fears of commitment and desertion. "Let courage be in your love! With your love, you should throw yourself at him who makes you afraid!" (*Thus*, I, Old and young women).

The Psychology of the Orgiastic

The mythological father of the Chinese civilization, the Yellow Emperor, saw sexuality as a prism which reflects human nature. "Whoever wants to understand the head, should explore the tail." Nietzsche concurred: "The degree and type of the sexuality of a man extend all the way to the ultimate peak of his spirit" (*Beyond*, IV, 75). Sexuality is the highest interest and achievement of the individual: "The tremendous importance the individual accords to the sexual instinct is not a result of its importance for the species, but arises because procreation is the real achievement of the individual and consequently his highest interest, his highest expression of power" (*Will*, III, 680).

From Sex to Meta-Sex

Nietzsche, for the most part, did not discuss sexuality in terms of behaviors, but as a central shaping force in art, culture, and life itself; and thus, we can say that he moved from sex to "meta-sex," from the concrete to the abstract and metaphoric, and from psychology of sex to the "psychology of the orgiastic as an overflowing feeling of life." The orgiastic, symbolized by Dionysus, is "the triumphant Yes to life beyond all death and change . . . through procreation, through the mysteries of sexuality" (*Twilight*, Skirmishes, 10). In other words, the Dionysian and the orgiastic together stand for the essence of the humanly unique erotic (the meaning ascribed to sexuality), in distinction from the biological sexual (act), shared by all mammals:

> The word "Dionysian" means: an urge to unity, a reaching out beyond personality, the everyday, society. . . ; an ecstatic affirmation of the total character of life as that which remains the same, just as powerful, just as blissful, through all change; the great pantheistic sharing of joy and sorrow; the eternal will to procreation, to fruitfulness. (*Will*, IV, 1050).

We will encounter Dionysus again in the chapter on self-creation (chapter 8), where he will resurface as "the genius of the heart." Nietzsche had "Dionysus of the Greeks" stand for "the religious affirmation of life, life whole and not denied or in part," explaining that typically, "the sexual act arouses profundity, mystery, reverence" (*Will*, IV, 1052). Thus, the Dionysian, as shown in the ancient Greek culture, stands for unrestricted and unsuppressed sexuality: "For the Greeks the sexual symbol was, therefore, the venerable symbol par excellence, the real profundity in the whole of ancient piety. Every single element in the act of procreation, of pregnancy, and of birth aroused the highest and most solemn feelings" (*Twilight*, Ancients, 4).

Sex and Sensuality

Nietzsche commended chastity, a noble sexual taste, and eroticism that preclude brutality, morbidity, and prudence (*Will*, IV, 947). The sexual feeling as such is warmly acclaimed, having a special, benevolent, and rare character: "One being gratifies another by the pleasure he enjoys" (*Daybreak*, I, 76). Sexual feelings are good and natural, yet their translation into behavior must be noble and chaste, favoring sensuality over sexuality, the latter being sheer lust in search of release. The Dionysian, orgiastic, and ecstatic elements were not intended to serve as a manual for wild sex parties, but rather aimed to commend an enthusiastic mode of experience, an intense and energized style of action in all endeavors of life.

Sensuality starts with the senses, and Nietzsche praised artists because "they have not lost the scent of life, they have loved the things of this world—they have loved their senses" (*Will*, III, 820). Sensuality, "the scent of life," cannot be suppressed: "These people abstain, it is true: but the bitch Sensuality glares enviously out of all they do" (*Thus*, I, Of chastity). Sensuality constitutes a threat to all "spiritual" despisers of the body and the worldly; it is also a threat to what seems to be their opposite, the rabble "the ever-ready stewing-oven of lust." Unlike them, the "free hearts" and the "lion-willed" conceive sensuality as "the earth's garden-joy, an overflowing of thanks to the present from the future." For free and innocent persons, sensuality is a restorative "wine of wines," the highest happiness and hope, and a bridge "over the differences of men and women" (*Thus*, III, Three evil things, 2).

Modern Marriage

The current devaluation of marriage in the Western world, manifested by declining rates of marriages, increased rates of divorce, and the rise of unmarried cohabitation and single parenthood, bears out Nietzsche's claim that "modern marriage has lost its meaning—consequently it is being abolished" (*Twilight*, Skirmishes, 39). Nietzsche's treatment of marriage was marred by his belief in categorical differences between females and males, lack of personal experience, and difficulties in intimate relationships. In his view of marriage, there is no room for physical intimacy, earthiness, and sensuality, which he otherwise commended. His views on the topic are marked by ambivalence and criticism, neglect of the present in favor of the future, and male-centeredness, with little regard for female needs.

The best marriages are instruments to create the Superman—"you should create a creator"—and in order to reach such excellence, couples must set high standards separately and together: "You should propagate yourself not only forward, but upward!" (*Thus*, III, Spirit of gravity, 24). Nietzsche had only contempt for "superfluous" people, who fail to live up to his standards, "a saint and a goose mate together" (*Thus*, III, Old and new law-tables, 24). He felt that marriage was not for him, neither for thinking free spirits "[who] must, like the prophetic birds of ancient times, prefer to fly alone" (*Human*, VII, 426). He warned against the "the hazard of marriage," giving up a life of creation for the sake of convenience, living in an "aimless drama" (*Daybreak*, III, 150). Human love affairs are not rational and are often a result of faulty thinking (*Daybreak*, IV, 387). Yet his "rational" attempts to straighten out the situation by having indissoluble marriages (*Twilight*, Skirmishes, 39), not based on love (*Human*, VII, 389) or without sexual attraction (*Beyond*, IV, 120), together with outlandish proposals to solve resulting sexual frustrations (*Human*, VII, 421; *Genealogy*, III, 733; *Human*, VII, 424) fell flat on their face. Simply put, Nietzsche could not envision what is now taken for granted: a marriage of equals based on friendship, an attraction combined with rational considerations.

A Friendly Conversation

Although Nietzsche's views on love matches must be taken with a grain of salt, his views on communication in marriage can be taken wholeheartedly. He esteemed marriage as friendship and a long conversation in which the partners have to share and know how to do it. "The best friend will probably get the best wife because a good marriage is based on a talent for friendship" (*Human*, VII, 378). In good couple relationships aggression and friendship are mutually exclusive, and arguments are settled without anger and silence (*Human*, VI, 325) and thus, the question to ask before deciding to marry someone should be: "Do you believe that you will be able to converse well with this woman into your old age? Everything else in marriage is transitory, but most of the time during the association belongs to conversation" (*Human*, VII, 406).

Contractual Relationship

Another recommendation that can only contribute to a good marital relationship is approaching it in a non-romanticized way, as a contract between consenting adults. Marriage is a contract that must be honored and, therefore, it would be worthwhile to consider it carefully ahead of commitment, possibly with the help of trial cohabitation, a "small marriage." If the contract is not kept up, a divorce is preferable to bad marriage as "marriage breaking" is better than "marriage bending." Good marriages are a serious challenge; "it is a big thing always to be with another!" and bad marriages cause much suffering, leading to resentment and revengefulness, blaming the other for not being single anymore. "I want honest people to say to one another: 'we love each other: let us see to it that we stay in love! Or shall our promise be a mistake?'" (*Thus*, III, Old and new law-tables, 24).

If marriage is a binding contract, one should be realistic about what can be promised; one certainly cannot promise "love forever" as feelings change and are not voluntary. Honest wedding vows relate to behaviors such as generosity, consideration, and care, but not to feelings, love or faithfulness (*Human*, II, 58), in short, goodwill, patience, compatibility, and mutual care are presuppositions of this contract" (*Genealogy*, III, 732).

FORMS OF DOMINATION

Social institutions and establishments, such as state, economy, religion, and military, control and hold power over individuals. Nietzsche exhibited in his writings a wide range of attitudes to these issues, from adoration of the state to total disillusionment; from worship of military and wars to their denouncement and condemnation. This variability is, of course, open to interpretation: as self-contradiction, as a process of change and maturation that took place between early and late publications, and as coexisting different parts or voices in him. Here, I will take into consideration his disenchantment with state and military. His view of religion, in any case, was always critical and hostile, while economy, business, and industry were never at the center of his attention.

The Necessary Powerful and Evil State

As I see it, Nietzsche was actually making three related points all along. First, the state is powerful; it was born with an act of violence, it uses force to dominate its subjects and it is here to stay. Second, the state is necessary; it has important functions to execute, and without it, things would be much worse. Third, the state, "the cold monster," is a dangerous entity, often detrimental to individuals. In other words, the state is a necessary evil, and people must choose either to defend its necessary features or avoid its evil ones. This decision is not completely rational, as it is influenced by personal-temperamental factors. Nietzsche himself switched from the first option to the second, but he always rejected a third option, one chosen by anarchists, of fighting the state and attempting to abolish it. If the state is a necessary evil, it follows that democracy or the parliamentary system cannot be a panacea or a value to cherish, but rather remain only a means for the state's smooth functioning, the lesser of other evil systems of ruling.

The Iron Clamp

To remind you, in describing the origins of the state in an act of one-sided violence, Nietzsche commented, "What has he to do with making contracts! We do not negotiate with such beings" (*Genealogy*, II, 17). With this remark, Nietzsche practically demolished the "social contract" myth of the creation of the state—no more tales of people getting together and deciding on peaceful ways to guarantee their shared interests and no more slogans of "by the people and for the people." Thus, Francis Ford Coppola's film trilogy *The Godfather*(1972), about a Sicilian mafia family in New York, can be understood as a metaphor for the state, according to which belligerent outsiders invaded and took control of peaceful communities; lived off their toil, gradually reinforcing their hold, settling in and intermingling; and in this process ultimately making rules, using punishment, and offering protection and benefits. The invaders strove later to maintain deterrence power and respectability (*The Godfather: Part II*), and as they became more established they aimed for legitimization, leaving their dubious past well covered (*The Godfather: Part III*). The state, of course, underwent some additional changes and became more bureaucratically complex. Moreover, the state became the custodian of morality. "Morality is based on force, which unites individuals into a state, later it becomes a custom and free obedience" (*Human*, III, 99). The story of the state's coming into the world can also be told differently, this time without "the bad guys" but in terms of an evolutionary process: "Here again we see the degree to which nature, in order to bring society about, uses pitiless inflexibility to forge for herself the cruel tool of the state—namely that conqueror with the iron hand." (*Greek*)

An Idol and a Lying Monster

Nietzsche started as a supporter of the state, believing that development is possible only under conditions of permanence and continuity (*Human*, V, 224) and that the preservation of "something longer-lasting than an individual" such as the *polis*, justifies, in the name of morality, the imposing of limitations on individuals (*Will*, III, 730). We can only admire how he outgrew the "instinct for nation and state" and became a champion of individuality and a critic of the state. Nietzsche drew our attention to the price and implications of living in the state, called by Zarathustra the new idol and "the cold monster" (impersonal, unfeeling, and dangerous). The state, an expert in managing masses, took, after his death, the place of God. With the birth of state, older forms of association, such as communities and tribes, disappeared; old codes of ethics vanished; and the state masquerading as the patron of morality took over, spreading lies in terms of good and evil. The state, in need of admiring and dedicated masses, used the media and dispensed honors and benefits to make people loyal to it (*Thus*, I, The new idol).

Everything about it is false; its use of rhetoric is misleading, with its biggest lie being "I, the state, am the people." The state is an injurious entity, "a place where everyone drinks poison loses himself, where slow suicide is called life" and not surprisingly, it is hated wherever people, not yet turned into governable subjects, still exist (*Thus*, I, The new idol). Similar warnings had appeared already in Nietzsche's early essay on Schopenhauer, where he argued that the state is not concerned with truth but rather with what is useful to it, "whether it is truth, half-truth, or error" (*Untimely*, Schopenhauer, 8). And he accused it of propagating a false doctrine, that it is humankind's highest goal and that everyone's highest duty is to serve it, a doctrine that is "a relapse not into paganism but into stupidity" (*Untimely*, Schopenhauer, 3).

Citizens of the ancient Greek state, actually smaller than modern small cities, knew each other and experienced themselves as being part of the *polis*. The modern anonymous state in contradistinction is experienced as a distant external powerful body. The state is power hungry, "for the state wants to be absolutely the most important beast on earth; and it is believed to be so too!" (*Thus*, II, Great events). Power in the hands of politicians is dangerous, as they will use any measure to maintain and increase it: "Power likes to walk on crooked legs" (*Thus*, I, Academic chairs of virtue). The problem and humanity's hardest misfortune are that the promise of political power does not usually attract the best candidates for positions of leadership; "the powerful of the earth are not also the first men. Then everything becomes false and awry and monstrous" (*Thus*, IV, Conversations with the Kings).

The cocktail of state, economic, and military interests is an especially poisonous one. "Nowadays the crudest and most evil forces, the egoism of the money-makers and the military despots, hold sway over almost everything on earth." These powers cooperate in order to dominate and shape what they consider as hostile forces, aiming to replace the church as an object of idolization (*Untimely*, Schopenhauer, 4). Thus, the state is not us; it is actually our enemy. "Destroyers are they who lay snares for the many, and call it state: they hang a sword and a hundred cravings over them." This being the case, we must learn to keep our distance from it. "Only there, where the state ceases, does the man who is not superfluous begin" (*Thus*, I, The new Idol, 11).

From Bad to a Little Better

The state, despite its shortcomings, is here to stay exactly as it should. And yet it comes in different shades, from bad to worse, and Nietzsche distinguished between new and old concepts of government, which brings us back to the illustrious *The Godfather*. Following invasion and a settling-in period, the self-made rulers conspired to portray the relation between government and people in a more favorable light, "as if two separate spheres of power, one stronger and higher, the other weaker and lower were negotiating and coming to agreement." In a later stage, just as the mafia invested in Los Vegas casinos to become to all appearances legitimate business, the state concocted a new concept, "that government is nothing but an organ of the people, and not a provident, honorable 'Above' in relationship to a habitually humble 'Below.'" Most of us indeed, would prefer to meet a hotel owner dressed in a suit and tie, rather than encounter, in a dark alley, a gun-carrying gangster. Nietzsche pointed out that this new image ultimately influences the political reality and that the relationship between rulers and ruled keeps changing. Thus, all that is left to do in the meantime is to hold on to our suspicions, stay on guard, and wish for the continuation of slow changes for the better (*Human*, VIII, 450).

Psychologists tend to consider childrens' relations with their parents, with siblings and peers, and the relations between their parents, as models of relationships in their adulthood. Nietzsche looked further, reminding us to take into consideration the reality of state and government in which individuals live. He saw the relation of government and citizens, usually taken for granted, as a model with far-reaching implications, patterning the interactions of teachers and pupils, managers and workers, parents and children and officers and soldiers (*Human*, VIII, 450).

The Failings of Democracy

Nietzsche's sober perception of government is relevant to the topic of democracy and the parliamentary system, which are highly praised and cherished by many. He is often portrayed as an anti-democrat, which is nowadays almost like declaring someone a heretic in the Middle Ages. In fact, although he was not democracy's greatest admirer and his reservations became more pertinent with time, he still recognized its advantages. Democracy undoubtedly is not the worst system of government, certainly better than some theocracies and military dictatorships (which often masquerade as democracies). Nietzsche rejected the value of equality, but he never doubted the formal value of equality before the law--that one's person vote should be equal to those of others. He did not question the idea of representation, which already existed in ancient Greece, and he saw the democratization of Europe as a positive step, which separated us from the Middle Age (*Human*, Wanderer, 275), and the boring democratic institutions have the advantage of being "quarantine arrangements" to fight the "ancient pestilence, lust for tyranny" (*Human*, Wanderer, 289).

The relative advantages of democracy should not blind us to the shortcomings of the parliamentary system of government: an inferior quality of decision making; lack of consideration of minority interests; collusion with the press in the project of turning the herd animal into master (*Will*, III, 753). Democracy is a matter of false choice, in which the public is given permission to choose among a few predetermined options, something which flatters voters, who see themselves as independent and individual, while, in fact, they remain a herd attacking those with different opinions (*Gay*, III, 174). We must choose candidates from a list we did not compose; who run with an agenda we could not influence; who after winning the election, do what they feel like doing, claiming that everything is done in our name and for our sake, until the next elections, when the story starts anew. The parties and candidates translate principles to populist slogans, "great frescoes of stupidity" (*Human*, VIII, 438) and lower their level of discourse to suit the unsophisticated easily courted voters with demagogy, defamations and TV, radio and newspapers ads (unknown in Nietzsche's day) paid for by interest groups and rich supporters.

Nietzsche did not delude himself about the irreversibility of his political culture and institutions; he knew that there is no point in resisting or trying to change the system and that one must accept it as if adapting to changes in the landscape in the aftermath of an earthquake. Those who "want to be the architects of their own fortune and misfortune" have nothing to expect from a system, which is practically a dictatorship of the majority, who vote without any serious deliberation or self-criticism, but sway with popular and populist catch words. It is only to be hoped that the narrow-minded majority should not demand "that everyone should live and act according to their standard" (*Human*, VIII, 438). If it was up to him, Nietzsche would have preferred to try out different kinds of leadership, to experiment with society-building. He wrote, "human society: that is an experiment, so I teach—a long search: it seeks, however, the commander!–An experiment, O my brothers! And not a 'contract'! Shatter; shatter that expression of the soft-hearted and half and half!" (*Thus*, III, Old and new law-tables, 25).

The Machine, Work, and Money

In his *Genealogy of Morality* Nietzsche suggested that society and morality were developed in prehistory out of economic transactions and the practice of debt; and thus, economy was conceived as a building force, a catalyst for the creation of culture. In modern times, however, economy became a negative force, which destroys culture and dominates and hinders individuals. "What was personal contest for the Greeks, war victory and justice for the Roman, is judged in terms of supply and demand, not according to one's needs but according to the consumer's" (*Daybreak*, III, 175).

Work is based on the biological drive to exist. "What can we find, in the toil and moil of all the millions, other than the drive to exist at any price?" (*Greek*). However the introduction of the notions of "dignity of man" and "dignity of work" gave us a respectable way to hide from ourselves the fact that we have become virtual slaves of money and work. Only persons who wake up and disengage themselves from the rat race, "who are then immediately preoccupied with the fine illusions of artistic culture," can be saved from the unnatural "practical pessimism" (*Greek*).

Restless Gluttony

We have become a society of consumers, and Nietzsche, who did not know about triple and super-sized burgers and the current plague of obesity, used the metaphor of food to describe our limitless appetites. He described the meals consumed by affluent people in fancy places, joined also by educated persons whose "tables groan under the weight of the dishes," and the more the better (*Daybreak*, III, 203). The gluttony of hyper-consumption requires money, which calls for more work. Money has become the measure of all things, just having it is not enough; it must be more than what others have, and it must be flaunted openly. Money came to represent "power, glory, pre-eminence, dignity, and influence" (*Daybreak*, III, 203). The giving-in to these worldly instincts and the constant search for advantages is what separates common types from nobility (*Gay*, I, 3).

In ancient Greece only slaves had to work while we have become workaholics, for whom efficiency and production are virtues; we are ashamed of reflection, and we think "with a watch in one's hand." We are afraid to miss out on something, and prefer "to do anything rather than nothing," without joy and relaxation, always on a lookout for gain, and in the meanwhile missing rituals and lively conversations. Nietzsche commented on impoverished writing style: "This is how people now write letters and the style and spirit of letters will always be the true 'sign of the times'" (*Gay*, IV, 329). We can only guess what he would have said about today's e-mails, Twitter, and Whatsapp. We are enslaved by our social need for comparison with others; by our out-of-control consumerism, by the Moloch of money, and by the social atmosphere of "time is money," which delegitimizes leisure, reflection, and idleness. Consumerism increases satisfaction and adaptation to existing conditions, giving rise to a "stationary level of mankind," and turning persons into specialized utility, "machine in the service of economy."

The market economy is built on the assumption that increased expenditure of the population increases its welfare, while in fact it actually brings exploitation, diminishes independence, and makes people powerless and valueless (*Will*, IV, 866). Self-reflection, quiet contemplation, and a feeling of wonder, "a genuinely religious life" that demands leisure and disengagement from the hassles of work and money-making, has almost disappeared (*Beyond*, III, 58). Modern workers, "the impossible class," are unable to consider the alternative of "a philosophy in rags"—a life of the spirit and intellectual interests, with few material needs (*Daybreak*, III, 206).

Cogs in a Machine

Technological changes have turned us into factory workers and functionaries in large organizations. "The press, the machine, the railway, the telegraph are premises whose thousand-year conclusion no one has yet dared to draw" (*Human*, Wanderer, 278) and of course, the internet, TV, and cell phones can be added to the list. We have become a "culture of big cities, newspapers, feverishness and pointlessness" (*Will*, III, 748) and this transformation is taken for granted: "It does not appear . . . altogether to be a shameful thing to be utilized as . . . the screws of a machine and the stopgaps, as it were, of the human spirit of invention." Nietzsche ridiculed the argument that higher wages could be a proper compensation and cure for such "impersonal enslavement," and he wished that workers would not cooperate with the "madness of nations which desire above all to produce as much as possible, and to be as rich as possible" (*Daybreak*, III, 206).

The wheels of the machine keep rolling in science too, ruining life, importing dehumanized and impersonal "clockwork and mechanism," and applying the "false economy of the 'division of labor.'" Scientists became workers and modern scientific activity has become a means to support culture, a means to produce barbarism (*Ecce,* Untimely, 1). Psychology is certainly not an exception in this regard. A scientist today, works as a slave; his study is not an occupation but a necessity, and scientists are narrowly focused and in a hurry, "agitated and breathless running to and fro," without time to examine important life issues that arise in their work, and without room for positive impact on culture, not to mention salvation (*Untimely,* Strauss, 8).

The machine (the economic system) turns individuals into uniform products, exchangeable with each other, lacking uniqueness, and without creativity. The model of the machine enables centralization and cooperation of masses and is therefore applied in political parties and the military (*Human,* Wanderer, 218). The standardization of persons unprepared for autocracy eventually "engenders a counter effect, a despairing boredom of soul, which teaches them to long for idleness in all its varieties (*Human,* Wanderer, 220). We have two options left, to wait for the inevitable "counter movement" (*Will,* IV, 866) to come out, or opt out, moving to places where it is possible to be more independent, getting organized to protest against capital and machine or, if worst comes to worst, die (*Daybreak,* III, 206).

War, Military, and Nationalism

War and military service, which disrupt life and efface individuality, are obviously significant "forms of domination." The military, the ultimate machine, turns people into uniformed soldiers; life is endangered and lost in wars and much suffering and destruction is inflicted on soldiers and civilian populations. Nationalism joins the military and wars as means of mind control, making citizens fearful or hateful of other nations and willing, out of loyalty to their nation, to obey authorities, kill, and get killed. The military, like all other organizations, has its own self-interest of growing, gaining power and benefits; Generals are not any different from politicians or other professionals with a particular mindset. I believe that these assertions would be agreeable to most of my readers and that Nietzsche, who wished to tame the monster of the state and prescribe a severe diet for the economy of consumerism, would have subscribed to these assertions wholeheartedly. However, on the issue of war and military more than others, he zigzagged between using war as a metaphor to praising the real sanguineous thing with extreme pronouncements that can hardly be whitewashed, thus offering a treasure of justifications and encouragements to the supporters of the military and warmongering.

Nietzsche's endorsement of the military can be explained by a combination of factors: following Heraclitus, he believed that opposition or agonality is the basic force of change and that positive things can come out of a conflict. He saw peace as a hindrance and believed that danger, war, adventure, and conquest can elevate humanity to higher levels (*Gay*, V, 377). His social criticism and the evaluation that the prevailing culture was decadent, together with his reservations about democracy, led him to prescribe war as therapy for these ills, a recommendation supported by his notions of manliness and his ideals of the Will to Power and the Superman. His typical Prussian upbringing, which glorified wars and made youngsters willing to serve the "Fatherland" and if necessary sacrifice their life to it, alongside a military service that consisted of trauma, exhilaration, disappointment, pain, and little heroism or glory, must have made their contribution too. Furthermore, he admired strength passionately and abhorred weakness, which was clearly expressed in the hallelujah he sang in *Genealogy of Morality* to the brave fighting societies, warriors-beasts-lions, in search of spoil and victory. He felt deep contempt for the disgusting, weak, and domesticated humans, a mediocre "teeming mass of worms" (*Genealogy*, I, 11). In modern times, Conan the Barbarian would probably have been his favorite hero.

Against Nationalism

Although Nietzsche retained some ambivalence about the military, his position on nationalism was more decisive. Starting as a Prussian patriot, he outgrew this infatuation, and in the aphorism titled *Peoples and Fatherlands*, he criticized pan-Germanism and patriotism and called for the unification of Europe (*Beyond*, VIII, 256). Similarly in his autobiography he criticized the German nation and its Will to Power, directed at building the Reich. He rejected the conception of Germany as a race, its anti-Semitism and nationalism, "this national neurosis from which Europe is sick" (*Ecce*, Books). The striving for a position of dominance among other states, the "great politics," only results in wars, readiness for wars, and the sacrificing of youth on the "Altar of the Fatherland" (*Human*, VIII, 481). Whatever were his feelings about wars, he believed the moment nationalism was uprooted, the military and wars would crumble.

The state, in the name of morality, patriotism, and pity, is skillful in distracting and seducing us away from our duties to ourselves, "to lose our own way and flee into the lovely temple of the religion of pity." War from the perspective of individuals is an opportunity to give up their own goals, "a detour to suicide with a good conscience" (*Gay*, IV, 338). The more we can curb the sickness of nationalism—the less we see our nation as better than others. The more skeptical we are about the rhetoric of patriotism, loyalty to the nation, state, and country, the wars will lose the oxygen they need to burn on. Unfortunately most people refuse or are unable to have such second thoughts and ask themselves whether they need actually be patriots of an arbitrarily drawn area on a map and whether they owe allegiance to any particular institutions or governments, "all that is not you." Nietzsche made it clear, and I would like to quote again, "Orient and Occident are chalk lines drawn before us to fool our timidity" (*Untimely*, Schopenhauer, 3).

Far from the Madding Crowd

The first step in avoiding the clutches of institutionalized domination would be to "know your enemy" and Nietzsche tried to open our eyes, in order to see how the state, religion, economy, and the military operate and impact us. The second step would be to internalize as an antidote Nietzsche's teachings on individuality and nobility, discussed at the beginning of the chapter. The third step would be the adoption of an attitude and policy of disengagement, lying low, to escape the system's radar. Nietzsche, using the voice of Zarathustra, expressed the intense feelings that mass society and the political system aroused in him:

> Foul smells their idol, the cold monster . . . break their windows and leap to freedom. Watch them clamber, these swift monkeys! They clamber over one another and thus drag one another into the mud and the depth. They all want to get to the throne: that is their madness—as if happiness sat on the throne. (*Thus*, I, The new idol)

The state is a necessary evil, and the most one can hope for is "a spirit of enlightenment and progressive development." This is paradoxically prevented by the very attempts to change the political system by revolutionary means (*Human*, VIII, 463). We should thus strive for "as little state as possible," which can be understood as a political libertarian position or as a personal rule of distance-keeping (*Human*, VIII, 473). As far as Nietzsche was concerned, involvement in politics and economics was seen as quite a vulgar activity. "Political and economic affairs are not worthy of being the enforced concern of society's most gifted spirits" (*Daybreak*, III, 179). Accordingly, he suggested that enlightened people should not take their duties towards the state too seriously and reduce commitments, expectations, and exposure to the media. "For he who has the *furor philosophicus* within him will already no longer have time for the *furor politicus*" (*Untimely*, Schopenhauer, 7).

The select few persons who can maintain a sense of self-determination by avoiding politics might even enjoy the fact that they are not like the many that keep following the latest news edition. They do not care too much about "the happiness of the many"; they take the political game with a grain of salt, and have their own ideas of happiness," for their goal cannot be embraced by any clumsy hand with just five fingers." And yet, occasionally they might come out of their isolation and speak their minds, which others usually will not listen to or understand anyhow. Nietzsche concluded his "advice column" for the spiritually higher persons in a poetic tone of reconciliation, possibly suggesting that this is the way of the world, that there is no place for alarm, that for great souls the earth remains free and in many places "the odor of tranquil seas blowing about them—are still empty for solitaries and solitary couples" (*Thus*, I, Of the new idol). Again, in a similar mood he reassures us that humanity is a temporary phenomenon anyway, and only nature will remain forever: "Soon afterwards, it is quiet in the forest again, so quiet that one can again hear clearly the buzzing, humming, and fluttering of the innumerable insects that live in, above, and below it" (*Human*, VIII, 438).

THE CULTURE COMPLEX

Buddha proclaimed in the first noble truth that "life is suffering" and taught the way of detachment from life; Nietzsche went the opposite way, recommending living life to the fullest, with passion and in a "grand style" (*Antichrist*, 59). For him (as it was for Buddha too), suffering was not merely an academic issue and his way of coping, going on living with the many kinds of suffering he had to bear, actually made up the building blocks of his psychology, philosophy, and conception of culture. Nietzsche pointed out however, that the issue is not the very fact of physical or mental suffering, but rather how they are understood. "What really raises one's indignation against suffering is not suffering intrinsically, but the senselessness of suffering" (*Genealogy*, II, 7) and similarly, "Man's problem is *not* suffering itself," but the lack of answer to the crying question, "*Why* do I suffer?" (*Genealogy*, III, 28).

Culture and Crisis

Culture is the product of the ways individuals and groups interpret their own suffering and give it meaning and value, through institutions, art, social practices, and world views. Yet culture, the solution of a problem, becomes a problem itself when it fails to fulfill its function of maintaining the illusion that life makes sense and is worthwhile. The failure is due to competing cultures and harmful social, technological, and political developments. This dysfunction occurs in mature, late cultures, in which people become weaker not because of troubling conflicting opposite drives and values, but rather due to contradicting traditions and origins (*Beyond*, V, 200). When integration is lost, when we have a hodgepodge collection of dispersing parts rather than an organic whole, we move from culture to non-culture—to decadence, where "life no longer dwells in the whole," where "the whole no longer lives at all: it is composite, calculated, artificial, and artifact" (*Case*, 6).

Cultural fragmentation and decadence are the opposite of growth, individuality, and nobility. Yet one cannot exist without the other. "Growth goes along with disintegration and fading away; suffering, a sign of decline, is found in periods of advance; forward movements coexist with pessimism and growth with nihilism" (*Will*, I, 112). This convolution of solutions becoming bigger problems than the ones they were supposed to solve operates in the life of persons as well. Thus Nietzsche implied that the life of individuals and groups is, in fact, a progression from one crisis situation to another. He found that modern culture stopped being a "stimulant to life," became decadent, and entered a crisis stage.

Nietzsche felt that non-academically involved philosophers (like him and Schopenhauer), must be critics of culture, "the bad consciences of their age," ones who apply "the knife of vivisection to the chest of the virtues of the day," in order to promote human greatness (*Beyond*, VI, 212). He hoped that with an understanding of the current culture and its impact on individuals, and with striving for different goals, the crisis would become an opportunity for the rejuvenating of culture and the emergence of more independent and creative individuals, "virile noble natures" (*Antichrist*, 58). A full cure of the crisis is not viable now; "I am still waiting for a philosophical physician in the exceptional sense of that word–one who has to pursue the problem of the total health of a people, time, race or of humanity" (*Gay*, Preface, 2) and until this physician arrives, Nietzsche can only offer a diagnosis and some recommendations. It is up to us to decide what snares of culture to avoid and how to guide our life; it up to us to decide whether to be heroic or not. "What makes one heroic?—Going out to meet at the same time one's highest suffering and one's highest hope" (*Gay*, III, 268).

The Varieties of Culture

As with other terms, Nietzsche used "culture" in at least two contradictory senses. He actually used the two in one sentence, in criticizing modern Europe as an "enfeebled humanity" suffering from overcultivation, which must be cured by war, "lest, by the means of culture, it should lose its culture and its very existence" (*Human*, I, 477). This pairing of identical words with different meanings was repeated in his writing about *The Danger Facing Our Culture*: "We belong to an age whose culture is in danger of perishing through the means to culture" (*Human*, I, 520). Culture can be conceptualized as either private, a characteristic of an individual, or public, a quality of societies and human collectives. In both cases, it can be either autonomous or imposed by outside forces.

Autonomous Cultures

Nietzsche considered the cultures of ancient Greece, the Roman Empire, and the Renaissance, to be autonomous cultures par excellence, embodying the values of nobility, heroism, high culture, reason, self-respect, and self-sufficiency. A culture is measured not only by its ideals but by the way it acts, the integrity of its values and actions, its internal coherence and harmony, its originality and uniqueness, in short by its "higher unity" (*Untimely*, History, 4). Such a culture, be it the culture of an individual or of societies encourages having a vision and shaping the self and the environment, in its light: "This is the fundamental idea of culture, insofar as it sets but one task for each of us: to further the production of the philosopher, of the artist, and of the saint within us and outside us, and thereby to work at the consummation of nature" (*Untimely*, Schopenhauer, 5).

Establishing such a culture is a creative act which combines diverse and contradictory elements, one of which is cruelty. "Almost everything we call 'higher culture' is based on the spiritualization of cruelty, on its becoming more profound: this is my proposition." Culture is the integration of the "savage animal" with the divine, and this is what makes the grandest achievements so alluring (*Beyond*, VII, 229).

Imposed Cultures

Externally imposed culture, a direct threat to autonomous culture, is employed by powerful larger organizations aiming to shape and control individuals to serve their own interests. The "forms of domination" described in the preceding section are the backbone of imposed culture. The aim of such cultures in the modern world is "to breed and tame a civilized animal, a *household pet*, out of the beast of prey 'man'" (*Genealogy*, I, 11). Imposed culture, is a tool of state and society, and it acts behind a screen of smoke; "'culture' from first to last teaches one to lose sight of realities and instead to hunt after thoroughly problematic, so-called ideal goals" (*Ecce*, Clever, 1). What culture calls "better" is actually more governable, "more comfortable, more mediocre, more indifferent, more Chinese [uniform], more Christian" (*Genealogy*, I, 12). The danger of imposed culture is that "it will produce an animal that takes taming to be an end in itself," with no goals beyond that (*Genealogy*, I, 9).

Between Two Cultures

Tensions exist between the two kinds of culture, and Nietzsche argued that autonomous culture and state are antagonists, one thrives when the other declines. "All great ages of culture are ages of political decline: what is great culturally has always been apolitical, even anti-political" (*Twilight*, Germans, 4). He described this process as "resurrection of the spirit," a revival of the spirits which takes place at politics' sickbed. "Culture owes its highest achievements to politically weakened times (*Human*, VIII, 465).

Individuals and societies alike develop a culture in response to basic problems of existence; public culture consists of institutions and shared myths; private culture consists of habits, worldview, and lifestyle. Nietzsche, who had an ascetic upbringing (Protestant ethics and Prussian mores), identified, experienced, and suffered from symptoms of decadence, nihilism (depression), and resentment (victimhood and helplessness), and these very symptoms were used to characterize the society and culture of his times. Nietzsche was well aware of the interplay between private and public cultures and he identified a vicious cycle, arguing that nihilistic and decadent (depressed and demoralized) individuals, suffering from the lethal combination of "profound nausea" and "great pity" and "will to nothingness" have a destructive influence on the whole collective (*Genealogy*, III, 14). Living with and between two cultures, is not a simple challenge: "How can the individual be adapted to so many and manifold claims of culture without being disquieted and destroying his personality, in short, how can the individual be initiated into the counterpoint of private and public culture, how can he lead the melody and at the same time accompany it?" (*Human*, V, 242).

The Genius of Culture

Nietzsche saw a viable culture as an organic whole, an amalgam of contradictory elements, put together with a pinch of creativity. The "genius of culture," both private and public, is expressed in the following beautiful image. Incidentally, "'falsehood" and "selfishness" in this quote are not negative attributes, but rather closer in meaning to creativity and originality:

> If anyone wished to imagine a genius of culture, what would it be like? It handles as its tools falsehood, force, and thoughtless selfishness so surely that it could only be called an evil, demoniacal being; but its aims, which are occasionally transparent, are great and good. It is a centaur, half-beast, half-man, and, in addition, has angel's wings upon its head. (*Human*, V, 241)

Culture and Mass Culture

Four processes threaten to destroy modern culture: the fast rate of changes, "haste and hurry now universal," and the loss of contemplation and naturalness; the decline of religion, leaving behind "swamps or stagnant pools"; the rise of materialism, "contemptible money economy," and with it a decline of love and goodness; and finally, the collusion and betrayal of the intellectuals, who are aware of the dangers and do nothing about them. "The educated classes are no longer lighthouses or refuges in the midst of this turmoil of secularization; they themselves grow daily more restless, thoughtless and loveless. Everything, contemporary art and science included, serves the coming barbarism" (*Untimely*, Schopenhauer, 4).

The Market-Place

Zarathustra drew the last man as an illustration of modern soul, and the market-place was made a symbol of mass culture. In the market-place persons are like flies, buzzing, seething and stinging. "Where solitude ends, there begins the market-place; and where the market-place begins, there begins also the noise of the great actors, and the buzzing of the poison-flies" (*Thus*, I, The flies of the market-place). In our consumerist culture, things, including ideas and aesthetic products, are measured by monetary value, which is determined to a large degree by the way they are packaged and presented and by the work of go-betweens, impresarios, advertising agencies, and public-relations experts. In this world, the image of things is more important than the things themselves, "representers" are more important than creators, and people no longer have a concept of quality and greatness. "Around the devisers of new values revolves the world:—invisibly it revolves" (*Thus*, I, The flies of the market-place).

In order to sell, there must always be new merchandise, new "in" products and celebrities. Things must be presented in an exaggerated manner; they are always the best, the newest, the most advanced; "full of clattering buffoons is the market-place,—and the people glory in their great men! These are for them the masters of the hour." This is a world of black and white, of crude generalizations, without room for qualifications and reservations, with pressure to adapt to such thinking, "Alas! You would set your chair between For and Against?" (*Thus*, I, The flies of the market-place).

Public Opinion and the Media

Nietzsche saw newspapers as danger to culture and a tool of manipulation by "superfluous people," who are interested in money and power only. "They vomit their bile and call it newspaper" (*Thus*, The new idol).

Newspapers were a monster; what kind of a monster will the media be with the addition of movies, TV, and internet? Public opinion is the negation of private opinion, and it serves as a referee of truth, values, and taste; it mobilizes and shapes; changes fashions but also makes nations go to war. Public opinion is what makes us members of a herd, particles in a mass, one of many identical others. We have thus become barren creatures who evade their own genius, who always look to see what others are doing to fit in. We became "completely exterior, without core, a tattered, painted sack of clothes, a ragtag ghost that cannot provoke even fear and certainly not sympathy" (*Untimely*, Schopenhauer, 1). People who are ruled by public opinion, hide behind social conventions, and disregard their uniqueness were considered by Nietzsche as pseudo-persons, and he wondered, "But what is it that forces the man to fear his neighbor, to think and act with his herd, and not seek his own joy?" And the answer was simple laziness, "taking things easily." Our combined shortcomings made our times "an age that rests its salvation on public opinion,—that is, on private laziness."

Overload of Information

What was true in Nietzsche's times is more so nowadays, when electronic media technologies change quickly and modern persons are bombarded by information of a wide scope and fast pace. They suffer from overload, as all those who try to stay up to date in their profession know. Their diet is too rich and they cannot digest it properly, making them oversensitive, irritable, exhausted, superficial, and paralyzed. Moderns hardly initiate actions and are usually activated by outside impressions, which puts them in a defensive position, trying to assimilate, interpret, or reject data implosions: "Cosmopolitanism in foods, literatures, newspapers, forms, tastes, even landscapes. The tempo of this influx is *prestissimo*; the impressions erase each other; one instinctively resists taking in anything deeply, to 'digest' anything; a weakening of the power to digest results from this" (*Will*, I, 71).

In such hectic conditions of life, attempts at integration fail; conflicts between bits of information are common and after repeated onslaughts of information, habituation takes place. A second nature is created, weaker, more restless than the first, less in touch with reality; where there is a lack of correspondence between internal conflicts and external realities, a situation unknown to the ancients: "modern man finally drags a huge crowd of indigestible rocks of knowledge around inside him, which then occasionally audibly bang around in his body, as it says in fairy tales" (*Untimely*, History, 4).

The ailments of modernity can be cured, and Nietzsche prescribed two deceptively simple and quick medications for those who do not wish to belong to the masses and refuse to be victims of public opinion: they must not look too much for comfort, they have to follow their consciousness which proclaims, "Be yourself!" and realize that "all you are now doing, thinking, desiring, is not you yourself" (*Untimely*, Schopenhauer, 1). They must draw limited horizons, a buffer against information overload. This first cure will be discussed in detail when I present Nietzsche's thoughts on self-creation (chapter 8) and the second one will be reviewed in the exploration of his life wisdom (chapter 6).

The Ills of Modern Men and Women

Nietzsche depicted the "last man" (*Thus*, Zarathustra's prologue, 5) as an icon of modern culture. I have already commented that his characterization was harsh, full of contempt, with no shred of empathy; and yet perhaps he had to shock us in order to get our attention. The last man cares only about being like others and about satisfying the hunger for material goods, without any longing for achievements of spiritual nature. Liberal democracy, egalitarianism, and mass culture brought about the "modern" morality of resentment and a culture devoid of aesthetic and non-materialistic values.

European Buddhism

The moderns adopted a European version of Buddhism, in the form of "morality of communal compassion." Dreams of messianic justice for all, tolerance and forgiveness of everything, thus became the highest morality (*Beyond*, V, 202). Their (and our) exaggerated tolerance, compromising and avoidance of clear-cut positions is the result of the combination of laziness and cowardliness. Nietzsche stood for the opposite, a robust formula for happiness which substitutes resignation with passion, determination and aspirations, "a *Yea*, a *Nay*, a straight line, a goal" (*Antichrist*, 1).

Semi-Barbarism

The persons "of the present" are unauthentic and sterile scarecrows, wearing masks to hide their internal emptiness. They are proud to be "complete realists, a without belief or superstition," not realizing that belief is necessary for creation. They lack intellectual capital and easily adopt and discard intellectual fashions; they "are half open doors at which grave-diggers wait" (*Thus*, II, Immaculate perception). Modernity is the new semi-barbarism, made up of a chaotic mishmash of fashions and styles, without any order, hierarchy, and style. Its lax slogan, "everything goes," leads to devaluation of the classics, loss of standards of excellence, and even hostility to perfection, maturity, and nobility in human art and culture (*Beyond*, VII, 224). Semi-barbarism is the bedfellow of a smug cultural philistinism, and moderns consider their period the best there ever was in history; they feel that they know everything there is to know; they do not engage in self-criticism and have an inflated self-image. A typical modern "fancies that he is himself a son of the Muses and a man of culture"; moderns do not produce culture, but are only its indiscriminate consumers (*Untimely*, Strauss, 1). They lost the healthy instinct of knowing what is real and right, not seeing the difference between "the quick and the dead, the genuine and the counterfeit, the original and the imitation, between a God and a host of idols" (*Untimely*, Strauss, 12).

Without Myth and Roots

Myth is the power that unifies cultures, supplying a context and focus for creativity. "Only a horizon defined by myths completes and unifies a whole cultural movement." Myths function as "unnoticed omnipresent demonic guardians," accompanying the upbringing of youth, enabling persons to interpret, in the light of myths, their life and struggles. The "mythical foundation" anchored in religion is also used by the state to maintain solidarity among its subjects. However with the decline of religion, the power of the myths dwindled. With our "cultural pluralism" or "multiculturalism" (terms unknown in Nietzsche's times) we lost a significant tie with one tradition; we have become rootless, without "the mythical home" and "the mythical maternal womb" of our existence (*Birth*, 23).

Masks and Roles

Show and impression management prevail in modern life; we don't have time, we hustle, we run away from ourselves and yet want to appear as self-content. "We live in fear of memory and of turning inward" (*Untimely*, Schopenhauer, 5). We are expected to have a profession, and a profession necessitates playing a role; a role becomes character, and art becomes nature; "people confound themselves with their role, becoming victims of a good performance." Such role playing extends to other areas in life, turning us all into actors who believe they can easily improvise, try out, and play all roles, "and all nature ceases and becomes art" (*Gay*, V, 356).

The masquerade takes a heavy social toll because whenever actors are considered masters, the real social architects, planners, and builders of society step down; and whenever connection with traditions withers, individuals stop seeing themselves as "one stone of many in societies' building" (*Gay*, V, 356). On the individual level, playacting causes additional loss of individuality, instincts, and self-trust; the actors become quixotic, swamped in their subjectivity, "masks and shadows," no more independent, but clones of each other (*Untimely*, History, 4).

What are we supposed to do with the above list of failings? We can always make a questionnaire out of it, with a score from one to five on each item, and call it the semi-barbarism questionnaire and, as is common in modern psychology, title it the SBQ. More seriously, we must remember that despite some overgeneralization, Nietzsche presented us with the worrying results of a CT scan he performed on our life's circumstances. He wanted the new doctors of the soul to have a clear view of morality, society, and culture and suggested ways to understand psychological problems in the context of society and culture and not in clinical-pathological terms only.

Are they supposed to share it with their clients, to take their blinders off? What if the person consulting them is religious, nationalist, a party member, a newspaper freak, in short, the latest model of the last person? We are moving now from Nietzsche's science (knowledge and wisdom) of psychology to the science and art of Nietzschean counseling and therapy. In art, there are no clear-cut rules; the new doctor of the soul must decide, what, with whom, and when to share, question, or hint; just as she must decide whether to share something about her life. Moreover, one can only hope that the Nietzschean therapists are not Nietzschean, that is to say, they know that his is only one perspective, and they must have others too, all of them integrated in their unique mixture, delivered in their singular style.

NOTE

1. Ernest Jones, *Sigmund Freud: Life and Work* (London: Hogarth Press, 1953), p. 421.

II

Psychotherapy

SIX

The Path of Wisdom

In the second part of this book, we will deal with Nietzsche's psychotherapy. Here too, he wrote about things he knew personally well: He suffered and felt pain almost daily, and depression for him was not a matter of academic study, but rather a personal descent into hell. "I too have been in the underworld, as was Odysseus, and I will often be there again" (*Human*, Assorted, 408). Similarly, when he wrote about solutions for problems in living, he described his own attempts, and when he taught "how to become who you are," he described his own experience.

Nietzsche saw his writings as a garden and a building. The psychotherapy part of my book will be dedicated to the further reconstruction of the main cornerstones in the building of wise living, changing and solving problems in life, and for this purpose I took the liberty to assemble stones that were scattered around in Nietzsche's writings: "The philosopher believes that the value of his philosophy lies in its totality, in its structure: posterity discovers it in the stones with which he built and with which other structures are subsequently built that are frequently better—and so, in the fact that that structure can be demolished and yet still possess value as material" (*Human*, Assorted, 201).

Do I have to repeat myself and say that Nietzsche's writings are multifaceted and multi-layered and not one integrated system? He was uncongenial to all systems of thought, and it holds true for his psychotherapy too. Do I have to remind you that he did not use explicitly the word "psychotherapy" and that he never divided his psychotherapy into themes and kinds? I will begin here with *The Path of Wisdom*, consisting of teachings and advice on the art of living, which can be considered as Nietzsche's guidance, consulting or preventive psychology, aiming to increase successful coping and build up resiliency. I will continue (chapter 7) with Nietzsche's "clinical psychology," directed at understanding and solving problems in living, ameliorating spiritual suffering, and relieving symptoms. I will conclude with his teaching on creating the self, self-design, or life-sculpting, what is popularly termed "self-actualization" (chapter 8).

TWO TIGHT-ROPE WALKERS

In an unforgettable metaphor, Zarathustra encountered two tight-rope walkers, trying to walk on a rope stretched between two towers. One tower, I would say, is when we are born; the other is when we die. One walker was serious and measured; the other danced his way cheerfully; one slipped and fell to his death; the other made it easily to the end (*Thus*, Prologue, 6). Zarathustra, so it can be understood, used this powerful image to say that dangers and maneuvering with life and with ourselves are the essences of being human. "Man is a rope, fastened between animal and Superman—a rope over an abyss" (*Thus*, Prologue, 4). This image also suggests that there are different ways to carry on.

Nietzsche, who shared with us his philosophy of life and scale of values, realized that values cannot be mandated and that people seeking happiness must find their own values independently, "for individual happiness springs from one's own unknown laws, and prescriptions from without can only hinder it" (*Daybreak*, II, 108). He could not teach us what to do in life, but he had much to offer on the question of how to do what we chose and how to conduct our life, as there are wise and unwise ways of doing it. He teaches how to climb and cross over on the rope of life. Differently put, he is actually instructing us, in the tradition of the ancient Greek, Roman, and Biblical wisdom books, how to live wisely: "If we are sensible, the only thing that need concern us is that we should have joy in our hearts. Alas someone added, if we are sensible the best thing we can do is to be wise" (*Human*, Wanderer, 300, 7).

Living Wisely

The "someone" in the above quote, is probably Nietzsche himself, who did not see happiness and joy as the ultimate goal in life. A prerequisite for being wise is not being stupid, as the two are not mutually exclusive. Another precondition is having an idea or picture of wise living, or in other words, a positive model of optimal functioning, or "mental health," to use the words of the new *psychologica*. Nietzsche went on to present desirable and undesirable behaviors, traits, and attitudes for living and he began with a basic requirement: "A man, who will not become master of his irritability, his venomous and vengeful feelings, and his lust, and attempts to become master in anything else, is as stupid as the farmer who lays out his field beside a torrent without guarding against it (*Human*, Wanderer, 65).

Failure to overcome the passions is one kind of stupidity, and forgetting our purpose is the "most frequent form of stupidity" (*Human*, Wanderer, 206) and thus, we choose a vocation as a means to an end, but then forget the end and let the means take over. An additional form of stupidity consists of lack of familiarity and insight into our needs and preferences, and consequently, making wrong decisions in time management, choice of friends, leisure activities, diet, and life habits. "This is what transforms the earth for so many into a 'vale of tears'" (*Human*, Wanderer, 6).

The title of the present chapter is taken from a long aphorism which includes, in a nutshell, much of Nietzsche's instruction on wise living. If we disassemble the quote into smaller units, we will find the principles involved in walking the path of wisdom. The same points also constitute an outline of a counseling and therapy handbook, designed for the new doctors of the soul:

> 1. Self-reliance and inner directedness. 2. Self-forgiveness, avoidance of self-criticism, self-forgiving, and progress in small steps. 3. Consecration of chance and turning constraints into opportunities. 4. Positive acceptance of what already happened, seeing older mistakes as instructive, and understanding problems in terms of human evolution. 5. Love of art and culture, including religion, as sources of wisdom, combined with an awareness of their shortcomings. 6. Avoidance of simplifications and generalizations, learning the history of issues and all their sides, and being familiar with the game of using two scales, "on the one hand—on the other hand." 7. Learning the past and extrapolating from it into the future. 8. Love of knowledge, utilization and integration of life's experiences: "You have it in your power to merge everything you have lived through—attempts, false starts, errors, delusions, passions, your love and your hope—into your goal, with nothing left over." 9. Seeing oneself as a microcosm in the macrocosm of environment and culture: "You are to become an inevitable chain of culture-rings." Understanding the culture one lives in, and accepting or rejecting its influences according to one's needs. 10. Listening to nature and learning its ways of operation. 11. Accepting old age and death calmly and without anger: "You encounter both old age and wisdom on one ridge of life—that is how nature wanted it" (*Human*, V, 292).[1]

The Greek Lesson

In an early collection of reflections on philology, Nietzsche heeded his own advice to learn from the past and drew from the Greek ancient world his model or ideal of the wise person: characterized by bodily health and agility, penetrating observation of daily matters, a sense of freedom, belief in good upbringing, ardor for excellence, love of the arts, respect for leisure, and a "sense for free individuality, for the symbolical" (*Philologists*, 104). The wise Greeks had a certain "child-like *naiveté*," and did not experience shame or bad conscience. They were sincere, passionate, and open like artists; individualistic, proud, and ambitious, not inclined towards conventionality (*Philologists*, 106).

The Greeks were "enemies of shyness and dullness," tolerant of pain, risk takers, with "insight into misery despite their bright and genial temperament," with an ability to see the profound and glorify mundane things. They could be vicious without suffering from guilt-feelings and easily forget what already transpired; they had an ability to understand, get along in, and influence their human environment, using envy and jealousy to their advantage (*Philologists*, 107); they were not moderate and cautious but rather alert and overly stimulated, with "fervor of the will" (*Philologists*, 108).

EARTH, ANIMAL, AND BODY

Zarathustra is the prophet and advocate of animality, earthiness, and corporality—the opposites of morality, idealism, and spirituality. "My ego taught me a new pride, I teach it to men: No longer to bury the head in the sand of heavenly things, but to carry it freely, an earthly head which creates meaning for the earth!" (*Thus*, I, Joys and passions). He urged us repeatedly to "remain true to the earth, and do not believe those who speak to you of super-terrestrial hopes! They are poisoners, whether they know it or not" (*Thus*, I, Prologue, 3). He was not looking forward to the kingdom of heaven because "we have become men, so we want the kingdom of earth" (*Thus*, IV, The ass festival, 2). Earthiness demands to bring lofty virtues down to earth, to the body and life, "that it may give the earth its meaning, a human meaning!" (*Thus*, I, The bestowing virtue, 2). The body means flesh, blood, and instincts, and not mummies and phantoms (*Thus*, III, The spirit of gravity, 2) and similarly, "to the discerning man all instincts are holy" (*Thus*, I, The bestowing virtue, 2).

The Human Animal

Studying Nietzsche's psychology of morality (chapter 4), we learned that humanity has undergone a few waves of socialization and moralization. At first, the fierce animality of humans was broken, to make them more self-conscious and more manageable, and much later, with the advent of Judaism and Christianity, the human body was bowdlerized for similar reasons, making it of secondary importance to the fictions of soul and spirit. For this purpose, the enemies of life targeted sexuality and "threw dirt on the origin, on the prerequisite of our life." (*Twilight*, Ancients, 4). Zarathustra attacked the despisers of the body and the denigrators of the earth, who see basic bodily functions as unclean. "To the clean are all things clean," but also, "to the swine all things become swinish!" and he called the latter "backworldsmen," because they see the world from the backside as a filthy monster (*Thus*, III, Old and new tables, 14). Only with the acknowledgment of the "splendid animal" in us can the "well-constituted and complete man" be achieved. (*Will*, IV, 1045).

Enemies of Life

Religion is not the only enemy of life; it is joined by a variety of other idealists and transcendentalists. Nietzsche urged us to be deaf to the metaphysical peddlers and indifferent to all theoretical questions and speculations that cannot be answered and really do not matter. Not having final answers should not hinder us from living. "We have no need of these certainties about the farthermost horizons in order to live a full and efficient human life, any more than the ant needs them in order to be a good ant." He called the popular questions of the goal of life and what happens after death "a bag of tricks," which only reinforces guilt feelings and fear of punishment. Nietzsche suggested that "we must once more become good friends of 'everyday matters,' rather than concern ourselves with "the problems of the dogmatic philosophers, be they idealists, materialists, or realists" (*Human*, Wanderer, 16).

The Sick Animal

Our animality, a biological fact, cannot be erased. Animals have different natures: some are grazing cattle (*Untimely*, History, 1); others are wild beast of prey (*Genealogy*, I, 11); and human animals are "more ill, less certain, more changeable, more insecure than any other animal" (*Will*, II, 258). Living and acting against our nature has disastrous effects, and the divorce from our animal nature makes us sick animals. Looking at humans from the animal perspective, Nietzsche figured that "they consider him the insane animal, the laughing animal, the weeping animal, the miserable animal" (*Gay*, III, 224). The attempts to turn persons ashamed of their instincts into angels resulted with the loss of animals' joy and innocence; with distasteful life and "upset stomach and that furry tongue" (*Genealogy*, II, 7). Rather than trusting their internal "divine animal"—their instincts—the sick animals depend on "the piled-up jumble of scholarly data" and turn to societal prescriptions for guidance, continually playing roles and wearing masks as "educated man, as scholar, as poet, as politician" (*Untimely*, History, 6).

Return to Nature

Nietzsche aimed to change the way we live, think, discuss, and study human life,, not in idealistic terms but in naturalistic ones. His motto was

Homo natura, a natural person; his call was the return to the body, to nature, to the original text, "the terrible original text" by peeling off layers of moralization, mystification, and religious doctrines. He urged us to stop listening to the "old metaphysical bird-catchers" who play an alluring tune, "thou art more! Thou art higher! Thou hast a different origin!" (*Beyond,* VII, 230). Alas, bird-catchers and birds do not die, they just keep on changing; Nirvana, enlightenment, spirituality, and all other otherworldly notions are still in circulation. We should come to terms with our animality, and give up abstractions and mystifications in favor of the near and the tangible (*Will,* II, 231). This is not a simple challenge, and Nietzsche wondered, "Error has turned animals into men; might truth be capable of turning man into an animal again?" (*Human,* IX, 219). Once we return to our nature, to animality, to the body, we will become "free born birds" that can easily fly anywhere they desire, always with freedom and the sunshine around them (*Gay,* IV, 294). In order to fly, we must identify, challenge, and discard the influences of education, society, and culture, which include the fantasies of "God, soul, virtue, sin, Beyond, truth, eternal life." Only after we get rid of these lies will we be able to return to "the fundamentals of life" (*Ecce,* Clever, 10).

The "fundamentals," the natural biological functions, "whatever originates in the stomach, the intestines, the beating of the heart, the nerves, the bile, the seed," cannot be judged in moral terms. Our physiological sensitivities, illnesses, and "the whole contingency of that machine about which we know so little," have nothing to do with good or evil, God or the devil (*Daybreak,* I, 86). In place of guilt and shame, Nietzsche praised "the vulgar element in everything that gives pleasure" and he acclaimed the model of Southern Europe, as was evident in Pompeii where "everything appears as poised and self-assured as anything noble." After all, we are animals like any other animal and should "run about freely" (*Gay,* II 77).

The Wisdom of the Body

Nietzsche rejected the dualistic concept of body and soul (chapter 1) and his psychology is based on the wisdom of the body. He despised and rejected the "sick and dying," who invented "things of heaven" (*Thus,* I, The Afterworldsmen). Zarathustra-Nietzsche posited that "there is more wisdom in your body than in your deepest philosophy": "The body is a great intelligence, a multiplicity with one sense, a war and peace, a herd and a herdsman. The body has a great intelligence; the little intelligence called spirit is just the body's instrument. The body doesn't say 'I'- it performs it" (*Thus,* I, The despisers of the body).

For this reason, one must take good care of the body, and, first of all, be in a good physical shape and keep moving. "My most creative moments were always accompanied by unusual muscular activity. The body is inspired: let us waive the question of the 'soul'" (*Ecce*, Thus). Also, "remain seated as little as possible; trust no thought that is not born in the open, to the accompaniment of free bodily motion nor one in which your very muscles do not celebrate a feast" (*Ecce*, Clever, 1). Other life habits, proper diet, rest, and fresh air are not less important. One must know one's body, even "the size of one's stomach," and treat it appropriately, in order to preserve mental functioning and creativity (*Ecce*, Clever). So many psychotherapists start with the soul, never bothering to inquire about and encourage basic bodily fitness and proper diet, while, in fact, it is the body which should be the point of departure, "the right place is the body, the gesture, the diet, physiology; the rest follows from that" (*Twilight*, Skirmishes, 47).

Higher noble types are at their best when heir reason is suspended and they succumb to instincts and behave like an animal risking its life to protect its young, or an animal following a female in heat, without thinking about danger or death. Being blind to our instincts, we seek moderation in pleasures, but miss intensity, "that pleasure of the rider on a fiery steed!" (*Gay*, IV, 870). This poetic image recognizes the exhilaration of passion and the dangers involved in opening up to our instincts, in letting the "heart displace the head," when strong pleasurable or unpleasurable feelings "reduce the intellect to silence or to servitude" (*Gay*, I, 3).

Innocent and Free Hearts

The voice of the healthy body is honest and pure and "it speaks of the meaning of the earth" (*Thus*, I, The afterworldly). Zarathustra invited us to listen to this voice and liberate ourselves from inhibitions set upon sensuality, lust for power, and selfishness, for "these three have hitherto been the best cursed, worst slanted and slandered,—these three I will weigh in a humanly good way" (*Thus*, III, The three evils, 1). These three are the antidotes to asceticism and chastity, meekness and passivity, unselfishness and unassertiveness. The rabble and the despisers of the body see sensuality as "the ever-ready stewing-oven of lust"; while for innocent and free hearts it is "the earth's garden-joy, an overflowing of thanks to the present from the future" (*Thus*, III, The three evils, 2).

The lust for power, a natural instinct of domination, with its awful, necessary, constructive destructiveness, is an agent of change that questions conventions, "the earthquake that breaks and breaks open everything rotten and hollow." It is a universal lust, appearing in many forms, changing lives and history (*Thus*, III, The three evils, 2). We should similarly respect "the sound, healthy selfishness which wells up out of a mighty soul," a soul with a strong handsome body, which sees self-delight as virtue; banishes cowardliness, worry, complaining and catastrophic thinking; rejects timidity, humbleness and unassertiveness; and sees willingness to tolerate mistreatment and inability to defend oneself as befitting the nature of slaves (*Thus*, III, The three evils, 2).

PLAY, DANCE, AND LAUGHTER

Nietzsche used a variety of metaphors to describe different phases and aspects of human life—children, camels, lions, and centaurs too. Some metaphors, like warriors, artists, and sages, represent our adult parts; others, like play, dance, and laughter, stand for the child in us. "Childish" play, dance, music, and laughter overlap conceptually and experientially, and they are different from their "adult" parallel routines of work, walking, talking, and somberness; they are not task-oriented, but rather *autotelic*, something that is engaged in for its own sake, with the reward inherent in the activity itself. With them, time is experienced differently and it freezes or moves faster. Zarathustra described himself as the dancer, the laughing prophet, and "one who loves jumping and escapades" (*Thus*, IV, The higher man, 18) and he saw life without them as tasteless. "And let that day be lost to us on which we did not dance once! And let that wisdom be false to us that brought no laughter with it!" (*Thus*, III, Old and new law-tables, 23).

The Eternal Child

The child is the last and highest stage in the transformation from camel to lion to child (*Thus*, I, The three metamorphoses) and indeed, when Zarathustra became a child he no longer had anything in common with the "sleepers" (*Thus*, I, Prologue, 2). Adults, making a sharp distinction between childhood and adulthood, think that "fairy-tales and games belong to childhood." But life is too short for such pedantry and it is better to maintain the attitude of children, looking at their games as work, and at their fairy tales as truth (*Human*, Assorted, 270). The Greek *pais paizon* [a child playing] became for Nietzsche a motto, almost like the Latin *amor fati*, and in his notes he wrote that in "childlike" play, those who are powerful enough turn the useless into an ideal. Likewise, *pais paizon* is the essence of God's "childlikeness" (*Will*, IV, 797). The child stands for "innocence and forgetting, a new beginning, a game, a wheel rolling on its own, a prime movement, a sacred Yes" (*Thus*, I, The three metamorphoses). A child also stands for "the capacity of being small," the ability to experience the world freshly and directly without the scaffolding of words and concepts, an ability that we must regain: "We must be as near to flowers, grasses, and butterflies as a child, that is, not much bigger than they. We adults have grown up beyond them and have to stoop to them" (*Human*, Wanderer, 51).

We should not become intellectual squares, set in old and customary ways of thinking. "Mature adulthood: that means, to have rediscovered the seriousness one had as a child at play" (*Beyond*, IV, 94). And Nietzsche added in his autobiography, "I know of no other manner of dealing with great tasks than as play: this, as a sign of greatness, is an essential prerequisite" (*Ecce*, Clever, 10).

A Dancing Star

One of Nietzsche's most poetic and popular aphorisms, often seen printed on T-shirts is "I tell you: one must still have chaos in oneself, to give birth to a *dancing star*" (*Thus*, I, Prologue), a saying which reminds us of the Biblical God creating light out of chaos (*Genesis*, I, 1–2) and of Nietzsche's image of God the creator as a child at play. We also sense that he was talking about himself, giving birth to books, his dancing stars. Nietzsche's dance represents enjoyable lightness, movement, and harmony in thinking and creating with art and ideas. "Our first questions about the value of a book, of a human being, or a musical composition are: Can they walk? Even more, can they dance?" (*Gay*, V, 366). The same goes for the ultimate creator. "I should believe only in a God who understood how to dance" (*Thus*, I, Reading and writing). Dance must appear effortlessness and graceful: "It is the stillest words which bring the storm. Thoughts that come on doves' feet guide the world" (*Thus*, I, The stillest hour).

Subscribing to science has a negative side-effect, as it "deprives us of more and more pleasure through casting suspicion on metaphysics, religion, and art, sources of joy to which mankind owes almost all of its humanity." We should, therefore, for our health, be able to look at things from the perspectives of art and religion as well. "A higher culture must give man a double-brain, as it were a brain with two chambers, one for the reception of science, the other for that of non-science" (*Human*, V, 251). Dancing between different perspectives is a sign of strength and flexibility (*Human*, V, 278); dance is a specific way of approaching intellectual and artistic pursuits, coping with life and dealing with problems; it is something that can be learned, a skill that must be built up gradually: "He who wants to learn to fly one day must first learn to stand and to walk and to run and to climb and to dance—you cannot learn to fly by flying!" (*Thus*, I, The spirit of gravity, 2).

The Olympian Vice

Nietzsche toyed with the idea that the Olympian gods practice philosophy, and it was clear to him that in doing it, they knew how to laugh at the most serious things. "Gods delight in making fun: even where sacred actions are concerned, it seems they cannot stop laughing" (*Beyond*, IX,

294). If we are not God or one of the gods, we should at least be like them. Moving from the Olympus down to earth, Nietzsche talked about laughter as an earthly consolation: "you should first learn to laugh, my young friends, if you want to remain pessimists; perhaps then, as laughers, you will someday send all metaphysical consolations to the devil—and metaphysics first of all" (*Birth,* 7).

We are the "comedian of the world," and the joke is on us, for we fail to see how humorous is our view of ourselves as the most important goal of existence. "If a God created the world, he created man to be his ape, as a perpetual source of amusement in the midst of his rather tedious eternities." How tragicomic are our gestures of suffering; how vain is our belief that we are so unique and above all living things. How we delude ourselves that the end of life on earth would be a cosmic disaster. Nietzsche advises us to see ourselves and our suffering in proportion. We "ants in the forest" are even smaller than we thought, and smaller than we could ever imagine; what is our life in comparison with the whole large "ocean of birth and decay" of the universe? In no way can we be the aim and the purpose of existence (*Human,*Wanderer, 14). Looking at the world philosophically and humorously, from an Olympian perspective, soaring above and beyond our personal problems, our individual life, and the whole human race enables us to be astonished at nothing and gain equanimity: "Many species of animals have already vanished; if man too should vanish nothing would be lacking in the world. One must be sufficient of a philosopher to admire this nothing too (*Nill admirari*) (*Will,* II, 302).

One must climb high, to have a broad perspective and maintain one's distance, in order to take things in proportion (*Thus,* I, Reading and writing). Describing the higher man, Nietzsche added, "Be of good courage, 'what does it matter!' 'How much is still possible!' Learn to laugh at yourselves as a man ought to laugh!" (*Thus,* I, The higher man, 15). It would be better for us to see, with a shrug of the shoulder, the absurdity of it all, and with this view Nietzsche was completely in tune with Qohelet (Ecclesiastes), his compatriot in the republic of geniuses, who so often said: "Vanity of vanities; all is vanity" (*Ecclesiastes,* I, 2).

The Olympian vice helps us take things in stride, but it also helps to deal more effectively with life's problems. Psychotherapists, the old doctors of the soul, with their sad nodding, humming, and obligatory empathy, too often reaffirm the tragic view of life's problems held by their clients. A new soul doctor, a Nietzschean therapist, might ask, "Can you see the joke, the absurd and comedy, in this situation?" Our bearings with other people easily create situations of strife and hurt. Our old mammal brain is ready to charge angrily or run desolated to hide in a cave; yet there is a better way: "He who wants to kill most thoroughly—laughs. One kills, not by anger but by laughter" (*Thus,* IV, The ass festival, 1). A straight line is the shortest one, but in life, it is not always the best one. "All good things approach their goal crookedly. Like cats they arch their backs, they purr inwardly at their approaching happiness—all good things laugh" (*Thus*, IV, The higher man, 17).

The Delight in Masks

Masks of conformity, lack of authenticity, and social role playing, worn against one's own convictions, demolish one's integrity (*Daybreak*, III, 149); masks worn in order to advance one's interests in the framework of existing social constraints are a different matter. The ability to pretend, change appearances, and wear masks, exemplified by actors and artists, is basically a coping and adaptation mechanism found as mimicry in the animal world (*Gay*, V, 362). Masks are natural, desirable and unavoidable, inherent to all ideologies, attitudes, and language, as there is always something not explicitly stated. In other words, every text has a sub-text, "Every philosophy also *hides* a philosophy; every opinion is also a hiding place, every word is also a mask" (*Beyond*, IX, 289).

Profound and ingenious spirits need masks (*Beyond*, II, 40) as a tool of maneuvering and self-expression. Having a larger repertoire of needs and possible satisfactions with many ways of self-expression, they are proficient in the language of mask and gesture. In this case, a mask is not a cover for something hidden or forbidden, but the result of playing one role and option out of many in an inner multiplicity. This richness was appreciated in ancient cultures, together with "delight in masks and the good conscience in using any kind of mask!" (*Gay*, II, 77). Wearing a mask, one can show feelings he does not have; pretend that she does not have unconventional feelings or thoughts; or hide one's pain and suffering in a noble manner. Unfortunate people, out of stupidity, consider the expression of pity as the ultimate good, and it is, therefore, advisable to show pity but not to have it (*Human*, I, 50). Nietzsche was probably referring to himself, when he suggested that in some cases, out of respect and consideration, people should not be unmasked:

> There are free, impudent spirits who would like to hide and deny that they are broken, proud, incurable hearts; and now and then even foolishness is a mask for an unholy, all-too-certain knowledge. Hence, it follows that it's part of a more sophisticated humanity to have reverence 'for the mask' and not to pursue psychology and curiosity in the wrong place. (*Beyond*, IX, 270)

CHANCE AND ACTION

Nietzsche's personality theory (chapter 3) seems to carry a paradox of action: on one hand he discredited the power of the will and maintained that we cannot read and know our innermost needs; not only that, we are also ruled by the forces of chance. On the other hand, he wanted us to become ourselves and even strive towards higher goals. If so, how is action possible without willing and without knowing what is it that we want; or in other words, how can we conduct ourselves intelligently and solve problems in living? The paradox of action is not only a conceptual problem in Nietzsche's theorizing; it is also a central problem in life, in self-changing and psychotherapy, where people ask for help in changing what appears to be up to them, but still they cannot change by themselves. Understanding the intricacies of chance and action is thus an important tool in the practice of the new doctors of the soul.

Nietzsche illustrated the problem of action with the issue of choosing a profession and a calling in life. Most people are "square pegs in round holes," who lack capacity and miss satisfaction because they were led by chance, with little reason and exploration of other options entering their decision. Later, they stayed on course, only out of convenience and practical considerations, "for wisdom on earth has almost always had something of the weakness of old age and lack of vigor about it" (*Philologists,* 1). He described the paradox again, claiming that people in "the midst of the great whirlpool of forces," mislead themselves into believing that the whirlpool is rational with a rational goal. Yet, as limited as it is, we must use our analytic abilities to the utmost, as putting ourselves in the hands of fate alone, will only leave us in the lurch (*Philologists*, 181).

We will deal with the paradox of action, by accepting it with the wisdom of Oedipus; by approaching it both empirically and poetically, with our "double brain"; by playing better the dice of chance; and finally in understanding willing as a tool. "Always do what you will—but first be one that can will!" (*Thus,* III, Virtue that makes small). If the will is a tool, like with all tools, we must know how and when to use it, when not to use it, and what are its limitations.

Wise Oedipus

Nietzsche associated Oedipus not with a conjectured psychological complex,[2] but rather with wisdom. Oedipus understood that we are not responsible for our dreams and hardly responsible for our waking life and accepting his wisdom is not easy at all. "The complete irresponsibility of man for his actions and his nature is the bitterest drop which he who understands must swallow" (*Human,* II, 107). We learned (chapter 2) to question the existence of some simple substratum of a voluntary inducing agent (such as consciousness, ego, motive, will, strength, or energy) behind actions. We also learned (chapter 3) not to delude ourselves as to the degree of control we have over our lives. We are not masters of our thoughts; consciousness, is not the "directing agent" and we cannot thoroughly understand our actions—"all actions are essentially unknown" (*Daybreak,* II, 116; *Gay,* IV, 335; *Beyond,* II, 32). Consequently, if we want to accomplish anything in life, we must, first of all, know our limitations and admit that we are quite clueless about our wishes and cannot carry them out by fiat.

Our Double Brain

We are with limited powers indeed, and here comes a tall order: We must nevertheless continue to believe that we know exactly what we want and that things are up to us. Nietzsche looked at these two facets with "a double-brain, as it were a brain with two chambers" (*Human,* V, 251), one cold and scientific, the other experiential and poetic. We saw that despite his reservations, he continued to talk about souls and spirits in order to connect with his readers, who could not be expected to tolerate the scientific arctic emptiness of no will, no consciousness, no ego and no personality. We, the new psychologists, will do like him—attack these concepts when they hinder the way, and use them when it drives a point home. With his scientific brain's chamber, he saw that "the world is not an organism at all but chaos" and that our notions and beliefs are only temporary resources for life (*Will,* III, 711). The world is chaotic, without "order, arrangement, form, beauty, wisdom, and whatever other names there are for our aesthetic anthropomorphisms." Nature is without laws, purposes, or accidents; it is with necessities only (*Gay,* III, 109).

The aphorism *Will and wave* comes from the second chamber of the brain, with a "spiritual," poetic, or "as if" perspective, reintroducing willing and purposes through the backdoor. Nietzsche watched the waves in a stormy sea—the way they rush to the cliffs and return back and still try again, as if their soul was searching something, continuing their advance vigorously. He ended this beautiful description with the words, "So live the waves, —so live we, the willful—more I do not say" (*Gay,* IV, 310). What he did not say explicitly is that although the poetical description is not factual, it is psychologically truthful and necessary. The tree of knowledge and the tree of life are different. "Probability, but no truth; the appearance of freedom, but no freedom—these are the two fruits by virtue of which the tree of knowledge cannot be confounded with the tree of life (*Human,* Wanderer, 1).

We can only see the world in our own human terms. Geophysical explanations are scientifically valid but experientially barren. It feels natural to describe the waves in the same terms we experience and understand ourselves, as willing and striving entities. Such an understanding is aesthetically uplifting and inspiring, making us feel one with nature. If we are wise, we should keep the two trees in our garden, enjoy their fruits, and know when to pick from each one of them.

Nietzsche's distinction between "the cause of an action generally, from the cause of an action in a particular manner, say, in this direction, with this aim," still leaves willing a place. He explicated his meaning by using the metaphor of "the match in relation to the barrel of gunpowder." Such matches are our aims, purposes, and callings, which are only directing forces, "the steersman and not the stream" (*Gay*, V, 360). The size of the gunpowder barrel is indeed not up to us, and its contents are unknown. However, it will detonate only with a match, which is experienced as wishing and willing a particular end (*Will*, II, 260). Such willing includes life plans and desired projects, and it is in this sense that he instructed, "Will a self, so you will become a self" (*Human*, Assorted, 366). He believed that no significant achievement can occur without it "and no artist would create his picture, no field marshal his victory, and no people its freedom, without previously having desired and striven for them in that sort of unhistorical condition." Nietzsche described this preparatory focused and driven condition as a state of falling in love, and he cited Goethe's words about the active person who "loves his deed infinitely more than it deserves to be loved, and the best deeds happen in such an excess of love that they would certainly have to be unworthy of this love, even if their worth were otherwise incalculably great" (*Untimely*, History, Foreword). The answer to a paradox is a paradox: we cannot will a self simply by command, but we cannot also become a self without willing it, by wishing, preparing, and trying—in short, if the barrel is empty, no match will help; yet the gunpowder will not explode by itself.

A Roll of the Dice

Being skeptic about the notions of will and purpose, Nietzsche thought that it is quite plausible that ultimately there is only one domain, that of "stupidity and hazard," and that "those iron hands of necessity that shake the dice-box of chance continue their game indefinitely." Sooner or later, it is probable that some of those throws will fall according to what we wish or find desirable, and then, out of vanity, we conceive these chance events as consequences of our willing and efforts (*Daybreak*, II, 130). Out of conceit, we usually attribute desirable occurrences to our own skills, talents, and willpower, and at the same time look for external explanations for failures. "No victor believes in chance" (*Gay*, III, 258). How can we act without realizing that there is a stronger force acting on us? Chance had already appeared as the main feature of human existence in Nietzsche's first book, where he quoted Silenus's words to King Midas, "Oh, wretched ephemeral race, children of chance and misery" (*Birth*, 3). Chance has a central place in Zarathustra's discourses and throughout Nietzsche's writings. He treated chance with both parts of his brain, as poet and thinker. In his autobiography, Nietzsche credited chance and accident in his own life and discoveries, "for everything epochal in that life came to me by accident, never by recommendation" (*Ecce*, Clever, 3). No philosopher before him dealt with chance to the extent he did; very few psychologists considered it after him.

Chance rules everything, and thus the astounding human phenomenon emerging from semi-beasts was described as the "most unexpected and most thrillingly lucky rolls of the dice in the game played by Heraclitus's 'great child,' whether he's called Zeus or chance" (*Genealogy*, II, 16) and similarly, "rationality appeared by chance accident as well" (*Daybreak*, II, 123). Following Darwin he wrote, "There is no purpose in nature—vision was not the intention behind the creation of the eye, it appeared by chance" (*Daybreak*, II, 122).

We Are Polyps

We cannot read ourselves and know all the drives and needs which make us who we are; we can only be understood as persons in a given environment, and Nietzsche used the nonglamorous metaphor of a polyp to drive his point home: We are no more than a polyp extending arms into our surroundings. Some of them find nourishment (reinforcement) by chance, and some, again by chance, do not, and wither in a process of extinction (*Daybreak*, II, 119). From arms let us move to hands; the hands needed to grab an opportunity we stumbled upon. "To recognize the active force, the creative force in the chance event" (*Will*, III, 673) is ultimately more important than the talent itself. With geniuses like Raphael, artistic vision is superior to craftsmanship, and what counts most of all is "the five hundred hands needed to tyrannize the *kairos*, 'the right time,' to seize chance by the forelock!" (*Beyond*, IX, 274).

Once we accept the "wantonness and foolishness," the irrational power of chance, rather than resist and fight this giant (*Thus*, I, The bestowing of virtue, 2), we will see Zarathustra's precept as blessing. "Above all things stand the heaven of Chance, the heaven of Innocence, the heaven of hazard [or coincidence], the heaven of wantonness" (*Thus*, III, Before sunrise). We will then see human existence differently, "for the earth is a table of the gods, and trembling creative new words and the dice throws of the gods" (*Thus*, IV, The seven seas, 3) and gain under the rule of Lord chance, "freedom and celestial serenity," beyond judgment with "an azure bell above all things" (*Thus*, III, Before sunrise).

Zarathustra taught his disciples to welcome and love chance. "My doctrine is: 'Let chance come to me: it is as innocent as a little child'" (*Thus*, III, On the Mount of Olives). He taught them to take chances and work with them. "I am Zarathustra the Godless: I cook every chance in my pot. And only when it is quite cooked do I welcome it as *my* food" (*Thus*, III, The virtue that makes small, 3). He taught his disciples to accept miscarried throws of the dice in stride, to play and mock, and avoid seeing themselves as failures if what they attempted failed (*Thus*, IV, Of the higher man, 14). Taking chances means running an experiment. "Thinkers should see their actions as experiments, success or failure are above all results-answers." The results of an experiment do not depend on us, and, therefore, there is no room for remorse or regret—feelings which suit subordinated fearful mentalities (*Gay*, I, 41). It is interesting or even perplexing that psychotherapists, in general, those who do not know Nietzsche, disregard chance altogether, do not prepare their clients to work with chance, and never suggest tossing a coin or throwing dice.[3]

Tools for Action

Nietzsche derived his principles of action from the observation of animals, from the realization that we are controlled by our environment and that we can more readily change the environment than change ourselves. To these he added the military-based approach of discipline and training. If we are weak, he reasoned, we must outsmart the enemy that is ourselves and sometimes know how to declare victory rather than experience defeat.

Like Animals Do

We must go to the animals, observe their ways, and learn from them. They do not examine their conscience, consciousness, or unconsciousness; they do not act because they want to act; they simply obey their instincts and respond to their environment. An action is the result of the meeting of persons and environments. Animals do not deliberate too much and they act swiftly and decisively: a fox sees a rabbit and leaps to grab it; a rabbit sees a fox and runs for her life. The moment an opportunity arises is not the time to contemplate, hesitate, and wish, but rather act. Nietzsche's famous formula for his happiness, "a Yes, a No, a straight line, a goal" (*Twilight*, Maxims, 41), can be understood as "if you have a chance, either go for it decisively or forget about it all together." Although swift instinctual acting can often be dangerous, Nietzsche recommended that we dare and adopt "the life of wild animals, for the forests, caves, steep mountains, and labyrinths" (*Thus*, IV, Science).

Many of Nietzsche's ideas were seeded in his first book, "Knowledge kills action; action requires the veils of illusion: that is the doctrine of Hamlet" (*Birth*, 7). Later, he suggested that "the decisive value of an action resides precisely on that which is not intentional in it." Intentions and awareness do not cause actions but only accompany, sometimes even garble them (*Beyond*, II, 32). Becoming conscious is an effort, strain, and discomfort for the organism (*Will*, II, 440), and the price of self-examination is deterioration in the quality of our moral decisions, compared with instinct-based thinking and action (*Will*, II, 440). Passions that once were not tolerated and considered evil can actually become guiding virtues (*Thus*, I, Joys and passions). The less conscious, the more we can listen to our own instincts and passions, the better it is: "We must, in fact, seek the perfect life where it has become least conscious (i.e. least aware of its logic, its reasons, its means and intentions, its utility) . . . the demand for a virtue that reasons is not reasonable" (*Will*, II, 439).

Training the Will

The will can be trained, and Nietzsche prescribed gymnastics of will strengthening, necessary for maintaining a joyful sense of self-mastery. Training must be continuous. "Every day on which we have not at least once denied ourselves some small thing is turned to bad use and a danger to the next day" (*Human*, Wanderer, 305). Training of the will must be gradual, progressing from light to heavy demands, establishing an experience of commanding and subsequent performance—experiences which build up a self-perception of efficacy; "one is a cause oneself, only when one knows that one has performed an act of will" (*Will*, II, 136). In order to maintain this sense of efficacy, it is also important not to demand what cannot be guaranteed to happen (*Beyond*, I, 19).

Discipline and habits, in addition to instincts and passions, enable us to act without too much deliberation: Is it Sunday or Tuesday? Get up at 06:40 and go to the gym. Is it Monday, Wednesday, or Friday? Go out jogging. Is it Thursday or Saturday? Get up only if you have to. True, on one hand, "a life entirely devoid of habits" is intolerable; on the other hand, habits limit one's spontaneity and turn us into their slaves. Nietzsche's solution of the dilemma was "I love brief habits" (*Gay*, IV, 295), habits for delimited periods, habits with vacations from them. He recommended swiftness in action, otherwise, hesitations, "shyness and ticklishness" might set in, "for I think it is best to do with profound problems as with a cold bath—quickly in, quickly out." He even anticipated objections to such an approach, sometimes raised by insight therapists against action-oriented ones, and answered them in advance, "That one does not thereby get into the depths, that one does not get deep enough down is a superstition of the hydrophobic" (*Gay*, V, 381).

Being Done

Granted that we cannot will to change ourselves, we polyps are nevertheless influenced and shaped by the environment we live in. Our living conditions and surroundings are more under our control, and we can, for example, decide where to live, with whom to associate, how to spend our free time, and what to eat. Nietzsche's psychology is characterized by materialism and environmentalism (chapter 1) and he argued that humans suffer from a serious grammatical mistake of mixing up the active and the passive. People who say that they have no idea what they are doing, or what they ought to do, actually express what is true for everybody: "Be sure of this: *you are being done!* at every moment!" (*Daybreak*, II, 120).

Thus, if you want to change yourself, change your environment appropriately or at least avoid what might impact you in undesirable directions. Writing about the connection between domestic peace and peace of soul, Nietzsche suggested that "the mood in which we usually exist depends upon the mood in which we maintain our environment" (*Daybreak,* IV, 283). We should maintain an adequate sustainable environment, and this is to my mind the reason that he, who hated politics and abhorred crowds, dealt so much with social issues and culture. This is why, despite his praise of selfishness, he commended contribution to others, as changing others eventually changes oneself. The human environment includes, of course, intimate relationships, and this is also the reason for his emphasis on friendship and choice of the right kind of friends, ones not only good for having a good time, but ones that will help us become who we are. This is also the reason for choosing partners for life who can be first of all good friends, who can reinforce existing patterns but also influence us in unexpected ways.

Nietzsche described a common situation of "combat of motives," of having different competing options to choose from. Whereas people believe that they perform a logical process of comparison and evaluation, and make their choice in light of anticipated consequences, what actually determines their decision is precedents, encouragement of significant persons, and the love of comfort and dislike of effort (*Daybreak,* II, 129). Environments influence us by the mechanisms of imitation, social comparison, and expectation. He described the development of empathy by means of bodily imitation of the expressions and gestures of others (*Daybreak,* II, 142). Humans have a "thirst for equality" expressed either negatively as a desire to diminish others to one's level, using spying and tripping up; or positively, by raising oneself to the level of others by helping them and recognizing their virtues (*Human,* VI, 300). Thus Nietzsche had a thirst for equality with Wagner, whom he befriended, but also with Schopenhauer, whose writings he only read. Figures of identification fortunately do not have to be alive, and there are many and different ones to choose from.

When significant others believe in us and expect the best of us, we can rise to the occasion and show "simplicity of style" in everything we do (*Gay,* III, 226). The same process takes place between parents and children, teachers and students, and between partners in intimate relations. Each side develops expectations and at the same time tends to fulfill the expectations of the other side, "for man creates for himself the ideal of woman, and woman molds herself according to this ideal"(*Gay,* II, 68). The same process takes place, of course, between clients and therapists.

Outsmart Yourself

If direct willing is not an option, one must use indirect means and rather than commanding—that is to say, one should try to outsmart oneself. As the self is a multiplicity of competing forces, one can play the power game of internal *realpolitik* and maneuver between competing forces and use the old method of "stick and carrot." Nietzsche hinted at a "divide and conquer" ploy, by calling for "the development of effective 'under-wills' or under-souls" (*Beyond*, I, 19). Thus, because my will is weak, I demand from myself to put on running shoes and apparel and go out for five minutes only. On some occasions I have returned home five minutes later and was very happy; most times, the roads, the weather and other runners made me continue.

Backwards Willing

We move now from future-oriented willing to past-oriented backward willing. Nietzsche used a metaphor of a steersman, boat, and stream. Chance and the stream push the boat, while the steersman is convinced, after the fact, that it was his willing and doing which did it (*Gay*, V, 360). Willing after the fact, is the gist of Ledru-Rollin's saying upon seeing a crowd surge past him in Paris during the French Revolution, "There go my people. I must find out where they are going so I can lead them."[4] This willing is not simply an illusion; it is a means of creating an integrated coherent identity and having a sense of efficacy. Zarathustra taught that "the Will is a creator," and that such "backwards will" is not a small matter at all, as it is an act of creation, redemption, reconciliation and acceptance of the past; putting together everything that was fragmented, enigmatic, and haphazard. Through this backward creating will, "it was" is transformed into "But I willed it thus! So shall I will it" and by so doing one creates the future (*Thus*, III, Old and new law-tables, 3; *Thus*, II, Redemption). We will meet this kind of will again, in the discussion of *amor fati* (chapter 7) and Eternal Recurrence (chapter 8).

UNTIMELINESS AND HORIZONS

Nietzsche's teachings on action and creating the self show that it is difficult, if not impossible, to create and change ourselves by command, by sheer willpower. Being products of our environment, we can do it much easier indirectly by choosing the kind of environment that will best bring us closer to our objectives. We should, therefore, examine the effects of the environment we live in and determine whether they are advancing us or holding us back. We should, if we care about what becomes of us, be selective, set limits and horizons, preventing exposure to what is detrimental to us.

The good Europeans exemplify the surpassing of the limited local, national, and chauvinistic perspective to become citizens of the world. Obviously, we live in a given place and a given time. Environments are usually understood in terms of place, but Nietzsche, with his theme of untimeliness, sensitized us to their time dimension as well. Nowadays people do not merely live in a given time; they are chained to it with optic fibers: we consume the latest news, fashions, models, and gadgets; we have turned into media junkies, assaulted by an explosion of information, transmitted by fast immediate digital means. Our magic words are "now" and "new"; the past is *passé,* give us the *dernier cri.*

Untimely People

I am thinking about the few persons I know who could be described as untimely.[5] They have an historical-cultural reference point to evaluate the present; they do not read the books everyone is talking about and have no use for the latest "in" authors and authorities. They have an almost personal relationship with historical and literary figures who symbolized for them important, human eternal issues. I am not sure whether they have chosen to be untimely or just developed into it; and I wonder whether it is possible to be both untimely and earthy. I assume that it is not a matter of total timeliness or total untimeliness, but rather a matter of proportions. People also differ in the degree to which their own past, present, and future play a role in their life. It is quite possible that the formula for becoming untimely is to study and be immersed since childhood in classical texts, such as Homer's *Iliad* and *Odyssey* or the Bible, which enables a continuous dialogue with them later in life. It seems to me that untimeliness is found among bright, imaginative, and idea-loving people; I suspect that it will exist to a lesser degree in those who as children were attractive, great athletes, and socially popular.

Untimely Nietzsche

Nietzsche the teacher of untimeliness was untimely himself. He wrote four *Untimely Meditations* and the main chapter in his *Twilight of the Idols* is titled *Skirmishes of an untimely man*; he felt that he did not write for his times. "My time has not yet come either; some are born posthumously" (*Ecce,* Books, 1). And he described the circumstances of the conception of the idea of the Eternal Recurrence in August 1881, writing on a sheet of paper the postscript, "Six thousand feet beyond man and time" (*Ecce,* Thus). Nietzsche's stance on untimeliness, like the rest of his psychology and philosophy, was influenced by his life experiences, schooling, and temperament. He studied in a prestigious rigorous boarding school, where the students did not just study Greek and Latin, but also read, wrote, and spoke these languages. Later in his studies, he continued to be fascinated with ancient cultures and texts and became a professor of philology.

Present, Past, and Future

Untimeliness, like Janus the double-faced god, has one face looking at the past, and another at the future. It was apparent to Nietzsche that philosophers must exist in contradiction to the ideals of their day. Becoming the "bad consciences" of their age, they are oriented to the tomorrow and the day after it (*Beyond*, VI, 212). Philosophers need peace and quiet from everything that has to do with "today" (*Genealogy*, III, 8) and in order to become timeless they ought to fight everything that makes them the children of their time (*Case*, Preface). Overidentification and involvement with one's times, "a consumptive historical fever," is a disease that must be diagnosed and treated. Only those who are not "citizens of this time" can raise their time to life (*Untimely*, Schopenhauer, 1), and only opposition to one's age, based on comparison with ancient times, can bring about beneficial changes (*Untimely*, History, Foreword). Untimeliness is a new morality, an antithesis to the willingness of people to betray their own conscience and be mobilized by state and nation and even risk their life in unnecessary wars: "Live in concealment in order that you may live to yourself. Live ignorant of that which seems to thy age to be most important! Put at least the skin of three centuries betwixt thyself and the present day! And the clamor of the present day, the noise of wars and revolutions, ought to be a murmur to thee!" (*Gay*, IV, 338).

Nietzsche's disenchantment with his own times had already appeared in his first book, where he lamented the loss of roots, secularization, adoption of foreign influences, deification of the present, "everything *sub specie saeculi* [under the aspect of the times, or the spirit of the age]" (*Birth*, 23). He conceived of ancient Greece as a cultural apex, because it had qualities favorable to the development of the individual (*Philologists*, 192) and thus, looking backward and studying the ancients, turns them into a point of reference, for the evaluating of the present (*Philologists*, 18). We will pick up the topic of untimeliness again when we discuss life's mission (chapter 8), but we already realize here that Nietzsche is not a proponent of the "living in the present," preached relentlessly in the new *psychologica* and by gurus of self-help. Living in the present and living in the moment are entirely different, and only the latter can attain happiness and make others happy too. Living "on the crest of the moment" is a matter of focusing, an ability to forget what was and to be fully engaged "standing on a single point, like a goddess of victory" (*Untimely*, History, Foreword).

Zarathustra wanted us to have some standards of quality, helping us choose and not just pick up whatever comes our way (such as emotionally charged special news editions and commentary, or a variety of "reality" TV shows). We should not let ourselves be manipulated by what our period and environment have to offer. Nietzsche gave us simple instructions on how not to be sucked in by the "maddening crowd": we should avoid trying to punish, improve, or change others as it is an almost impossible task to accomplish, and we ourselves are changed in the attempt. Instead, let us be concerned only with improving ourselves and learn to look away and keep a distance between the follies of others and ourselves (*Gay*, IV, 338). If we do not have a clear goal in mind, it would be better to wait and do nothing until it is found. Believers in life do not fling themselves at the moment; they have the capacity to wait and idle in the meanwhile (*Thus*, I, The preachers of death).

Horizons, Remembering and Forgetting

Freedom of spirit demands some self-determined, self-limiting horizons beyond which it will be impossible to see. We need such horizons around and within us, protecting ourselves from an implosion of stimuli and memories. Horizons are a principle of selection, a taste developed, where we impose our own criteria and values. Homes have walls around them, and in an aphorism titled *Feeling in the country* Nietzsche used a pastoral simile to make his point: "If one does not have stable, calm lines on the horizon of his life, like lines of mountaintops or trees, then man's innermost will itself become restless, distracted, and covetous, like the city dweller's character: he knows no happiness, and gives none" (*Human*, V, 290).

The human instinct for self-preservation, in charge of choosing appropriate conditions for living in matters of environment, nutrition, and recreation, is also involved in self-defense measures to avoid hearing and seeing, or being exposed to injurious input. "This is elementary prudence, the first proof that a man is not an accident but a necessity" (*Ecce*, Clever, 8). An informed selection is highly relevant today when the media floods people by visual depictions of violence, sex, fashions, and merchandise.

When too much effort in guarding one's horizons is needed, one should consider changing to another environment. "One must separate from anything that forces one to repeat 'no,' again and again." We should detach ourselves from situations which force us to give up liberty and initiative and become "a mere bundle of reactions." Information overload, when many waves of discordant information keep on impinging on the gates of memory, has a negative effect on the "soul of modern man," making it difficult to reach any integration (*Untimely*, History, 4). Nietzsche described some scholars as decadents, persons without horizons, who have become compulsive consumers of books rather than think for themselves (*Ecce*, Clever, 8), not realizing that wisdom is not a matter of quantity of information, but of an ability to select and utilize it. "I want, once and for all, *not* to know many things. Wisdom sets limits to knowledge, too" (*Twilight*, Maxims, 5).

Forgetting is an act of drawing internal limits or horizons, to preclude unwanted memories. It is necessary for life and action, and the ability to take lightly one's mistakes, enemies, and accidents. Strong natures can forget and recuperate (*Genealogy*, I, 10). Preoccupation with remembering and ruminating about the past, whether of individuals, nations, or cultures, like insomnia, is a destructive activity. It is better to draw from the past only useful information, internalize it, "transform into blood," and discard and forget everything else. Survival, forceful action, optimism and satisfaction, all depend on an instinct and an ability to draw a horizon around us, a clear line separating between what to remember and what to forget (*Untimely*, History, Foreword).

How would it feel to live without horizons at all, "in the horizon of the infinite"? This is a state of giving up concepts and theories, a state of non-duality and wholeness, which most persons cannot tolerate. Nietzsche compared it to a little ship that left the land behind, to sail into the ocean, sometimes feeling "that it is infinite, and that there is nothing more frightful than infinity." Relinquishing one's horizons can be an irreversible act. "Alas, if homesickness for the land should attack you as if there had been more freedom there, and there is no 'land' any longer!" (*Gay*, III, 124).

SOLITUDE AND DEATH

Children are taught how to live with others, make friends, cooperate, compete, and compromise. They are usually not taught how to live alone or be lonely, which is conceived as an unfortunate aversive state, that one should do everything possible to avoid. Nietzsche was a teacher of solitude who outlined its benefits without forgetting its dangers. He also taught how to die well, usually not considered a topic that can or must be learned. Sadly, he could only demonstrate with his own life the accomplishments of creative solitude but not the achievement of dying well. And yet, by this very fact, he was still teaching that dying well is not always in our hands.

Between Loneliness and Solitude

Solitude can be best understood in comparison to loneliness: the former is a chosen state, entered and left voluntarily, the latter is an imposition, in which one is bound involuntary; one can be a weekend retreat, the other is a prison term. Persons who choose to adopt and experience a creative solitude are conceived by others as exotic and unique humans. Yet most people are simply lazy, and only a few are willing to detach themselves from the crowd, go against their inborn tendency to be conformist herd animals, and stand out as individuals. Not everyone is ready to pay the price of hardship and suffering involved in giving up the youthful wishes for "joy, safety, and honor." Solitude poses the danger of melancholy, but also the threat of solitude turning into a personal destructive icy trait of "a moral or intellectual hardening" in which ideals are given up; creativity and originality decline and culture becomes superfluous (*Untimely*, Schopenhauer, 3).

But Why This Solitude

Given the heavy price individuals pay for solitude, Nietzsche asked, "But why this solitude?" and he offered "the creative solitude within" as his answer: solitude, like untimeliness, basically seeing things differently from others, is a necessary condition for authenticity and creativity. He explains that being alone, with a remote perspective, far from friends and music, he can see the world clearly and positively (*Daybreak*, V, 485), and that "returning to his desert" is necessary to let the slow process of creation take its course until "water comes to light out of the well of my self." Solitude encourages encounters with one's own ideas, rather than drinking "out of everybody's cistern." Living with the many will lead to blending in and losing individuality, as they want to "banish me from myself and rob me of my soul" (*Daybreak*, V, 491).

Nietzsche "the Solitary" admitted that there is much boredom, dismay, and disgust in loneliness. Moments of deep communication with the self and with nature compensated for it and made him stronger. One who cannot stand boredom and runs away from it is running away from himself. "He will never drink the most powerful elixir from his own innermost spring" (*Human*, Wanderer, 200). Only those who can stand boredom and solitude will avoid being ridiculous, superficial, and bound "scribbling slaves," seemingly intellectuals, who follow their time's conventions. They are the opposite of free spirits, of "philosophers of the future," who could say with Nietzsche that "we are born, sworn, jealous friends of *solitude*, of our own most profound, most midnight, most midday solitude" (*Beyond*, II, 44). Creators are solitary stars: "Thus is a star thrown into the void and into the icy breath of solitude" (*Thus*, I, The way of the creator).

Good Solitude

Solitude brings out one's qualities; "in solitude there grows what any one brings into it—also the brute in one's nature" (*Thus*, IV, Higher man, 13). Some people cherish solitude, others stay clear of it: sociable natures feel best when they are able to share their experiences with others; solitary natures hate emotional displays and experience their joys and torments in silence (*Daybreak*, V, 524). Solitary natures are used to their solitude and they can "spin forth their monologue of a life in a calm, joyous mood, holding good conversations with themselves, even laughing." This should be accepted and respected, and there is no reason to pity them. When solitary persons start comparing themselves with more sociable ones, they open themselves to doubts and self-reproach, which can be helped by reassurance from others, making them think and feel better about themselves (*Human*, IX, 625). People should take their nature in consideration before deciding where to build their house. "If you feel great and fruitful in solitude, a life in society will diminish you and make you empty: and *vice versa*." Creators should pick a place to live and work, where they feel creative as if supported by a gentle loving father, "whether it be in the midst of the crowd or in a silent retreat" (*Daybreak*, V, 473). Once you decide to build your house in solitude, it would be best not to turn into a complete recluse, continue to take care of oneself, and have a net of friends available from time to time: "And have people around you who are like a garden—or like music over water in the evening, when the day is already becoming a memory. Choose good solitude, the free, high-spirited, easy solitude, which gives you also a right to remain, in some sense or other, still good yourselves!" (*Beyond*, II, 25).

The Finest Festival

Reader, have no fear! You are going to do it, whether prepared or not; whether you do it in style or not; whether you are going to like it or not; you are going to die anyhow. Knowing that we are going to die is perhaps what differentiates us humans from other animals, and fear of death is common to all of us. The great teachers of life tried to calm us: One said that when I am alive I am not dead, and when dead, I am not alive, and, therefore, it is not relevant to me. Another said that everything that is not up to me should not concern me at all. Nietzsche chose other ways to deal with the problem.

Thinking about Death

It is not the fact of death, but the way we understand it that matters, and the way people relate to death says much about them. "How one dies is indifferent, the whole way in which a man thinks of death during the prime of his life and strength is very expressive and significant for what we call his character" (*Human*, II, 88). There are many ways to look at death, and foremost among them is a refusal to think about it, occupying oneself with plans and future aspirations despite the fact that "death and the stillness of death are the only things certain and common to all in this future!" (*Gay*, IV, 278). It is also possible to embrace death as an essential, ever-present part of life, and this acceptance can be done in many ways: with poetic resignation ("How everyone's shadow, his gloomy traveling-companion stands behind him!"); with a daredevil approach ("Through the certain prospect of death a precious, fragrant drop of frivolity might be mixed with every life"); and finally as "druggist-souls" do, resentfully turning death into "a drop of poison, unpleasant to taste, which makes the whole of life hideous" (*Human*, Wanderer, 322).

The hour of death can be difficult indeed, but it is made worse by fears, preconceived notions, and superstitions "as if dying was of much consequence and meant the crossing of bridges of the most terrible kind." Rather than a mysterious crossing over to another world, and rather than a solemn serious "comedy of vanity," Nietzsche suggested turning death into a celebration, "a testimony concerning the living" (*Human*, Assorted, 88), and Zarathustra taught the "consummating death," the finest festival, which is turned into a stimulus, example, and promise for the living (*Thus*, I, Voluntary death).

Death Is Natural

Thinking of death as unnatural for relatively young persons or seeing death as an undeserved punishment ("This is not fair") just makes our coping more difficult, adding feelings of resentment and devastation. If we accept that "the total character of the world, however, is in all eternity chaos" (*Gay*, III, 109), and that there are only necessities (It happened because it had to happen.), it will be much easier to come to terms with reality, death included. Nietzsche the Overturner performed his magic again, advising us, "Let us beware of saying that death is opposed to life; the living is merely a type of what is dead, and a very rare type" (*Gay*, III, 109). If so, we must celebrate the fact that we (hopefully) lived and celebrate the fact that those close to us will (temporarily) continue to live.

Like Epictetus, who reminded his students that "the door is always open,"[6] Nietzsche believed that "the thought of suicide is a great consolation: by means of it one gets successfully through many a bad night" (*Beyond*, IV, 157). He objected to prohibition and forced prevention of suicide, which should be a person's individual decision. "There is a justice according to which we take a man's life, but no justice according to which we take his death: that is nothing but cruelty (*Human*, I, 88). He supported euthanasia and assisted death, which he designated as a "holy cruelty," as is evident in an account of a person holding "a sickly, wretched, misshapen child without life enough to die," calling to consult with a holy man, who advised to kill the child, as "it is crueler to let the child live" (*Gay*, II, 73).

The Golden Ball

Nietzsche, who looked at the world in aesthetic terms and not in moral ones, looked at dying as something that can be done either gracefully or not. Zarathustra taught the value of dying at the right time and praised "the voluntary death, which comes unto me because I want it" (*Thus*, I, Voluntary death). He saw this lesson as a gift, "a golden ball" passed on to his followers, teaching that prolonging life at any cost is not an advantage. One who lives on "too old for his truths and triumphs" is not an inspiring example, and thus the question is not length of life, but its quality. If life was a failure, a timely death can be its saving grace; if life was a success, a timely death can be its pinnacle. The time to practice the art of timely departure is at the height of one's success. "One must discontinue being feasted upon when one tastes best." One should be ready to die at the right time, after having a goal and an heir, and for their sake avoid hanging into life at any price (*Thus*, I, Voluntary death). Although Nietzsche himself did not have a successful death, his life was successful: he had a goal and we, the new doctors of the soul, are his heirs.

NOTES

1. I have summarized and added numerals to break up the quotation into separate components.
2. Sigmund Freud, "The Interpretation of Dreams," in *The Standard Edition of the Complete Psychological Works of Sigmund Freud (SE)*, vol. 5, trans. and ed. James Strachey (London: Hogarth Press, 1958), 261.
3. See in Uri Wernik, *Chance Action and Therapy: The Playful Way of Changing* (Hauppauge, NY: Nova Science Publishers, 2011).
4. Calman, Alvin R. "Ledru-Rollin and the Second French Republic," *Studies in History, Economics and Public Law* 53 (1922), archive.org/stream/ledrurollinsecon00calm/ledrurollinsecon00calm_djvu.txt, accessed June 22, 2014.
5. I especially have in mind my late teacher Professor David Flusser, who studied the Jewish sources of early Christianity.
6. P. E. Matheson, trans., *The Discourses of Epictetus* (New York: Heritage Press, 1968), 162, classics.mit.edu/Epictetus/discourses.1.one.html, accessed June 22, 2014.

SEVEN

Healing the Soul

I begin this chapter with a polemic (*A Polemic* was the subtitle of Nietzsche's *On the Genealogy of Morality*). I will then review ways of understanding mental suffering and principles and methods of mental help and change. I will conclude with a consideration of desired qualities of the doctors of the soul.

NIETZSCHE CONTRA FREUD

The heading "Nietzsche contra Freud" is, of course, a take on *Nietzsche Contra Wagner*. I have said in my introduction, that many of Nietzsche's psychoanalytically oriented commentators saw him as an early forerunner of psychoanalysis. I argue that this is only one possible interpretation, and I offer here an alternative one, claiming that Nietzsche stood for the exact opposite of the main psychoanalytic precepts. This is not a pedantic excursion into the history of ideas. Seeing Nietzsche through Freudian spectacles to my mind leads to a distorted view and a glossing over of his unique and original contributions.

I know that I am opening myself to the criticism that I use Freud as a straw-man and that my description does not do justice to current psychoanalytic formulations. Justice I cannot do, as there are too many versions and developments to be reviewed here. However, I am describing what was true in Freud's times, most of which remained the gist of current "dynamic" insight-oriented psychotherapies. I also admit that it is easier for me to highlight what a Nietzschean psychotherapy is not, rather than stating conclusively what it is. Incidentally, Freud himself was the first to appropriate Nietzsche to his ranks. In an interview held in 1927 in honor of his seventieth birthday, with G. S. Viereck, Freud called Nietzsche one of the first psychoanalysts and found it "amazing to what extent his intuition foreshadows our discoveries."[1] Interestingly, Freud invited Viereck, a German-American poet, writer, and pro-Nazi propagandist to write a book about him, probably not knowing that his next interviewee was going to be Adolf Hitler.[2]

Psychoanalysis in a Nutshell

It is difficult to give a conclusive statement on the basic tenets of psychoanalysis, as they kept changing and were open to different interpretations and emphasis by Freud himself and later by his disciples. Freud presented five points of view: topographic (the mental apparatus is divided into the systems of conscious, pre-conscious, and unconscious), dynamic (the theory of conflict between drives and prohibitions), economic (the theory of energy flow), structural (the psyche is divided into id, ego, and super-ego) and genetic (development proceeds through predetermined stages and disturbances in any of them cause psychological problems). Furthermore, human behavior and experience are mostly determined by unconscious and irrational drives. Attempts to bring these drives to awareness invites resistance in the form of defense mechanisms, chief among them is repression. The conflict between consciousness and unconscious-repressed contents is the reason for mental disorders such as neurosis, anxiety, or depression. In other words, manifest symptoms are caused by latent disturbances, such as repressed trauma or unresolved issues in childhood. Psychoanalysis, which literally means analysis of the psyche, whether done independently in self-analysis or in therapy with an analyst, focuses on bringing the repressed conflicts to consciousness, using the techniques of free association, interpretation of verbalization, and analysis of dreams, resistance, and transference. Consequently, insight into the meaning of the symptom is gained, enabling the patients to resolve the underlying conflict.

We can easily put aside Freud's genetic and economic positions, as they do not have anything in common with Nietzsche. Nietzsche recognized the significance of the child's unique upbringing circumstances (cultural factors, parental practices, and the parents' relationship) for the person's future well-being. Yet, he did not subscribe to any theory of universal developmental stages and complexes. Freud was a neurologist and naturally saw psychological phenomena in terms of anatomy and physiology and hence structures and energy. He was also a "child of his time" and the thermodynamic principles operating in the steam engine, the most advanced technology of his days, became a metaphor for his psychodynamics. Nietzsche was in this respect untimely. Although he was well-read in evolution theory and biology, being a philologist, he drew more from the metaphors of language, state, and society. Hence in his picture of human psychology there is a Will to Power but not energy.

A Matter of Style

Before we go on to examine whether something of Nietzsche can be found in the other three psychoanalytic points of view, I suggest that we refresh our memory about Nietzsche's critique of psychological terminology, reviewed in the section *The Language of Psychology* (chapter 2). Obviously, this is not a part of Nietzsche which Freud adopted: Nietzsche was concerned about "giving a false reality to a fiction," assuming that events are the result of things which are outside of them and thus, "an artificial and imaginary distinction is made between actions and what supposedly activates them (*Will*, III, 521). This mistake, he found, started with Descartes's argumentation, "There is thinking: therefore there is something that thinks" (*Will*, III, 484). Freud, on the contrary, "discovered" the something that thinks, inhibits, represses, and so on. Nietzsche, unlike him, described processes, without adding "doers to deeds." Freud used the pronoun "the" before "id," "ego," or "conscious," as if they were places, parts, and entities, while with Nietzsche, conscious or unconscious were adjectives only. The words "mind," "spirit," and "soul" were considered by him as hypothetical constructs, and he used them tentatively and interchangeably.

Freud and Nietzsche alike did not lack a sense of their own importance, originality, and the enormity of their contributions. However, Freud saw himself as a discoverer, while Nietzsche saw himself as an uncoverer. Viereck, in the interview with Freud, mentioned above, described Freud, "the father of psychoanalysis," as Oedipus who solved the riddle, the secrets of human conduct, "Freud is to psychology, what Galileo was to astronomy. He is the Columbus of the subconscious. He opens new vistas, he sounds new depths . . . deciphering the hidden meaning of the records inscribed on the tablets of the unconscious." Nietzsche, father of his books only, and not the chieftain of a movement, saw himself as Odysseus, entering the Circe's cave; a slayer of myths, who exposed the illusionary enchantments of God and morality. If Freud is seen as the person who solved the riddle, Nietzsche must be the one who tempered the enthusiasm. "Whoever looks into himself as into vast space and carries galaxies in himself, also knows how irregular all galaxies are; they lead into the chaos and labyrinth of existence" (*Gay*, IV, 322).

I am afraid that "discoverers" fare better in public opinion than "uncoverers" as Nietzsche was. "What defines me, what sets me apart from the whole rest of humanity is that I uncovered Christian morality" (*Ecce*, Destiny, 7). The two thinkers were presenting different kinds of truths and Nietzsche was perhaps contrasting himself with approaches similar to Freud's, when he wrote about "estimation of unpretentious truths":

> At first, one has scorn on his lips for unpretentious truths, as if they could offer no match for the others: they stand so modest, simple, sober, even apparently discouraging, while the other truths are so

> beautiful, splendid, enchanting, or even enrapturing. But truths that are hard won, certain, enduring, and therefore still of consequence for all further knowledge are the higher. (*Human*, I, 3)

The Use of History for Life

Freud is supposed to have said that "only a good-for-nothing is not interested in his past,"[3] and indeed psychoanalysis and related insight therapies explore the past to understand present difficulties, and by so doing heal the trauma and fixations that took place in childhood. Nietzsche, on the other hand, saw no advantage in an extensive exploration of the past: "Every past is worthy of condemning" (*Untimely*, History, 3). He dedicated his *On the Use and Abuse of History for Life* to find out whether and how a historical outlook supports life in the cases of cultures, societies, and individuals. He was skeptic about the validity of all historical-past explanations. "With regard to *origin*, everything human deserves ironic reflection: that is why there is such an *excess* of irony in the world" (*Human*, V, 252) and also, "through searching out origins, one becomes a crab. The historian looks backward, and finally he also believes backward" (*Twilight*, Maxims, 24).

While Freud sought the motives behind behaviors, Nietzsche examined how behaviors and actions were interpreted. "Motives are less important than the explanations-attributions given by people, and thus happiness or misery depend more on the explanation than on the motive (*Gay*, I, 44). He said specifically that there is no point in looking for "moral," that is, "dynamic," or "intra-psychic" explanations, and he directed us instead to physiological, environmental, and cultural (cognitions, beliefs, attitudes) factors. Compared with instincts, the value of states of consciousness, faith, and beliefs as psychological explanatory factors, is nil, "strictly speaking, the whole concept of intellectual causality is false" (*Antichrist*, 39). He underscored the idea that psychological problems cannot be explained by other psychological conditions by giving an example from his own life: not having any happy childhood memories had nothing to do with a lack of companionship, as in fact being in the same position as an adult did not prevent him from being cheerful and brave. The real curse in his early life was ignorance of physiology and mystifying "'Idealism,' which explain[s] all the blunders, the great aberrations of instinct, and the modest specializations which diverted me from my life-task" (*Ecce*, Clever, 2).

In addition to the distinction between motives and interpretations, Nietzsche differentiated between origin and function. It is impossible to deduct origins from functions, and knowing why something took place initially does not explain why it continues to exist nor does it change the facts themselves; the two are poles apart, with all heavens (*toto coelo*) between them. In other words, the original behavior-problem appeared in one context and continued in another context, with different functions and in different organized "system of purposes," and with a new interpretation (*Genealogy*, II, 12). Gaining insight into the origins of things is generally not a productive activity; it does not lead to significant gains, as past investigators hoped it would, and it distracts from the appreciation and understanding of immediate factors. The less significant the origins become, the more "things nearest to us, around and within us, gradually begin to manifest their wealth of colors, beauties, enigmas, and diversity of meaning, of which earlier humanity never dreamed" (*Daybreak*, I, 44).

Mechanisms and Routines

Psychoanalysts and devotees of psychoanalysis's derivatives discover in Nietzsche's writings discussions in terms of unconsciousness, repression, and other defense mechanisms, and they often quote Nietzsche's observation, "'I did that,' says my memory. 'I could not have done that,' says my pride, and remains adamant. Eventually—the memory yields" (*Beyond*, IV, 68). On the face of it, you have it all—conflict, guilt, repression into the unconscious, and if you want, denial too. Nietzsche, however, was not describing mechanisms of defense, nor pathological acts, but rather standard routine procedures of more or less conscious maintenance of a coherent, constructive picture of the self and the word, for the sake of survival. We cannot stop the running of our internal Photoshop® program and there is no possibility of seeing things as they objectively are. The same procedures take place when we are awake and in our dreams; "we only invent and imagine him with whom we associate—and forget it immediately" (*Beyond*, IV, 138). We can only see ourselves and the world through the medium of language, which is inherently based on selection, generalization, and distortion—that is to say, lying. This is our fundamental ingrained nature: the greatest part of our experiences is fabricated, and we can only think over any event as "inventors." Nietzsche tried to soften the blow to our vanity, suggesting that "one is much more of an artist than one is aware of" (*Beyond*, V, 192).

Another favorite example, considered as a proto-Freudian manifestation of repression and psychodynamic conflict, is found in Nietzsche's analysis of the origins of bad conscience, where he argued that instincts that cannot be discharged outside are internalized. "From this first grows in man what people later call his 'soul'" (*Genealogy*, II, 16). Taking heed from politicians who often claim "my words were taken out of context," I wish to clarify the context of this quote: Nietzsche was referring to a one-of-a-kind trauma—humanity's pre-historical transition from tribal morality of custom to the morality of law, enforced harshly and violently by the rudimentary state. In addition to criticism raised about this particular theorizing (chapter 4), it must be pointed out, that Nietzsche was referring to a collective development (similar to the invention of language) and not to what might take place individually and routinely; he was also referring to a normal temporary disease, which like pregnancy gave birth to psychological life and made social functioning possible. Besides, he was not describing repression, but rather external suppression, of the kind that still takes place in dictatorships, which is very painful and far from being unconscious.

The Royal Road and the One-Way Road

Freud believed that "the interpretation of dreams is the royal road to knowledge of the unconscious activities of the mind."[4] He described other roads too, assuming that the unconscious can be known and that in order to affect recovery it is essential that what was repressed will become open to awareness. The two thinkers concurred on the importance of unconscious processes, and indeed, Nietzsche accentuated the theme of the "ridiculous overestimation and misunderstanding of consciousness" (*Gay*, I, 11), criticized the exclusion of unconscious processes from the explanations of action (*Daybreak*, II, 129), and argued that "the greatest part of our spirit's activity remains unconscious and unfelt" (*Gay*, IV, 333). However, they continued the ride (to continue the image of a road) in completely different directions.

While Freud believed that he discovered the secrets of the unconscious and could show others how to decipher it, and psychoanalysts go from actions to expose the "psychodynamics" behind them, Nietzsche rejected the assumption of "the comprehensibility of human actions" (*Will*, II, 406). He asserted that our "general sensorium and supreme court," our directing agent and coordinator of bodily functions and behaviors, is not accessible to any conscious involvement or understanding because its operations do not take place with words at all. Our notions of pleasure or displeasure, what we experience as feelings, thinking, and logic, are no more than verbal cues or shadows, a reconstruction of what goes on in our "kingdom of instincts" (*Will*, III, 524). Thus, consciousness cannot change the primacy of instincts, just as birth-giving cannot change a baby's genetic endowment (*Beyond*, I, 3). In short, the expectation that it is possible to know what is inherently unconscious, by conscious means, as well as changing unconscious content by insight, is akin to expecting a puppet-on-a-string to wag the puppeteer.

Furthermore, Nietzsche argued that an examination of the origins and functions of consciousness makes it clear why it is not a reliable tool of self-understanding. It was developed as a means of communication with others, especially between leaders and followers, adults and children, in situations of life-threatening emergencies. "Consciousness does not really belong to man's individual existence but rather to his social or herd nature; that, as follows from this, it has developed subtlety only insofar as this is required by social or herd utility." Thus, although each human is obviously a one-of-a-kind unique individual, the moment we translate our experiences to consciousness and use language, we are unavoidably reduced to the "average," to what is common with others and easily comprehended by them. Nietzsche concluded that "we simply lack any organ for knowledge, for truth: we know (or believe or imagine) just as much as may be useful in the interests of the human herd, the species" (*Gay*, V, 354). What goes on behind the scenes "unconsciously" is inherently incomprehensible and inaccessible. Suffering and distress, therefore, must remain a riddle: "One simply knows nothing of the whole inner sequence and intricacies that are distress from me or for you. The whole economy of my soul and the balance affected by 'distress' the way new springs and needs break open, the way in which old wounds are healing, the way whole periods of the past are shed" (*Gay*, IV, 338).

Nietzsche would have said to C. G. Jung, Freud's former disciple, who exclaimed, "Until you make the unconscious conscious, it will direct your life and you will call it fate,"[5] that it will direct your life anyhow, and if you want to change your fate to some degree, you should better look elsewhere.

Turning Conscious to Unconscious

While in Freud's model of mind, unconsciousness is posited at the lowest level and consciousness is set at the top, Nietzsche saw it the other way around. Consciousness is the lowest and unconsciousness is the higher level. Nietzsche's response to Freud's "Where id was, there shall ego be,"[6] would have been "Where ego was, there shall id be." Our consciousness has its own limitations. "The chamber of human consciousness is small" (*Genealogy*, III, 18), and it is only a recent unfinished evolutionary development, which by itself, without instinctual dominance, would have led to human demise. Rather than being a regulating power (as Freud saw the ego), it operates "by perverse judging and dreaming with open eyes, by superficiality and credulity." Our overestimation of consciousness prevents us from realizing the task "to embody knowledge in ourselves and make it instinctive" (*Gay*, I, 11).

The animal functions are much more important for survival than "all our beautiful moods and heights of consciousness," which only serve the bodily affairs (*Will*, III, 674). The rationale of all education and morality (and I extrapolate it also to therapy) is "that one tried to attain to the certainty of an instinct." We should train ourselves to act without too much conscious deliberation. "In fact, this unconsciousness belongs to any kind of perfection: even the mathematician employs his combinations unconsciously" (*Will*, II, 432).

Self-Analysis and Navel Gazing

Freud and Nietzsche alike used the materials of their own lives to build their psychologies, and obviously having different lives, their psychologies are different. Freud's theories stemmed from a long process of self-analysis, the results of which found their way into his *The Interpretation of Dreams*[7] and *Psychopathology of Everyday Life*.[8] He believed that analysts should perform self-analysis and also be analyzed by other analysts, because of their own resistance, blind spots, and counter-transferences. In light of Freud's advice, "Look into the depths of your own soul and learn first to know yourself, then you will understand why this illness was bound to come upon you and perhaps you will thenceforth avoid falling ill,"[9] patients are expected to learn in therapy the skill of self-analysis, in order to gain awareness to their inner motivations and conflicts.

Nietzsche felt distaste for what he called "navel gazing" (*Will*, II, 426). Behind this feeling were personal reasons as well as substantial considerations. He disclosed how he was able to reject his own negative self-evaluations, "thanks to the uncontrollable mistrust of the *possibility* of self-knowledge . . . this entire fact is almost the surest thing I know about myself. Within me, there must be some kind of aversion to *believing* anything definite about myself (*Beyond*, IX, 280). All definite statements about the self, personality, or character, "I am so and so" or "this problem is because of that reason," could lead to a reification of the self and perpetuation of problems. The object of our self-examination should not be our personality, but rather our actions and habits which constitute "the history of every day." Rather than being self-conscious, Nietzsche commended familiarity with the environment we live in and awareness of the consequences of our actions. The question to ask is "are they the product of innumerable little cowardices and lazinesses or of your courage and inventive reason?" (*Gay*, IV, 308). In another place he cautioned, "One must not eye oneself while having an experience; else the eye becomes 'an evil eye'" (*Twilight*, Skirmishes, 7).

Nietzsche saw the enterprise of self-knowledge, or self-analysis as impossible, undesirable, and dangerous. He contended that "People can hardly observe, and especially not themselves. 'Everybody is farthest away—from himself', the maxim 'know thyself' is almost malicious" (*Gay*, IV, 335). He reiterated, "For us this law holds for all eternity: 'Each man is furthest from himself'—where we ourselves are concerned, we are not 'knowledgeable people'" (*Genealogy*, prologue, 1). Introspection is a sign of degeneration, and the psychologists of the future (which he invited us to join) have little patience for something that is equal to an instrument trying to know itself: "We are instruments of knowledge and would like to possess all the naiveté and precision of an instrument—consequently, we must not analyze ourselves, 'know' ourselves" (*Will*, II, 426).

Nietzsche admitted that it was quite an effort for him to overcome the temptation to introspect. However, out of self-preservation instincts, a great psychologist "never seeks himself; he has no eyes for himself, no interest or curiosity in himself." Thus, we must try to "shut our eyes to ourselves" (*Will*, II, 426), in other words, "a psychologist must turn his eyes from himself to see anything at all" (*Twilight*, Maxims, 35). We can understand Goethe's quote, "We can only truly respect highly the man who is not seeking himself" (*Beyond*, IX, 266)m as implying that self-analysis derails people from their real challenges, from action in the world. Ignorance of the self is bliss. "We don't know ourselves, we knowledgeable people—we are personally ignorant about ourselves. And there's a good reason for that" (*Genealogy*, prologue, 1). Nietzsche expressed his reservations and concerns about self-knowledge, more a disease than a cure, in a beautiful aphorism quoted already in these pages, saying that we cannot recognize and know ourselves; that humans are "a dark and hidden thing" always changing appearances; that it is dangerous and painful "to dig down into oneself in this way and to descend violently and directly into the shaft of one's being" (*Untimely*, Schopenhauer, 1).

The very presumption and attempt to "analyze" the self is human *hubris* in action, "for we experiment with ourselves in a manner we would not permit with any animal and happily and inquisitively slit the souls of living bodies open." Self-questioning bears more doubts about the self, practically becoming an act of self-violation. There are exceptions, as some people, "we nutcrackers of the soul, we questioning and questionable people," and Nietzsche among them, are perhaps by nature more introspective, and in some cases self-questioning might enhance living, only if they become worthy of being questioned through their actions (*Genealogy*, III, 9).

While psychoanalysts hail Socrates's statement, "the unexamined life isn't worth living,"[10] Nietzsche believed, like Sheldon Kopp, that "the unlived life is not worth examining."[11] Nietzsche saw our lack of transparency to ourselves not as a limitation, but as an essential human characteristic. Furthermore, he believed in setting horizons, in the importance of not knowing everything and not saying everything. We must develop and maintain a will to ignorance, as it is a necessary condition for the preservation and prosperity of life; "a great, firm dome of ignorance must encompass you" (*Will*, III, 609). There are things that should better be left covered. "We must leave many things in the Hades of half-conscious feeling, and not try to release them from their shadow-existence, or else they will become, as thoughts and words, our demoniacal tyrants, with cruel lust after our blood" (*Human*, Assorted, 374).

If Freud stands for depth, Nietzsche stands for superficiality, albeit a deep superficiality, with a purpose behind it, "the more superficially and coarsely it is conceived, the more valuable, definite, beautiful, and significant the world appears." The illusion of truth is over-esteemed while we should actually value more "the force that forms, simplifies, shapes, invents . . . only with a certain obtuseness of vision, a will to simplicity, does the beautiful, the 'valuable' appear: in itself, it is I know not what" (*Will*, III, 602).

SPIRITUAL SUFFERING

I have kept Nietzsche's somewhat poetical and tentative terms of soul and spiritual, which usually stand for the mind, psychological or mental. Most of the material in the present section is taken from the third essay, on the meaning of asceticism in Nietzsche's *On the Genealogy of Morality*. This essay is usually understood as a sociological discussion of asceticism and resentment, but I suggest reading it as a psychological investigation of mental suffering in general and depression in particular. Nietzsche saw it as one of "three decisive preliminary studies by a psychologist for a revaluation of values" and also as "the first psychology of the priest" (*Ecce*, Genealogy) and in fact, the words "psychology" or "psychologist" appeared in this book fourteen times.

The Normalcy of Pathology

It is the fate of humans to be sick animals, "less certain, more changeable, more insecure than any other animal." This sickness opened the door to the denial of life, heralded by the ascetic priests who waged war against passionate, instinctual, and powerful living. Having to navigate between our drives and the burden of concerns for the future, we become restless, disgusted, exhausted, tied-up, and fed up (*Genealogy*, III, 13). Nietzsche again overturned our assumption that the pathological is abnormal and is in need of explanation. He posited that on the contrary, given our existential condition, being a well functioning, reasonably happy person is almost the miraculous exception. "The more normal this pathology is among human beings—and we cannot deny its normality—the higher we should esteem the rare cases of spiritual and physical power, humanity's *strokes of luck*" (*Genealogy*, III, 13).

There is almost no escape from potential problems: "Wherever he turns, the individual realizes only too clearly his own shortcomings, his insufficiency and his incompetence." In addition, humans suffer from unreliable and conflicting beliefs and opinions that surround them; the unequal distribution of talents; the suffering and violence that humans inflict on each other, and finally the general lack of wisdom and knowledge (*Untimely*, Schopenhauer, 4). Vulnerable, mortal, and insignificant humans have many reasons for fear and anxiety, and three-quarters of their "energy and goodwill can be paralyzed and made unfruitful by it."

Only the fortunate ones succeed in keeping up appearance and project "self-confidence and mutual cheerful agreeableness" (*Human,* Assorted, 209). Such inherent deficiencies and unappealing life conditions hinder people's will to power, courage, and pride, and have a direct impact on their physiology. "Considered physiologically, everything ugly weakens and saddens man. It reminds him of decay, danger, impotence; it actually reduces his strength" (*Twilight,* Skirmishes, 20).

Suffering and Interpretation

Nietzsche viewed "spiritual suffering," not as an unavoidable fact, but as a false causal interpretation of other unaccounted and unformulated facts, "essentially a fat word set in place of a very spindly question mark." What is referred to as "spiritual suffering" and is not successfully dealt with "has nothing to do with the 'soul,' it's more likely something to do with his belly." He used the metaphor of digestion, to describe the ability to come to terms, forget, and work through experiences and occurrences, including negative ones, to go on with life safely. Those who fail, who because of physiologically and psychologically weaker systems are stuck in their past, suffer from "indigestion" and not recognizing this weakness, search their soul for explanations (*Genealogy,* III, 16). Nietzsche understood sicknesses, and especially those of the "nerves and head" as symptoms of a weak defensive system, heightened irritability, and salience of pleasure and displeasure (*Will,* I, 43. 7).

Albert Ellis,[12] the founder of Rational Emotional Therapy and one of the fathers of cognitive behavioral therapy, presented his ABC model of emotional reaction in the 1950s, showing that **A**ctivating events (failing an exam) are not the reasons for apparent emotional **C**onsequences (sadness and anger), as they are mediated by **B**elief systems (I am stupid, the teacher is unfair). Nietzsche would have suggested a somewhat different five factors model (*Genealogy,* III, 14–16), analyzing the suffering of our student in terms of a situational event (failing grade in an exam); cultural or family expectations (excellence in studies); physiological characteristics (such as intelligence, talents, resiliency); emotional consequences (distress, sadness, and anger); and finally interpretation (I am a failure, something is wrong with me). The cycle can start off with each of these factors, and thus the interpretation itself can turn into an activating event for further anguish over one's shortcomings (I have unresolved psychological issues). In other words, people must have explanations for their problematic feelings; however, the explanations found are often worse than the problem itself, thus the interpretation and not the complaint, the hidden beliefs and not the "fat words" are the appropriate targets for therapeutic intervention.

Suffering and Sickness

Nietzsche, who himself suffered from unexplained ailments, supplied a list of physiological problems that could be the cause of depression, among them gastritis and mineral deficiency. Yet when a medical explanation and cure of suffering is not found, an abstract explanation will not suffice, and people search for a rack to hang their emotional coat on and an agent that can be blamed. Such a resentful discharge of feelings grants some relief and serves as an anesthesia for their torment. The painful feeling is deadened and driven away by a more intense feeling, which can be triggered by a pretext close at hand, which suffering people have a need and a talent for inventing and enjoying. We can only imagine how the victims of their ire react and how the "sick" ones, in return, see it as a justification of their original bad feelings. Such people enjoy suspicions, rehashing old wrongs, and the poison of their anger. Their motto is, "I am suffering; someone or other must be to blame for that" (*Genealogy*, III, 15).

Suffering and Culture

Nietzsche saw psychological problems, as well as well-being, in the context of culture. He posited a direct link between cultural factors and individual psychological disorders. Thus, modern culture's overstimulation becomes a burden to susceptible persons, who are pushed closer to madness (*Human*, V, 244). Throughout his writings, Nietzsche described four modes of social and individual dysfunction, comprising of asceticism, nihilism-pessimism, resentment, and decadence. These modes, that is to say, patterns consisting of typical cognitions, feelings, and behavior tendencies, are reactions to change and distress in living, influenced by the confluence of social processes and individual physiological makeup. Each of them can be triggered by the other ones; be functional in supporting growth, or dysfunctional in becoming the ground for the development of disorders such as depression.

Ascetic and resentful individuals do not determine their values and wishes and are similarly oriented to others, rather than being self-oriented. Ascetics live under the curb of an external, metaphysical value system and aim to do what is morally right or good in the eyes of God, such as being humble, unselfish, and chaste. Consequently, they are guided by inhibitions, sin, and guilt (*Genealogy*, III, Epigraph). The resentful slavish person "always requires first an opposing world, a world outside them. Psychologically speaking, it needs external stimuli in order to act at all—its action is basically reaction" (*Genealogy*, I, 10). In this mode, life is conducted with a continuous reference to another individual or group held responsible for one's own misfortunes. Resentment is based on a feeling of helplessness, an inability to change the existing power structure, feelings of envy, blaming, and vindictiveness. Initially, it helps to boost self-worth and avoid demoralization; later it weakens and paralyzes self-recovery (*Ecce*, Wise, 6).

Nihilists and decadents alike, though for different reasons, exhibit an impairment of their determination and effectiveness. The psychological state of nihilism and insignificance (*Will*, III, 585), happens when belief systems and organizing schemes break down and the meanings, truths, and goals of life disintegrate (*Will*, I, 10A). Nihilists reject the world as it is and cannot believe in the possibility of change; therefore their existence (including actions, suffering, willing, and feeling) has no meaning, and their pathos is the one of "in vain" (*Will*, III, 585). This condition can easily deteriorate to pessimism, withdrawal, and suicidal thoughts (*Will*, I, 38). This is exactly the issue that Nietzsche targeted "against 'meaninglessness' on the one hand, against moral value judgments on the other" (*Will*, I, 4).

Unlike nihilism, decadence is a natural unavoidable development in the cycle of life: growth, maturity, and aging, but also decadence, sickness, deterioration, and elimination are all normal (*Will*, I, 41). Similarly, social phenomena like vice, prostitution, and distress cannot be eradicated. "A society is not free to remain young (*Will*, I, 40). Under a condition of decadence or "degeneration," value systems do not function effectively and life is run by environmental contingencies, accidents, and uncontrolled basic drives (*Will*, I, 44). Decadents are not motivated to change their condition (*Will*, I, 44), therefore there is no point in fighting it (*Will*, I, 43), and thus the only practical measure to take is containment, avoiding the spread of the process to healthier parts (*Will*, I, 41).

Depression Examined

Nietzsche characterized depression by a triad of inhibition, lethargy and self-loathing, and he paid attention to its facial expression, bodily language, emotions, cognition, and self-perception. Inhibition is an instinctual self-protective measure that takes place in degenerated lives (*Genealogy*, III, 13) and in situations of social disintegration, malnutrition, or mass diseases. It is a physiological process, which decreases liveliness and activity (*Genealogy*, III, 17). Lethargy includes lack of enthusiasm, listlessness, exhaustion, heaviness, and "the deep depression, leaden exhaustion, and black sorrow of the physiologically impaired." Depressed people do not like themselves; they feel dejected, disgusted, stuck with themselves, and full of self-contempt (*despectio sui*); they are full of deep sorrow, anticipating additional failures, wishing they could be someone else (*Genealogy*, III, 14). The combination of these three leads to a sorry existence, "the hygiene of the fakir," where willing, desiring, striving, and feeling love or hate are all diminished (*Genealogy*, III, 17). On top of these, a secondary pathology is developed, the consequence of living with depression, which invite the combined feelings of anger, resentment, and envy: "Here the worms of angry and resentful feelings swarm; here the air stinks of secrets and duplicity; here are constantly spun the nets of the most malicious conspiracies—the plotting of suffering people against the successful and victorious" (*Genealogy*, III, 14).

The Cures of Depression

Nietzsche described different psychological-moral-religious interventions, aiming at "alleviation of suffering, consolation and narcotizing." It is quite surprising to discover that the therapy techniques presented and the goals of "self-discipline, self-surveillance, and self-overcoming" (*Genealogy*, III, 16), are not that different from cognitive-behavioral therapy or "positive psychology" which became popular about 120 years later. Nietzsche, however, was not overly enthused with these techniques; he suggested that they are limited in their effectiveness, and at best can offer only temporary relief, as they fight suffering and unhappiness but not the cause, the essential sickness, not the assumptions about the world, nor the physiological ground of the problem (*Genealogy*, III, 18).

Besides, the healers themselves with their "priestly medication" are part of the same society and culture that bred the suffering, and Nietzsche, writing as a psychologist for other psychologists, explained that we must, therefore, distrust ourselves for "we are probably sacrificial victims and prey, as well, made sick by this contemporary taste for moralizing" (*Genealogy*, III, 20). This realization holds true for contemporary therapists: we are children of our times; we are shaped by a certain culture; we too are blind to our culture's implicit assumptions, which mold the ways we evaluate and help our clients.

Nietzsche reviewed different methods and principles of help: Therapist convince sufferers that pain is only the result of faulty reasoning, assuming that it will disappear the moment the error is recognized. Nietzsche had reservations about such a naïve challenging of emotions, commenting that it is "interesting enough, but too absurd, with too little practical significance, too full of cobwebs and loafing around" (*Genealogy*, III, 17). Rather than challenging feelings of emptiness and aimlessness by rational means, they can be deadened and deflected by means of emotional excitation, using among others, music, celebrating the misfortunes of others, enthusiasm or hatred for persons or periods, submerging oneself in work or a project, craving for knowledge, pathos, fanaticism, and mysticism. However, such gambits have negative side effects as they weaken the will and the ability to plan and accomplish; and they make people overly vain and easily humiliated (*Will*, I, 29). Intense feelings, especially ones that are aroused suddenly, can "remove the human soul for once from its entire frame." Being immersed in extreme terror, elation, lust, revenge, despair, triumph, or hate makes people forget their petty, small-minded disinterestedness, apathy, and irritations. Using this "pack of wild hounds" might also worsen the conditions of sufferers, changing depression to other negative feelings of guilt, sin, and fear (*Genealogy*, III, 20).

Another technique used to achieve equanimity and lower the intensity of pain is the reduction of one's level of activity by means of intentional starving of desires and physical well-being and by avoiding willing, fighting, and loving. This move, the reverse of excitation, can be construed in clinical, religious, or spiritual terms, as self-hypnosis, mindfulness, selflessness, sanctification, redemption, or nothingness. "The method requires rare powers, above all, courage, contempt for opinion, and 'intellectual stoicism'" (*Genealogy*, III, 17). This approach actually prescribes the symptom, telling persons who find it difficult to be active to reduce their activity and pay attention to other matters. And again, one can choose the opposite technique of activation, namely, being busy with work and assignment, leaving no room for depression. "For it is *narrow*, this room of human consciousness!" By focusing on something in the outside world, one stops paying attention and worrying about the self. Activation can be established by rigid habits, inflexible timetables, perfectionist standards, and meticulous following of orders given by a close person taking on the role of a taskmaster (*Genealogy*, III, 18).

Depressed people, due to their inhibitions, lethargy, and self-hate, tend to avoid pleasures. Consequently, the resulting poor diet of "reinforcements" and estrangement from other people perpetuates their depression. Prescribing "a small pleasure" is an efficient tool in combating depression, and the most accessible pleasure that can be recommended is "the pleasure in *creating* pleasure" for others, achieved by expressions of kindness, giving gifts, helping, complimenting, and encouraging. The very act of pleasuring others arouses "the strongest, most life-affirming drive, even if only in the most cautious doses—the *Will to Power*." Being helpful and considerate gives solace and increases feelings of superiority and happiness (*Genealogy*, III, 18). Martin Seligman's "Positive psychology"[13] prescriptions of showing gratitude to others can be seen as a later application of Nietzsche's principle of "the pleasure in *creating* pleasure." In addition, participation in a community or a congregation, built on the experience of "us" and a "will to mutual assistance," makes persons feel like effective parts of a larger group. "In the fight against depression, the *development of the herd* is an essential step and a victory" (*Genealogy*, III, 18).

Cognitive clarification and emotional excitation are contradictory measures, and so are activation, affiliation, and hibernation. Nietzsche taught that whatever the cure given, it must suit the sufferer. "One temperament finds it useful to be able to give vent to its disgust in words, being made sweeter by speech. Another reaches its full bitterness only by speaking out." For the latter, restraint is preferable, as it "improves . . . character and prevents it from becoming too acrid and sour" (*Human*,

Assorted, 44). What is medicine for one person can be poison for another, and, for this reason, one technique cannot suit all, and the therapist's judgment, the art of therapy, remains indispensable.

WAR, WISDOM, AND ART

Nietzsche's answer to the universal question of coping with suffering, pain, and illness consists of three paths, at times contradicting and at times complementing each other: fighting and persevering; accepting, justifying and reframing; and finally transforming and creating. To put it differently, he presents the ways of the hero-warrior-soldier; the way of the sage-philosopher-psychologist; and the way of the artist-musician-poet. To put it differently once more, I am going to review now what Nietzsche called life's school of war, the highest wisdom, and making things beautiful (aesthetic activity).

Out of Life's School of War

The metaphors of war and warrior go back to prehistory. The Chinese classic *The Art of War* by Sun Tzu (sixth century BCE)[14] was and still is a source of inspiration for soldiers, businesspeople, athletes, and for the conduct of life in general. It is a fruitful metaphor as different tactics and measures can be derived from it, such as guerrilla warfare rather than a frontal onslaught, spying and information gathering, deception and surprise attacks. In Nietzsche's case, the source of his hero-warrior-soldier images lies in the Hellenic world's adoration of life of combat and victory, already described in his early essay *Homer's Contest*. Since his high school days, Nietzsche was an avid student of Greek mythology, tragedies, and philosophy. He found himself close in mind to Heraclitus, and especially to his idea that everything is strife and endless contest (*Agon*) and this affinity was expressed in a short poem titled *Heraclitean*, starting with the line, "Only fights yield Happiness on earth, And on battlefields Friendship has its birth" (*Gay*, Prelude, 41). This metaphor combines different strands of meaning: love of confrontation and victory; having a goal more important than life; courage, strength, hardness, and perseverance; preparation, training, and discipline; and finally, an ability to command and obey.

A Soldier and Warrior

Nietzsche found all these elements in himself, and in a letter to Peter Gast (April 6, 1883)[15] he wrote, "You would not believe, dear friend, what an abundance of suffering life has unloaded upon me, at all times, from *early* childhood on. But I am a soldier—and this soldier, in the end, did become the father of Zarathustra!" He had to see himself as a warrior and become one in order to overcome his suffering, pain, and sickness. Getting rid of pain is a negative minimalistic motivation; maintaining the freedom to pursue one's goals is a positive one which grants endurance and courage. "If we have our own why of life, we shall get along with almost any how" (*Twilight*, Maxims, 12). Similarly, he described heroism as "going out to meet at the same time one's highest suffering and one's highest hope" (*Gay*, III, 268).

Nietzsche's lessons from coping with suffering were distilled into what became an often quoted motto, "Out of life's school of war: What does not destroy me, makes me stronger" (*Twilight*, Maxims, 8). Likewise, war is the great wisdom of profound persons in whom "through a wound the spirits increase, and vigor grows" (*Twilight*, Preface), and in the same spirit Nietzsche advised, "In times of painful tension and vulnerability, choose war: it hardens, it produces muscles" (*Will*, IV, 1040). The amount of resistance individuals and people must overcome, and the effort it takes to hold on, sometimes taking risks and being cruel to themselves, is a measure of their freedom. "The highest type of free man must be sought where the highest resistance is constantly overcome" (*Twilight*, Skirmishes, 38).

Russian Fatalism

Going to war with no chance of winning is not the cleverest idea. "How poisonous, how crafty, how bad, every long war makes one, which cannot be waged openly by means of force!" (*Beyond*, Chapter II, 25). We must be smart too, and beware of "The Appearance of Heroism.—throwing ourselves in the midst of our enemies may be a sign of cowardice" (*Daybreak*, IV, 299). Nietzsche saw inactivity as medicine for sicknesses of the soul: lying still and avoiding thinking is an inexpensive medicine, that when administered correctly can even become quite pleasant (*Human*, Assorted, 361). He used war and warrior metaphors, not only for frontal assault but also to teach "Russian fatalism." Illness puts one in a state of helplessness followed by resentment, and the sick person's best response would be in certain cases a disaffected fatalism with which "the Russian soldier, when a campaign becomes unbearable, finally lies down in the snow," ceasing all exertions, not willing to fight in vain. This hibernation or the way of the fakir is a wise decision, worthier than courage in facing death, as it reduces activity level, saves energy, and supports self-preservation (*Ecce*, Wise, 6).

The Highest Wisdom

While the "life's school of war" teaches fighting and overcoming, the highest wisdom teaches accepting and justifying. "To think of one's self as a destiny, not to wish one's self 'different' this, in such circumstances, is the very highest wisdom" (*Ecce*, Wise, 6). This wisdom, which Nietzsche also calls the highest form of affirmation, recognizes that pain, suffering, and sickness are an essential part of our life. "I, Zarathustra, the advocate of living, the advocate of suffering, the advocate of the circuit—thee do I call, my most abysmal thought!" (*Thus*, The convalescent, 1). Sickness is a fact of life. "Even Socrates said, as he died: 'to live—that means to be sick a long time: I owe Asclepius the Savior a rooster'" (*Twilight*, Socrates, 1).

That Which Was

Nietzsche highlighted the time dimension of trauma, in which the past intrudes upon the present, coming back as a ghost haunting and disturbing later on. "A leaf is continuously released from the roll of time, falls out, flutters away—and suddenly flutters back again into the man's lap" (*Untimely*, History, 1). Humans are historical creatures who live with memories of the past, which can become "an invisible and dark weight," an intruding and painful burden. The "it was" can turn to be traumatic, turning existence into "a past tense that is never over and done with," that only death can terminate (*Untimely*, History, 1).

The source of our mental suffering is obviously a painful event that already happened. Willing liberates; yet helplessness in relation to what has been done, the "it was" puts our will in chains. Time cannot run backward, and "that which was" becomes a stone we cannot roll. Nietzsche's remedy for trauma, in the spirit of Eternal Recurrence, is its acceptance and justification, not once but endless times. Zarathustra taught the art of redeeming and integrating the past "to compose into one and bring together what is fragment and riddle and dreadful chance in man—as poet, reader of riddles, and redeemer of chance" (*Thus*, III, Old and new law-tables, 3). He taught how to turn a painful "it was" into a building block, something that will transform our life in such a way that we will be able to say, from this point in time, that we are willing to repeat the "it was" again and again. I understand Nietzsche's idea of redemption or psychotherapy, not in terms of gaining additional insight into what happened, but rather creating the future by remolding "every 'It was' into 'I willed it so!'" (*Thus*, II, Redemption). In this redemption, one comes to terms with the past, the future, and the nature of time itself. "I love him who justifies the future and redeems the past: for he wants to perish in the present" (*Thus*, Prologue, 3).

Amor Fati

In an aphorism about Nietzsche's new-year wishes, the motto *amor fati* (love your fate) appeared for the first time. "I want to learn more and more to see as beautiful what is necessary in things; then I shall be one of those who make things beautiful." He wishes that *amor fati* will be his love, that affirmative outlook will be his manner, and that he will not fight what is ugly, neither accuse anymore (*Gay*, IV, 276). In other words, the full acceptance of reality without condemnation will enable its transformation into art and at the same time effect a personal transformation. "My formula for greatness in man is *amor fati*: that a man should wish to have nothing altered, either in the future, the past, or for all eternity." One should accept necessity, avoid covering it up with idealistic false notions, and actually love it (*Ecce*, Clever, 10). Nietzsche described such greatness, in terms of Eternal Recurrence, "the ideal of the most high-spirited, alive, and world-affirming human being." Such a person comes to terms with what was and, moreover, wants it to repeat into all eternity, "shouting insatiably *da capo* [Italian music term, which means repeating the previous part from the beginning]." With such an attitude towards hardships and difficulties with other people, one turns oneself into a necessity (*Beyond*, II, 56).

Reversing of Perspectives

The "highest wisdom" is about coming to terms with a given reality, and about seeing the whole picture and not only its disadvantages. Reversal of perspective is a play with our cognitive binoculars, in which we can change the focus, size, and lighting of what we look at and, in so doing, question the previous values and interpretations we assigned to phenomena, thus enabling reformulation or reframing. Nietzsche's life experiences trained him to view ideas and values from the perspective of the sick and, conversely, see the manifestations of an instinct for decadence, from the perspective of abundance and self-confidence, making him a skillful master with a "knack of reversing perspectives" (*Ecce*, Wise, 1). We cannot always change reality, but we can still be masters of changing the way we see it, what Nietzsche termed "the principle of belief." Reversing perspectives, *amor fati*, and turning what was into "I wished it so," are instances of this principle in action. If we cannot will things, it is possible to "lay some *meaning* into them," and then believe that they obey our will (*Twilight*, Maxims, 18). In this respect, he concurred with Epictetus, the stoic who taught that we are basically influenced by our interpretation of reality rather than reality itself: "When a misfortune strikes us, we can overcome it either by removing its cause or else by changing the effect it has on our feelings, that is, by reinterpreting the misfortune as a good, whose benefit may only later become clear" (*Human*, III, 108).

From the perspective of the tragic-Dionysian tradition, pain and pleasure cannot be separated, as pain and destruction are a consequence of the will to pleasure and the will to create (*Will*, III, 853, 3). Another turn of the binoculars' lenses and pain stops being a fact, but merely an interpretation of some complex physiological events, concepts invented to give the impression of understanding unclear conditions (*Genealogy*, III, 16). Nietzsche went on playing with his magical lenses and now we see things turned upside-down, and the problem is not sickness, which is a normal essential component of our soul, but rather the very wish to be healthy. The wish to be healthy itself is a weakness and a prejudice (*Gay*, III, 120). Health and sickness are not opposites, and it is possible to be healthy and sick at the same time. Health can be understood not as an absence of sickness but as a manner of energetic functioning which includes the ability to bear and overcome sickness, with an "overflowing, plastic, and rejuvenating power" (*Will*, IV, 1014).

Creativity concurs with suffering—the brightest and most brilliant parts of Nietzsche's writings coincided with bodily weakness and suffering (*Ecce*, Wise, 1). Failures, anxieties, deprivations, and mistakes are necessary just as their opposites; "the path to one's own heaven always leads through the voluptuousness of one's own hell" (*Gay*, IV, 338). Inability to endure one's suffering and doing everything possible to prevent and get rid of it encourages remissness and precludes happiness. "For happiness and misfortune are brother and sister, who grow tall together, or, as with you, remain small together (*Gay*, IV, 338). The two, health and illness, cannot be separated; the ability to tolerate sickness defines health, and illness is a trigger for a new learning, "as an instrument and fishhook of knowledge" (*Human*, Preface, 4).

Everything for the Best

Acceptance is indeed the highest wisdom, just as nonacceptance is the highest folly ("it's not fair"; "it should not have happened"; "why me?"), only adding resentment, bitterness, and perplexity to a bad situation. Nietzsche went beyond acceptance of pain as an inherent part of existence, to see it as an advantage, almost a blessing that must be justified, and yes, loved. He wrote about personal providence in the midst of "the beautiful chaos of existence" and about chance, which sometimes plays with us, leading us to beautiful unexpected places that we could not have found on our own. With this positive mindset, we should believe that what happens to us eventually works out for the best—as if it happened especially for us and, therefore, we should not wish to give it up. Providence, however, needs our help in interpreting and rearranging events in a way that would benefit us (*Gay*, IV, 277). Accepting what cannot be changed and moreover, seeing the potential advantages and opportunities involved in a given undesired situation, is a wisdom shared by other inhabitants of "the republic of geniuses" (*Untimely*, History, IX), among them Epictetus and his contemporary, Rabbi Akiva, the Talmudic sage. This highest wisdom also reverberates in the clichés that "every cloud has a silver lining and everything is for the best."

Suffering and Depth

Nietzsche, who had no option but to live with pain and suffering, tried not only to persevere, but attempted to accentuate their benefits, thus turning a constraint into an opportunity, and the list of advantages is telling: "Prophetic human beings are afflicted with a great deal of suffering . . . it is their pain that makes them prophets" (*Gay*, III, 316); without pain and sickness, the great suspicion which liberates the spirit and a philosophical examination of life, will probably be lost. In addition to this, he doubted whether pain improves persons, but knew that it makes them deeper. "Only great pain is the ultimate liberator of the spirit" (*Gay*, Preface to the 2nd Edition, 3). Those who know severe suffering become persons who know much about a terrifying world, about which others have no clue. "Deep suffering makes noble; it separates" (*Contra*, The Psychologist Speaks Up, 3). The ability to discover happiness in the midst of weakness of a recurring chronic sickness is a sign of the free spirit, who can remain grateful and see the bright side of things and even become less pessimistic (*Human*, Preface, 5). Suffering well arouses appreciation and not pity. "I love him whose soul is deep even in the wounding, and whom a little thing can ruin: thus he gladly goes across the bridge" (*Thus*, Prologue, 4).

MAKING BEAUTIFUL

To recap, we are exploring Nietzsche's answers to the question of how it is possible to go on living in the face of pain and sickness. The answers discussed so far were fighting (the school of war) and/or accepting and reinterpreting (the highest wisdom) one's hardship. His third answer was transforming this reality by aesthetic activity: converting wretchedness into beauty; being an artist and becoming a piece of art. What are the nature and the danger of pain, sickness, and suffering? They are salient phenomena which remove to the background, reduce, and belittle other previously satisfying activities and experiences. With longer periods of suffering, self-pity grows; senselessness, helplessness, and hopelessness set in. Consequently, the person breaks down or enters a state of "practical pessimism" (*Birth*, 7), in which the world and life become despicable. Here enters art, created and appreciated: "Without art we would be nothing but foreground and live entirely in the spell of that perspective which makes what is closest at hand and most vulgar appear as if it were vast, and reality itself" (*Gay*, II, 78).

The Poets of our Lives

Art strengthens our hold on life and the world. "Art is the fundamental metaphysical activity of Man; art is the highest form of human activity" (*Birth*, Preface). Art helps us make sense of the world and when pain becomes a prominent feature of our world, art can make sense of it too. If we want to be "the poets of our lives," we should learn from artists how to turn ugly, repulsive, and undesired things into their opposites of beautiful, attractive, and desirable, by changing perspectives, distancing, and framing (*Gay*, IV, 299). In this respect, aesthetic activity is closely related to the highest wisdom of interpretation and dreaming, which can be considered as an artistic activity. Art is thus an act of re-creation, necessary for recuperation like sleep, something that "prevents the bow from snapping" (*Untimely*, Wagner, 4).

A Will to Appearance

As far back as his first book, pain was made the basic fact of existence, "the sole ground of being," out of which emerged a need for "rapt vision and delightful illusion to redeem itself" (*Birth*, 4). Art is rooted in the Dionysian and the Apollonian: the former with a "primordial joy experienced even in pain" (*Birth*, 24) and the latter with a "primordial pleasure of mere appearance," and thus beauty arises "just as roses burst from thorny bushes" (*Birth*, 49). Art is the "cult of the untrue" and "the good will to appearance."

Keeping up appearances is a role to perform and a goal to achieve. People must not suspect that we are suffering and are under pain, as their pity will not help us. The credibility of our show can only strengthen us. I am thinking about Freddie Mercury's last album *Innuendo.*[16] He hid from others his terminal illness with AIDS, and sang, like no one else could, that he was "going slightly mad" and that "the show must go on." He was an artist to the last moment, turning his turmoil, pain, and anxieties into art.

The Hero and the Fool

Art gives us a measure of choice over situations that were forced on us. It gives us courage; "this triumphant state is what the tragic artist chooses, what he glorifies" (*Twilight*, Skirmishes, 24). Art helps by turning an unfortunate given suffering into an event experienced by a tragic-warrior; a hero redeemed by "states in which suffering is willed, transfigured, deified, where suffering is a form of great delight" (*Will*, III, 853, 2).

Art enables turning pain into something temporarily more distant, necessary, and more bearable. We can see the situation and ourselves differently, as heroes or as fools, and laugh about the situation in which we are (*Gay*, II, 107). Using humor and laughing at ourselves is a uniquely human capability, invented in response to deep suffering, "The unhappiest and most melancholy animal is as fitting, the most cheerful" (*Will*, I, 91).

Art as Solace

In ancient Greece, the role of all true tragedies was to give "metaphysical solace" and send the spectators home with the message "that despite every phenomenal change, life is at bottom indestructibly joyful and powerful" (*Birth,* 7) and again, "we may see the artistic buoyancy and creative joy as a luminous cloud shape reflected upon the dark surface of a lake of sorrow" (*Birth,* 9). Nietzsche understood the power of art to offer solace and make us beautiful in dealing with hardships in his early, unpublished essay *The Greek State,* where he saw art as something that enables life under the roughest conditions and escape from the trap of "practical pessimism."

The Standard of Art

Individual morality entails an aesthetic evaluation, asking whether a behavior is beautiful or not (chapter 6). Hence, aesthetic considerations can be our guiding principle in coping with pain, making us ask if the way we cope is beautiful and graceful, or not. Making something beautiful or seeing it as such is a human quality, implying a choice, and one can carry her burden in an inspiring, uplifting manner or in an unworthy demoralizing one. The way persons cope with pain and sickness and anticipate death impacts their own feelings and the feelings of others; their Will to Power, courage, and pride "all fall with the ugly and rise with the beautiful" (*Twilight,* Skirmishes, 20). We must be realistic: Art is not a solution for everyone, it is not a fast cure, and it does not guarantee health, happiness or release from pain. And yet "the slow arrow of beauty" offers something intangible, a longing, a wish to do something with one's pain and life, the satisfaction of shaping at least what is up to us in our own style, even if it is having a band play *Sweet Georgia Brown* at one's funeral. Nietzsche described this sad beauty as noble and serene, one that develops slowly and is found in our hearts. "What do we long for when we see beauty? To be beautiful" (*Human,* IV, 149).

PSYCHOTHERAPIA ACTIVA

Nietzsche's principles of wise living were also his principles of solving problems in living. He considered *Vita activa* superior to *vita contemplativa,* as the latter is based on fear, tiredness, and diminished appreciation of the pleasure in acting (*Daybreak,* I, 4). I believe that Nietzsche would have similarly upheld *psychotherapia activa* [active psychotherapy] and Zarathustra said it outright, "Only the doer learns" (*Thus,* IV, The ugliest man). Unlike Socrates and Plato and the later Protestant theologians, Nietzsche did not believe that faith leads to deeds and asserted that on the contrary, the formula to translate an idea into action is "works, first and foremost! That is to say, doing, doing, doing!" and only then can the corresponding faith appear (*Daybreak*, I, 22). Nietzsche rejected all moralizing systems which call to refrain from action, renounce urges, and overcome them; instead, he welcomed systems which energize persons and stimulate action and repetition of action until perfection is reached. With such an active goal-directed approach, what is undesirable and troubling is left behind, like falling yellow leaves, with no need for hateful confrontation, "Our doing must determine what we leave undone; in that we do, we leave undone" (*Gay*, IV, 304).

The feeling of remorse, guilt, and the accompanying rehashing of past hurts is a form of decadence. "This reopening of old wounds, this wallowing in self-contempt and contrition, is one more illness, out of which no 'salvation of the soul' can arise but only a new form of soul sickness." In such cases, when these negative feelings hinder recovery, "one must try counterbalancing it all by new activities, in order to escape from the sickness of self-torture as quickly as possible" (*Will*, II, 233). Yet given the paradox of will and the fact that we are a multiplicity (chapter 3), in which different parts might have different notions about which action to take, doing and acting are not such straightforward, simple matters. In addition, an action is a "problem for those who wait" and procrastination inconveniences many of us, who need luck and unpredictable triggers to start moving, sometimes waking up from our slumber too late (*Beyond*, IX, 277).

It is easier to "swing into action" by developing life fitness, taking small or slow steps, experimenting with different possibilities, examining the assumptions and distortions one has and imitating successful others. Additional action-promoting suggestions were examined in the discussion of chance and action (chapter 6). Describing all these action stratagems, Nietzsche did not even once suggest that understanding the reasons behind a problem might help to solve it, and instead he took the problems as a given as if concurring with Murphy's Law, "If something can go wrong, it will."

Life Fitness

A client arrives at therapy, and in many cases, at the end of the first session, the therapist will know quite a lot about the presenting problem and the family background; but most probably will know almost nothing about "prosaic matters" such as the client's physical fitness, diet, reading and music tastes, habits, social relations, and connection with nature. Had Nietzsche been this client's therapist, he would have zeroed in on these questions, first of all. "To counter any kind of affliction or distress of soul one ought in the first instance to try a change of diet and hard physical labor" (*Daybreak*, IV, 269). Nietzsche understood freedom as "facility in self-direction" and a psychological problem can thus be understood as a diminished facility and limitation of freedom, stemming from low fitness: "All fitness the result of fortunate organization, all freedom the result of fitness" (*Will*, III, 705). The pleasure derived from bodily prowess and from examining and discarding old conventions, and from new understandings and knowledge, grants feeling of power, superiority, and uniqueness. For this reason, improved physical and intellectual fitness offer a cure for depression (*Human*, V, 252).

Efforts to improve fitness must be based on the specific needs and characteristics of the person. "Each one has his own standard, often between the narrowest and most delicate limits" (*Ecce*, Clever, 1). Thus, proper nutrition is crucial, for "all prejudices may be traced back to the intestines" (*Ecce*, Clever, 1), and a suitable climate enhances creativity, for "none of us can live anywhere" (*Ecce*, Clever, 2). Fitness must be built but also maintained, and it is important to be aware of exhaustion, to take care to recuperate after a continued effort, and to renew strength possibly by reading, intimate relationships, and listening to music. He found that reading enabled him to escape from himself and recover from his earnestness (*Ecce*, Clever, 3), and encounters with Richard Wagner gave him "days of confidence, of cheerfulness, of sublime flashes, and of profound moments (*Ecce*, Clever, 5). He had a definite taste in music, and perhaps we should also have our own: "It should be cheerful and yet profound, like an October afternoon. It should be unique, wanton, and tender, and like a dainty, sweet woman in roguishness and grace" (*Ecce*, Clever, 7).

Thinking Differently

Interpretations have a crucial role both in the creation and amelioration of mental suffering. To remind you, I have compared Albert Ellis's ABC model with Nietzsche's implicit five factors model. Ellis is usually considered a pioneer of Cognitive Behavioral Therapy, but Nietzsche already stated before him, "We have to *learn to think differently*—in order, at last, perhaps very late on, to attain even more: *to feel different*" (*Daybreak*, III, 103). Nietzsche declared himself more than once a disciple of Dionysus. Yet he used, perhaps as a counterbalance to this god's passionate, almost feral ways, some of the prescriptions for cool-headed rational living stemming from the Stoic, Epicurean, and Cynic schools of thought. He saw his *Human, All Too Human* as a contribution and affirmation of "an intellectual cure, consisting in a course of anti-romantic self-treatment." Based on his experiences and insights, Nietzsche taught persons who wish to be free spirits, a "lesson in health that may be recommended as a *disciplina voluntatis*," in other words, how to train themselves to think in a constructive manner (*Human*, Assortment, Preface, 2).

In order to feel different, Nietzsche recounted how he taught himself to think differently by first analyzing his former, romantic unscientific pessimism, which magnified and interpreted his individual experiences as valid universal judgments. He then detailed how he challenged this thought by fighting it repeatedly and patiently, until he turned this perspective around, to reach the proposition that "a sufferer has no right to pessimism because he suffers" (*Human*, Assorted, 5). In addition to such a cognitive workout, Nietzsche prescribed a change of environment, which triggers new cognitions and feelings: "Just as a physician transfers his patient to totally strange surroundings, in order to displace him from his entire 'hitherto,' from his cares, friends, letters, duties, stupidities and painful memories, and teaches him to stretch out hands and senses to new nourishment, a new sun, a new future" (*Human*, Assorted, 5).

Self-Mastery

Suggesting techniques to overcome unsought urges, Nietzsche wrote about "self-mastery" and "self-control," terms usually found in behavior-modification textbooks. Behaviorists, grounded in learning theory, are usually unaware that Nietzsche, based on his theory of multiplicity, already suggested some of their practices. Nietzsche proposed "methods for combating the vehemence of an impulse." With today's epidemic of obesity and overconsumption of pornography, control of such impulses has become an urgent issue. His contributions go beyond techniques, and more importantly, they offer ways to understand and approach problem situations. In treating persons, who tend to feel guilt and shame about uncontrolled habits, a Nietzschean therapist will first of all reassure and emphasize their "innocence and irresponsibility" regarding the issue.

Nietzsche suggested to persons who wish to overcome an urge that they are actually not in control, and hence missing their goal cannot be considered a failure. "But the will to combat the violence of a craving is beyond our power, equally with the method we adopt and the success we may have in applying it." People are only the arena in which the fight goes on, and their intellect is no more than the "blind instrument" of rivaling powers (*Daybreak*, II, 109), one of which wants to terminate a behavior; the other wishes to continue it. In a situation like this, a frontal attack is useless, as failures increase demoralization, and it could be wiser to give up expectations for a one shot permanent solution. Mark Twain said, "quitting smoking is easy, I've done it hundreds of times;" in other words, the quitting and smoking parties fight for control and each of them has the upper hand for a while only. A final capitulation is not the rule: After a successful diet many regain their weight, and after detoxifications some persons relapse and return to their drinking habits. Containment of the problem is a more realistic goal, which calls for continuous monitoring and use of different successive ploys. Ultimately, some of them will work for different periods of time. Therapy becomes in this way an experiment and a game, and self-control becomes something playful.

Many Ways

Nietzsche offered six means, techniques, of coping with such urges. First is the avoidance of situations—in behavioral terms, stimulus control, where satisfying the impulse is initially possible, with gradually prolonged periods refraining from consumptive behavior. Second is the enforcing of a severe schedule of fixed times and places for satisfying an urge, thus regulating the drive in light of a self-made plan and not by the urge's natural ebb and flow. Third is to prescribe an unrestrained gratification to the point of disgust and satiation, while taking into consideration the danger involved in such flooding, which is like "the rider who rides his horse to death and breaks his own neck in doing so." Fourth is the use of an "intellectual trick" of associating the idea of the gratification with some painful (losing others people's respect) or disgusting thought (contact with bodily discharges). Much later, in 1986, such a technique was promoted by Joseph Cautela as "covert conditioning."[17] Fifth is the introduction of competing behaviors and satisfactions, which distract and redirect one's powers and interests into new directions, making the original interest less alluring. Sixth, one can weaken the urge's strength by the dangerous and possibly destructive weakening of the body and diminishing of liveliness, by means of self-starvation and sleep deprivation (*Daybreak*, II, 109).

High and Low Tides

In applying techniques of change, Nietzsche paid special attention to the issue of timing: it is important to evaluate whether to curb an urge at all and when and how to do it, as passions go through different phases. In an early phase, "they are merely disastrous when they drag down their victim with the weight of stupidity"; in a much later phase they "spiritualize" themselves (*Twilight*, Morality, 1). Sometimes the inner tide draws us to a thing; sometimes it draws us away from it (*Daybreak*, IX, 500), and he advised "using high and low tides" to find the right point for intervention.

Gently and Easily

Although passions can be stupid and bear negative consequences, they must be respected and not treated as an enemy to be exterminated. "An attack on the roots of passion means an attack on the roots of life" (*Twilight*, Morality, 1). Hence, changing should be done carefully, taking in consideration that what seems at first like a problem might have some vital function. Nietzsche criticized moral teachers who instruct a person "to get himself into his own power," explaining that such demands turn natural strivings and inclinations into threats, which invite oversensitivity, defensiveness, loss of trust, and disappointments. This kind of self-control turns a person to be "impoverished and cut off from the finest accidents of his soul!" preventing experimenting with the new and unfamiliar (*Gay*, IV, 305). Moreover, he did not believe in hard work in the areas of self-change, therapy, and all creative endeavors; a sound work should be produced with no more than three-quarters of the creator's strength, as otherwise it becomes full of tension. "All good things have something easygoing about them and lie like cows in the meadow" (*Human*, Assorted, 107).

Slow Cures, Small Doses, and Freezing

A chronic sickness of the soul, like those of the body, usually does not arise from one psychological or physiological trauma, but rather from "countless little-unheeded instances of neglect." A chronic lung infection, for example, could result from habitual shallow breathing and too little air supply to the lungs. The cure, in this case, consists of "countless little exercises in the opposite direction," making a rule to take long deep breaths every fifteen minutes, optimally lying on the floor, using an alarm clock as a memory aid. Such cures are "petty and slow, and he who wishes to cure his soul must also consider making changes to the very pettiest of his habits." Quite often people develop unsuitable habits, such as cursing at every inconvenience, which are installed by frequent repetitions, until the behavior rules the person performing it. The way to deal with such problem would be to institute another competing desirable habit like repeating ten times a day self-reassuring statements (*Daybreak*, V, 462).

The example of lung infection indicates that there is no single one-time dramatic reason for a problem, but rather many small discrete quite prosaic, unintentional actions. Accordingly, healing ought to proceed in the reverse route, resulting from the constant repetition of certain actions that promote correct health. Note that Nietzsche did not explore the reasons for shallow breathing, and as far as he was concerned, it simply happened, was repeated often enough, and turned into a disturbing habit. If breathing caused the problem, breathing (in a different manner) will cure it too, and breathing can become different with the help of environmental prompts as simple as a clock (or a smartphone nowadays).

Repetition and Freezing

Nietzsche realized that nothing of significance can be created in one stroke, and reckoned that changes in evaluations, our habitual moral outlook, must be established gradually and slowly, until they have gained prominence over the old ones; "the means to it must be given in the smallest doses but unremittingly over long periods of time!" The consequences of disregarding the principle of small doses can be seen in the political field, in which revolutions attempting to bring about a swift change in evaluations were only "a pathetic and bloody *piece of quackery*" (*Daybreak*, V, 534).

Humans tend to react emotionally, with suspicion and hostility towards persons who make arguments they are not ready to accept; "stupid so often becomes malignant" (*Human*, Wanderer, 39). Therapists' enthusiastic attempts to eradicate concepts backfire. Not being satisfied with "refuting it and drawing out of it the illogical worm that resides within," they go further to make an idea or behavior totally detestable. Under such a heavy onslaught and confrontation that is experienced as an insult and, therefore, mobilizes resistance, the idea keeps resurrecting and its kernel produces new shoots. Because "conceptions are very tenacious of life" and "one refutation is not a refutation," Nietzsche suggested that rather than directly confront what is objectionable, it should be put carefully and repeatedly on ice, to enable well-timed unthreatened consideration (*Human*, Wanderer, 211). He described how he illuminated the "underworld of ideals" not with pyrotechnics or pathos, but rather, "one error after the other is quietly laid on ice; the ideal is not refuted—it freezes (*Ecce*, Human).

Seeming Becomes Being

People are confronted with two kinds of psychological challenges: on one hand, controlling and changing dysfunctional habits, which was discussed above; on the other hand, adopting new desirable behaviors, such as an introvert's desire to act more warmly and openly with people, or a timid person's wish to act more assertively. Nietzsche looked at the issue of "not asserting our rights" and realized that exercising power demands effort and courage, and many fail to assert their rights out of fear and laziness, hiding behind the virtues of patience and forbearance (*Human*, Wanderer, 251). What can they do? His answer was in line with William James[18] and George Kelly's personal construct theory.[19] The three of them saw imitation, what is often seen as hypocrisy or dissimulation, as an important tool of change. He articulated this principle as "seeming becomes being," and remarked with a grain of irony, "The hypocrite who always plays one and the same role finally ceases to be a hypocrite." This takes place also in the professions and arts, where novices imitate and copy manners, expressions, and bearings of older hands. What works and succeeds gradually gains power over them. "If someone wants to seem to be something, stubbornly and for a long time, he eventually finds it hard to be anything else" (*Human*, I, 51).

Nietzsche considered "dissimulation as duty" because repeated dissimulations eventually sublimate themselves and turn into nature, into organs and instincts (*Daybreak*, IV, 248). Deception turns into honesty by means of two parallel processes: one is the result of efforts and preparation made to play a role well, in which the very acting changes people's hidden assumptions about themselves. The other is the feedback they get from their audience, "for men will believe something is true if it is evident that others believe in it firmly" (*Human*, II, 52). Adopting new and atypical forms of behavior might feel artificial or even ridiculous, and in order to overcome this obstacle, Nietzsche made it a point to occasionally behave more emotionally and with fewer inhibitions, "cultivate a little vice of emotion," which is the only way for self-overcoming (*Twilight*, Skirmishes, 28). Changing our habitual ways guarantees renewal and creativity, and thus if we find ourselves, we lose ourselves to find it again. "For a thinker it is a drawback to be bound to a single person all the time" (*Human*, Wanderer, 306). Play-acting for a long time and to excess, the reverse of our habitual behaviors, gives us a taste of our talents and pleasure in antithetical talents, "for the employment of excess as a cure is one of the more refined artifices in the art of living" (*Human*, Assorted, 365).

THE DOCTORS OF THE SOUL

All of Nietzsche's writings and especially the material reviewed in the present book is pertinent to becoming not just a soul doctor, but rather of the new (Nietzschean) kind. Nietzsche, the critic of culture, was also a critic of doctors of the soul, in other words, he was a critic of psychotherapy. Just as Zarathustra contrasted old with new law-tables, Nietzsche contrasted *psychologica* (chapter 1) with the new psychology, ascetic priests with the new doctors of the soul, and bound with free spirits. A Nietzschean psychotherapist would thus be a new soul doctor, a new psychologist, and a free spirit combined.

Nietzsche's discussion of the new doctors of the soul cannot serve as a *Vademecum* (a manual—literally, "go with me"), but rather as a blueprint for a *Vadetecum* (literally, "go with yourself"). He expected his readers not to follow in his footsteps but rather to follow their own selves (*Gay*, Overture, 7). Nietzsche used medicine, religion, education, and art as metaphors for diagnosing and healing cultures and individuals. In this regard, he followed the Pre-Socratic philosophers who combined the roles of educators, teachers, and physicians in one, and as such were able to describe and suggest solutions to the problems of their times.

The Nietzschean Therapist

Nietzsche was a psychologist and a soul doctor—"I, as physician and patient in one"—who explored the soul and took "a curative journey" (*Human*, Assorted, 5) and so was Zarathustra, who as a teacher of doctors of the soul recommended giving a personal example. "Physician, heal yourself: then will you also heal your patient. Let it be his best cure to see with his eyes him who makes himself whole" (*Thus*, I, Bestowing virtue, 2). Nietzsche treated Jesus as his alter-ego and described him as "savior and physician" and as another "physician of the soul" (*Human*, Wanderer, 83). He used in his writings the German *Arzt* (which according to the *Online Etymology Dictionary* derives from the Greek *arkhiatros* "chief healer," namely a court physician), usually rendered by Nietzsche's translators either as "physician" or "doctor." As the term "healer" has mystical connotations, and the term "physician" excludes those without a medical degree, I will prefer, as in the title of this book, the more inclusive term "doctor."

A Curative Journey

Nietzsche described the characteristic of doctors of the soul and the nature of the doctor-patient relationship. He started with a reservation, recommending, "If possible live without a physician." Going to a doctor of the soul involves the risk of developing dependency and turning into a passive follower of prescriptions, forgetting one's own goals, and thus becoming less responsible for oneself (*Gay*, IV, 322). Zarathustra in the same vein, warned against this tendency. "I am a railing alongside the torrent; whoever is able to grasp me may grasp me! Your crutch, however, I am not" (*Thus*, I, The pale criminal).

There is no substitute for self-reliance and if we wish to return to health, we must be ready "to burden ourselves more heavily than we have ever been burdened before." As his own patient, Nietzsche examined his own assumptions and struggled to change them (*Human*, Assortment, Preface, 5). The doctor of the soul thus can help, by helping others help themselves: "One should speak only of self-education" (*Human*, Wanderer, 267). In other words, doctors teach their patients to be their own patients. Nietzsche urged the new doctors of the soul to avoid thinking in terms of "punishing, blaming, and improving" and take in consideration that in using aversive means, they themselves might be unintentionally altered. It is crucial that a doctor will avoid direct confrontation, and in a way play judo: "let us rather go aside! Let us look away!" It is essential for doctors to be much more than a passive screen, to deserve and be able to use themselves as personal examples; "let us elevate ourselves all the higher! Let us ever give to our pattern more shining colors!" (*Gay*, IV, 321).

Unlike preachers of morality who try to persuade their patients that they are very sick and in need of a radical cure, new doctors of the soul do not accept on face value all reports of self-diagnosis, suffering, and pain, knowing well that quite often people tend to exaggerate and portray life as hard to endure. Sometimes they are in love with their complaints, although they have the means to cope with them. New doctors of the soul do not suffer from "therapeutic furor." They recognize self-healing abilities, that "in the greatest degree of pain, fainting takes place by itself." They oppose the idea that annihilation of passions and silencing the will bring happiness, and, therefore, reject "stoic or Buddhist reduction of liveliness," and they count on persons' powers of resiliency. "A loss scarcely remains a loss for an hour: in some way or other a gift from heaven has always fallen into our lap at the same moment—a new form of strength, for example: be it but a new opportunity for the exercise of strength!" (*Gay*, V, 326).

Nietzsche emphasized the doctor's authenticity, basic decency, and the issue of compatibility or chemistry between doctor and patient-follower. The doctor can be dangerous for the welfare of her patient. "You must be born for your physician, otherwise you are bound to perish because of your physician" (*Human*, IX, 573). The patient is not encountering an interchangeable technician, but rather a unique exemplar, unlike others, not suitable for everyone. Zarathustra's question is addressed at other doctors and patients alike: "This is my way, where is yours?" (*Thus*, III, The Spirit of Gravity). Nietzsche warned that "the most dangerous doctors are those born actors who imitate born doctors with perfect deceptive art (*Human*, VI, 306). Who does not know therapists who have no core ideas and values of their own and go through the motions, clinging to one popular technique or theory? Another potential danger lies in the doctor's inability to overcome his feelings of pity which will not only hurt himself, but also "paralyze him at all critical moments, undermine the foundations of his knowledge, and unnerve his helpful and delicate hand" (*Daybreak*, II, 134). In the same spirit, a doctor must assess if help is feasible at all. "To the incurable, one should not try to be a physician—thus Zarathustra teaches" (*Thus*, III, Tablets, 17).

Nietzsche rejected pity but was all in favor of the doctor's empathy, a condition of finding the commonalities between her and her clients, rather than labeling them as totally different or abnormal. "You will also want to help, but only those whose distress you entirely understand, because they have one sorrow and one hope in common with you." The doctor can help others out of "fellowship in joy," aiming for the goals she holds, in the same ways she helps herself: "I want to make them more courageous, more enduring, more simple, more joyful!" (*Gay*, IV, 338).

Doctor and Psychologist

A new soul doctor is also a new psychologist, one who is willing to give up the old psychologists' notions of the soul in favor of a new version of "'mortal soul' and 'soul as the multiplicity of the subject' and 'soul as the social structure of drives and affects'" (*Beyond*, I, 12). The old psychology was based on "moral prejudices and fears," while the new psychology, a "true physical psychology" recognizes the doctrine of "the mutual interdependence of the 'good' and the 'bad' drives" and moves "directly over and away from morality" (*Beyond*, I, 23).

Psychologists, contemplative beings by nature, often see themselves in the role of "a spectator and auditor before the great pantomime and concert of life." Nietzsche reminds the psychologist to also be "a real creator, and continuous poet of life." A doctor of the soul should combine observation and action, thinking and feeling, and thus become a creator of the new "whole eternally increasing world of valuations, colors, weights, perspectives, gradations, affirmations and negations," and in so being, become a model to others. Doctors of the soul sometimes underestimate the power they hold in creating values and they have to grapple with the fact that "we are neither as proud nor as happy as we might be" (*Gay*, IV, 301).

Doctor and Philosopher

Nietzsche awaited the philosophical physicians, who unlike common philosophers would have on their agenda "health, future, growth, power, life" rather than "truth." Such doctors and philosophers "pursue the problem of the total health of a people, time, and race or of humanity," seeing complains holistically, and not as discrete localized symptoms (*Gay*, Preface, 2). A doctor should be a philosopher in the original sense of the word, "a lover of wisdom" who learns from giants at the republic of geniuses, and the ones to whom Nietzsche kept relating in his writings were Schopenhauer, Goethe, Emerson, and the Pre-Socratic philosophers. A doctor should be an earthy philosopher, who knows that all "answers to the question about the *value* of existence" could always be understood as "symptoms of certain bodies," that is, they are subjective and should be evaluated by their implications for life (*Gay,* Preface [to 2nd ed.], 2).

Doctor and Educator

Nietzsche's third *Untimely Meditation* on *Schopenhauer as Educator* shed light on doctors of the soul from the perspective of education. An educator is not merely a classroom teacher, but rather a living or historical figure that due to his or her qualities enables the student-patient-disciple to discover and release what is his or her core, dismantling conventions and overcoming traditions: "Your true educators and formative teachers reveal to you what the true basic material of your being is, something in itself uneducable and, in any case, difficult of access, bound and paralyzed: your educators can be only your liberators" (*Untimely*, Schopenhauer, 1).

An educator facilitates the process of self-discovery, not through introspection, but rather by the examination of the past formative encounters with educators, the identification and strengthening of positive strengths, and the harmonious development of all aspects of one's personality. These processes are set into motion by a personal example of the educator and the nature of the relationship which includes admiration and love, and, in fact, Nietzsche felt that Schopenhauer was a friend, a mentor, a loving father, "*as though* it were for me he had written" (*Untimely*, Schopenhauer, 2).

Spiritual Advisers

The new doctors of the soul are all of the above, philosophers, psychologists, artists, educators, and to some degree, or occasionally, priests-confessors. Furthermore, they aim not merely at relief and consolation, but rather at a transformation and they operate in light of this principle: "It is the means of consolation which have stamped life with that fundamental melancholy character which we now believe it possesses" (*Daybreak*, I, 52).

Writing about *The future of the doctor*, Nietzsche described some desired features of psychotherapists, addressed as "spirit doctors, the so-called spiritual advisers." In addition to the basic requirement of being well trained and staying up to date, the soul doctor must also have other qualities: communication skills in adapting the message to the person and "drawing the heart out of his body"; resiliency and toughness ("masculinity") which dispels despondency ("the worm-eaten spot in all ill people"). A soul doctor must also be a diplomat and a negotiator, a secret agent and a lawyer, who understand the secrets of the soul. In short, "a good doctor today needs all the tricks and privileges of all the other professions." With the right attitude and abilities, such doctors can go beyond being "medicine men." Through their work with individuals, they can make a far-reaching impact: increase productivity, promote a positive mood and good will, decrease guilt and villainy, culminating in "spiritual-physical aristocracy," which ultimately effects a larger societal change (*Human*, V, 243).

Writing about *The future of the doctor*, Nietzsche described some desired features of psychotherapists, addressed as "spirit doctors, the so-called spiritual advisers." In addition to the basic requirement of being well trained and staying up to date, the soul doctor must also have other qualities: communication skills in adapting the message to the person and "drawing the heart out of his body"; resiliency and toughness ("masculinity") which dispels despondency ("the worm-eaten spot in all ill people"). A soul doctor must also be a diplomat and a negotiator, a secret agent and a lawyer, who understand the secrets of the soul. In short, "a good doctor today needs all the tricks and privileges of all the other professions." With the right attitude and abilities, such doctors can go beyond being "medicine men." Through their work with individuals, they can make a far-reaching impact: increase productivity, promote a positive mood and good will, decrease guilt and villainy, culminating in "spiritual-physical aristocracy," which ultimately effects a larger societal change (*Human*, V, 243).

NOTES

1. George S. Viereck and Sigmund Freud, "An Interview with Freud," in Th. Reik, C. Staff, and B. N. Nelson, eds., *Psychoanalysis and the Future* (New York: National Psychological Association for Psychoanalysis, Inc., 1957), www.psychanalyse.lu/articles/FreudInterview.pdf, accessed June 22, 2014.
2. Tom Reiss, *The Orientalist: Solving the Mystery of a Strange and Dangerous Life* (New York: Random House, 2005), 288-89.
3. Quoted in Suzanne Bernfeld, "Freud and Archeology," *The American Imago: A Psychoanalytic Journal for the Arts and Sciences* 8 (1951): 111.
4. Sigmund Freud, "The Interpretation of Dreams," 608.
5. Carl G. Jung, "Christ, a Symbol of the Self," in *Collected Works of C. G. Jung*, trans. R. F. C. Hull, Vol. 9 ii (Princeton, NJ: Princeton University Press, 1970), 70.
6. Sigmund Freud, "New Introductory Lectures on Psychoanalysis," in *The Standard Edition of the Complete Psychological Works of Sigmund Freud [SE]*, in *SE*, Vol. 22.
7. Ibid.
8. Sigmund Freud, "The Psychopathology of Everyday Life" in *SE*, Vol. 6.
9. Sigmund Freud, "A Short Account of Psycho-analysis" in *SE*, Vol. 19: 191–209.
10. Michael C. Stokes, *Apology of Socrates* (Warminster, UK: Aris & Phillips, 1997), 38a.
11. Sheldon B. Kopp, *If You Meet the Buddha on the Road, Kill Him! The Pilgrimage of Psychotherapy Patients* (Ben Lomond, CA: Science and Behavior Books, 1972).
12. Albert Ellis, "Rational Psychotherapy and Individual Psychology," *Journal of Individual Psychology* 13 (1957): 38–44.
13. Martin E. P. Seligman, *Authentic Happiness: Using the New Positive Psychology to Realize Your Potential for Lasting Fulfillment* (New York: Free Press, 2002).
14. Samuel B. Griffith, trans., *Sun Tzu: The Art of War,* (London: Oxford University Press, 1971).
15. Christopher Middleton, trans., *Selected Letters of Friedrich Nietzsche* (Chicago: University of Chicago Press, 1969), 211.
16. Queen, Audio CD, *Innuendo* (Hollywood Records: 1994).
17. Joseph R. Cautela and Albert J. Kearney, *The Covert Conditioning Handbook* (New York: Springer Pub., 1986).
18. William James, *The Principles of Psychology* (New York: Dover Publications, 1950).
19. George Kelly, *The Psychology of Personal Constructs* (New York: Norton, 1955).

EIGHT

Creating the Self

We are moving now from principles of wise living, spiritual suffering and solving psychological problems to shaping life and creating the self; we are moving from necessity to choice, from coping to initiating. We will enter now Nietzsche's garden and discuss the nature of the creator, life with a cause and a task, and being a free spirit. He used the metaphor of a tree to describe himself. "For a tree to become tall it must grow tough roots among the rocks" (*Thus*, III, Before Sunrise), and "because we ourselves keep growing, keep changing, we shed our old bark, we shed our skin every spring, we keep becoming younger, fuller of future, taller, stronger" (*Gay*, V, 371). He described his writing as trees and himself as a garden, in which they grow: "Still are my children verdant in their first spring, standing nigh one another, and shaken in common by the winds, the trees of my garden and of my best soil" (*Thus*, III, Involuntary bliss).

GARDENS AND WILDERNESS

Architects and gardeners are creators, masters, and their own lawgivers, and we can, if we so desire, aspire to be like them. Nietzsche reminded us that if we do not want our life to be a collection of accidents, we do not have much time left: "We possess only a short-lived today to show why and to what end we evolved." We must, therefore, take charge, and refuse to take conventions for granted. "Why cling to this clod of earth, this way of life, why pay attention to what your neighbor says?" We must find our own way, because "nobody can build the bridge for you to walk across the river of life, no one but you yourself alone." There are many paths, bridges, and demi-gods to help us, but there is only one way that is going to be ours, and ours alone (*Untimely*, Schopenhauer, 1).

The fascination with gardens, palaces, nature, and the desire for riches are based on the wish "to remove disorder and vulgarity from sight and to build a home for the nobility of soul." This is also the reason for other cultural activities such as traveling, reading, listening to music, watching theaters, and visiting museums. The majority of "weak and the self-discontented" people seek cultural exposure either to escape from themselves or somehow to be changed by it while stronger persons prefer to shape themselves according to their own design and can do away with foreign influences (*Will*, IV, 941).

Branching Paths

Nietzsche described two approaches to life, one passive and descendant—just living and moving along; the other active and ascendant—doing something with one's life. These lines of life are ours to choose and they function as our egoism's "canon for the value" (*Twilight*, Skirmishes, 33). Wagner's development exemplified these lines—once his ruling passion was clear to him, it took charge of his nature, "from that time on there was an end to fumbling, straying, to the proliferation of secondary shoots" (descending line); instead, he started progressing according to his artistic plans (ascending line) which became "a single inner law." It goes without saying that passion without talent and intelligence cannot accomplish much (*Untimely*, Wagner, 2). An ascending line is not about reaching some end point, but rather about perpetual change, growing like trees, in accord with the nature of life, "not in one place, but all over, not in one direction, but equally upwards and outwards as inwards and downwards" (*Gay*, V, 371).

The Wilderness

Giving style to one's nature is "a grand and rare art" worthy of those who examine themselves, with an ingenious plan, and who "have palaces to build and gardens to lay out." It is unworthy for "weak characters who have no power over themselves, and hate the restriction of style," consequently ending with "wild, arbitrary, fantastic, confusing and surprising" results (*Gay*, IV, 290). Most people live undisturbed in a state of wilderness without a life plan. If they are educated, they exist as persons of learning, whose "buildings are carted together not constructed" (*Untimely*, History, 7). They take the way of least resistance; because that is the way they are, because this is the way they were brought up to be: Role players without a clue to their own individual needs (*Daybreak*, III, 178; *Gay*, V, 356). This is what society expects them to do, by glorifying work, offering security and easy satisfactions, making them more governable (*Daybreak*, III, 173). They are accidental travelers in life without any higher necessity; unfocused, with average talents, "trashy concerns," and lacking a life calling (*Philologists*, 12). Rather than being architects, people yield to a life of service and help to others. The hilarious situation in which "everyone serves somebody else," leads to none of them having an object in existence (*Philologists*, 12). There are many other distractions in addition to our neighbors' many cries for help, presented in the guise of morality; "I know there are hundreds of respectable and laudable methods of making me stray from my course" (*Gay*, IV, 338).

To Cultivate or Not

Only "active, successful natures," persons who do not act according to the maxim "know thyself," but as if inspired by the motto "will a self, and so become a self" (*Human*, Assorted, 366), can have a life-plan and try to execute it. Change is possible, "the doctrine of the exchangeability of character" is false, and we are not a "complete *fully-developed fact*." Living with or without a life-plan is not an either-or decision, and we can choose whether to cultivate the shoots of our drives "as a beautiful fruit tree on a trellis" or just let the plants grow and compete among themselves and add only little embellishment and tidying-up. We can also choose to do nothing and enjoy the wilderness, despite the trouble it might give (*Daybreak*, V, 560).

In his notes, Nietzsche offered potential self-designers a list of eight questions, based on "typical forms of self-formation." It can be assumed that in practice, people do not design themselves as rationally and in details, as architects do, before the construction of a building commences. Chance factors and temperament play a large role in the unfolding of life, and yet these questions can help persons decide if they wish to take the project of self-creating upon themselves. The variables Nietzsche noted included: multifariousness vs. simplicity; happiness seeking vs. happiness indifference; self-demanding vs. self-contentedness; agreeableness vs. disagreeableness; risk taking vs. prudence; goal-directedness vs. goal-avoidance; respect and power seeking vs. depreciation seeking; and finally, leadership vs. subservience (*Will*, IV, 909). He considered giving style to one's nature to be an art and described its envisioning and implementing in terms befitting an artist with brush and paints in front of an easel (*Gay*, IV, 290). If self-design consists of turning oneself into a piece of art, the final product can be judged in terms of trends and styles, and Nietzsche indeed mentioned "French, English, Dutch or Chinese fashions" in gardening (*Daybreak*, V, 560). I suggest seeing Nietzsche's themes of becoming what one is, the genius of the heart, the free spirits, and other related themes, as a gardening manual and a catalogue of gardens' fashions. In other words, he is offering us a compendium of possible life-tasks and projects and an arsenal of tools, aids in accomplishing them. He left it to his readers to choose, mix and match from these models-plans according to their understanding and inclinations. In any case, because all people are unique, even when they adopt similar models, each individual garden will be unequaled. I will start with the manual and continue with the catalogue.

THE GARDENER'S MANUAL

This manual for gardeners of the self, is appropriate for advanced gardeners only: who already have met the "paradox of action" (chapters 3 and 6) and nevertheless did not give up on acting; who will do what depends on them to become who they are, still facing the possibility that it is a complicated project with some questions remaining unanswered. To begin with, how can we do anything about becoming who we are if indeed we confront "a brazen wall of fate; we *are* in prison, we can only *dream* ourselves free, not make ourselves free" (*Human*, II, 33). To continue, why should we be concerned at all about what we become, granted that "the voluntary is absolutely lacking . . . everything has been directed along certain lines from the beginning" (*Will*, II, 458). In other words, how can we think about "giving style" when, "the single human being is a piece of *fatum* from the front and from the rear, one law more, one necessity more for all that is yet to come and to be" (*Twilight*, Morality, 6)? These queries are underscored by Nietzsche's conception of the "innocence of becoming," which implies that we will become what we are, whatever we do, "one will become only that which one is (in spite of all: that means education, instruction, milieu, chance, and accident)." A person's vices or virtues are not causes of what one becomes, but consequences of early environment and constitutional factors, and for this reason, the idea that we "*ought* to be thus and thus" (*Will*, II, 334), is as pointless as the idea, "a tree as he ought to be" (*Will*, II, 332).

Despite these quandaries, gardeners do not despair easily, and must continue doing their best. They know that they must begin by examining the piece of land they want to cultivate and check what grows there naturally. The answer to the question of "who we are" is not a direct one and cannot be found inside us. We should not examine our entrails because a person is a "dark and veiled thing" and the very inward drilling is dangerous. All the needed information can be found in our nature, manifested in what we did and continue to do: our friends, our aversions, our gestures, our memories, books and handwriting, all tell a story about us (*Untimely*, Schopenhauer, 1). We can thus ask ourselves what we liked until now, what excited us, what advanced us, and what might be worthwhile to do in the future, "for your true nature lies, not hidden deep within you, but immeasurably high above you, or at least above that which you normally take to be yourself" (*Untimely*, Schopenhauer, 3).

In my reading, gardening, architecture, art, and music are central themes in Nietzsche's work, and he used them to teach principles of self-design, turning ourselves into a pleasing piece of art by adding a second nature and giving up parts of the first nature; sometimes hiding what cannot be discarded; often using reinterpretation; always using, "long exercise and daily labor at the task" (*Gay*, IV, 290). The different principles of self-creation can be reduced to three guidelines: combining diverse elements into a unique unified organic structure; being what one is, that is to say, authenticity or correspondence with one's nature; finally, discarding foreign non-authentic materials, which I will call "the Michelangelo principle."

Becoming a Living Unity

A worthy piece of art, literary, graphic, or musical can be expected to be a harmonious whole, in which inner tensions are integrated in a creative and original way. The same artistic-aesthetic criteria are applied by Nietzsche to cultures and individuals alike. "True culture must, in any event, presuppose unity of style" (*Untimely*, Strauss, 2). Culture is at its best as a "single living unity" rather than dissolution into "inner and outer, content and form," and promoting culture would mean promoting this "higher unity" (*Untimely*, History, 10), an idea also phrased succinctly as "multiplicity in unity" (*Beyond*, VI, 212). Such unity is lacking in modern culture, and this lack of integration moved Nietzsche to proclaim that it "is no real culture" in comparison with the Hellenic one, which was "no mere aggregate," but rather an organized chaos (*Untimely*, History, 10). The moderns failed to synthesize their diverse and conflicting standards and values, consequently suffering from unrest, doubt, and paralysis of will, missing in their body and soul "balance, a center of gravity and perpendicular poise" (*Beyond*, VI, 208).

A Unique Harmonious Organization

Nietzsche proposed that pleasing landscapes and a pleasant human character have in common "beneath all their multiplicity, a simple geometrical shape," also described as a "mathematical substratum" (*Human*, Wanderer, 115). He held up Napoleon as an example of "a single drive worked through to the end with perfect consistency," one which had the characteristic, found in antiquity, of "simple construction and the inventive elaboration and variation of a single motif or of a few motifs" (*Daybreak*, IV, 245). This is not the case with "inverted cripples," whom Zarathustra despised, "men who lack everything save for one thing, of which they have too much." Such persons are "fragments and limbs and terrible accidents—but no men!" In reaction to this sorry sight, he proclaimed, "And it is my art and aim, to compose into one and bring together what is fragment and riddle and dreadful chance (*Thus*, II, Redemption). This is also the task of a great architecture of culture and the self, "to force opposing forces into harmony, through an overwhelming aggregation of the remaining, less incompatible powers, yet without suppressing or shackling them" (*Human*, V, 276).

Morality of Mature Individuals

The aim of the gardener (or to use other metaphors, the architect, artist or musician) should be "to make a whole *person* of oneself and keep in mind that person's *greatest good* in everything one does," an objective which Nietzsche considered as "morality of the mature individual." Such a morality necessitates attunement with one's needs, overcoming pitying impulses and distracting activities made for the sake of others, be they persons, state, or occupation (*Human*, II, 95). A piece of art ought to have a unity of style indeed, but "living unities" are also assessed according to their forcefulness and the nature of their inner organization, "as regents at the head of a community" and their capabilities of "obeying and commanding" (*Will*, III, 492). The highest man is one that can put together and rule the greatest sum of drives under the condition of unity (*Will*, IV, 966), an ability which contributes to greatness. "I believe that it is precisely through the presence of opposites and feelings they occasion that the great man, the bow with the greatest tension, develops" (*Will*, IV, 967).

Nietzsche expected gardeners to appraise their strengths and weaknesses, fit them together until a pleasing artistic plan is reached, and continue adding and detracting elements as needed, in a process of daily cultivation. This is a task suitable for strong characters, who can tolerate the restraints of style. "A human being should attain satisfaction with himself, whether by means of this or that poetry and art" (*Gay*, IV, 290). Gardeners, like artists, cut out unwanted elements and look at their project from different perspectives, distances, filters, and frames. "We want to be the poets of our life—first of all in the smallest, most everyday matters" (*Gay*, V, 299).

Becoming What One Is

Because of their laziness, people "seem like manufactured goods, unimportant, and unworthy to be associated with or instructed." Those who refuse to belong to the mass must give up their comfort and listen to their conscience which tells them, "Be yourself! All that you are now doing, thinking, and desiring is not really yourself" (*Untimely*, Schopenhauer, 1). Nietzsche asked again, "What does your conscience say?—"You shall become the person you are" (*Gay*, III, 270). The subtitle of *Ecce Homo*, Nietzsche's autobiography, *How one becomes what one is,* raises the reader's expectations that the secret of self-actualization, acclaimed profusely in humanistic psychology and self-help books, is going to be revealed at last. This is the promise sought by many people who seek to "find themselves," as if they lost their core true self somewhere; often believing it will be revealed to them in far away "spiritual" lands or mountaintops.

Not Knowing What One Is

Nietzsche the Overturner saw the issue of becoming what one is differently, as can be seen in his personal answer to the question of "how I became who I am": Firstly, he reversed the direction of the arrow of time, arguing that one can only look retrospectively, and think how "I became what I am now," and not prospectively, "how I will become what I am supposed to be." Secondly, he moved the emphasis from essence to action: What you are is what you did and did not do, and Nietzsche, who serves as our example, saw his life as identical with his life-task of "transvaluing all values." Thirdly, he moved it away from the realm of will and intention, stating that one cannot want to become someone or something, as the very trying, makes accomplishment impossible. On the contrary, "the fact that one becomes what one is, presupposes that one has not the remotest idea of what one is" (*Ecce*, Clever, 9).

Self-making is a matter of "bringing forth," a process of spiritual pregnancy with an idea or a project, without willing or doing, but rather waiting patiently, taking care of one's needs for creativity, "letting the embryo come to maturity" (*Daybreak*, V, 552). The reason for letting things take their own course is that doubts, mistakes, "deviations and aberrations," chance events and opportunities, might well contribute to the process of becoming. In addition, what is based on *nosce teipsum* [know yourself] is liable to produce misunderstandings, "narrowing and mediocratizing" of the self. Until the moment of fruition, the process must be internal, "the long secret work and artistry of my instinct," and this work must be protected and remain undisturbed and free from the mores and imperatives of society. "Beware even of every grand word or attitude!" (*Ecce*, Clever, 9). Nietzsche quoted Oliver Cromwell, "a man never rises higher than when he does not know where his way can still lead him" (*Untimely*, Schopenhauer, 1), and the way that cannot be known in advance obviously cannot be prescribed. "Nobody can build the bridge for you to walk across the river of life, no one but you yourself alone" and adhering to the guidance of "demi-gods" (writers of self-help books?) is harmful: we must realize that ours must be a unique way, suitable for us alone and when it is found, we should not ask "where does it lead?" but simply "go along with it" (*Untimely*, Schopenhauer, 1).

Self-Love and Egoism

Self-creators are on one hand, persons of action who realize that "know yourself" and understanding of past actions are impossible demands. On the other hand, they are, "selfish, with a unique distinguished self-created ideal," who resolve, as self-directed persons, to limit themselves to purify their opinions and values, to determine what is good for them and avoid a moralistic judgment of their actions (*Gay*, IV, 335). Self-creators must start with learning and caring about themselves, a skill that can be learned from artists who know how to put and observe themselves on a stage, "from a distance as something past and whole" (*Gay*, II, 78). Caring and loving ourselves means giving ourselves a priority over others (*Ecce*, Clever, 9), putting "your own salvation above everything," because "there are no institutions which you should prize more highly than your own soul" (*Philologists*, 21).

In order to be an egoist, one must have an "ego," that is to say, being a person who rejects "socially constructed" fictional definitions of the self (*Daybreak*, II, 105), one who overcomes socialization's prejudices of overestimation of blame and underestimation of value (*Human*, Wanderer, 262). Nietzsche must have felt that he had to save egoism and selfishness from a society that does everything it can to remove, denounce, and curb their beauty and cheerfulness. He retorted that selflessness "has no value either in heaven or on earth" (*Gay*, V, 345), that the ancient philosophers taught that living according to the rules and expectations of others is not the way to achieve happiness; while those who write their own rules, the thinkers, "are the happiest of all" (*Gay*, IV, 328). Actions should originate, not with what others think, but instead with a logical self-examination of one's complex motivations; "the most essential thing is the feeling 'who am I? Who is the other in relation to me?'" (*Will*, II, 365).

To Love and Respect

Egoism alone is not enough, and it must be joined by self-love and self-respect. Yet self-love and love of others, without self-respect, is soon marred by contempt (*Will*, IV, 920). Respect, reverence for ourselves, and a good ear for our instincts will preclude future regret for failing to listen to one's needs, or not enjoying what life had to offer (*Will*, IV, 918). Self-love, the ability to be with oneself, like all kinds of love must be learned, and it develops in the same way that we get acquainted with and begin to like new music: We have to listen to the whole piece, identify the melody and main themes, get used to some of its strange chords until we feel that they are necessary, and continue listening until its charm is found (*Gay*, IV, 334; *Thus*, III, The spirit of gravity, 2). We must especially appreciate our "dissonances," our non-harmonious and non-integrated elements (*Gay*, IV, 319). Yet, in order to listen, we must have free time not filled up with busy work, and for this reason, Nietzsche often extolled idleness, which is also "the parent of psychology." Self-love also means daring to believe in oneself and one's intuitions. "He who does not believe in himself always lies" (*Thus*, II, Immaculate perception).

Self-respect and self-love are only preconditions for action: "The most personal question of truth" is not who am I or why am I here, but rather,

"What am I really doing? And why am I doing it?" (*Daybreak*, III, 196). Similarly, Zarathustra taught, "Of what account is happiness? For long I have not aspired after happiness, I aspire after my work (*Thus*, IV, The honey offering). Striving to be what one is, like striving for heroic life, must pass a simple test as to whether it implies a practical activity. The question to ask is how "a new set circle of duties may be derived from this ideal and how one can proceed towards so extravagant a goal through a practical activity" (*Untimely*, Schopenhauer, 5).

The Michelangelo Principle

The reverse side of the coin of "be who you are" is "do not be who you are not!" Our consciousness must be freed of imperatives: "Beware even of every grand word or attitude!" (*Ecce*, Clever, 9). In his notebooks, Nietzsche added the metaphor of sculpting to the ones of gardening, music, and architecture, to describe the challenge of self-creating. This is not for everyone, certainly not for idealist fools, who are not "lofty and hard enough to be permitted to shape *men* as artists," and ruin the "most beautiful stone" (*Beyond*, II, 62). Self-creators abide by the dictum "Always a sculptor!" and Zarathustra found that the image of his vision slumbered within a stone, which he set to release, "now rages my hammer ruthlessly against its prison. From the stone fly the fragments" (*Thus*, II, The blissful isles). Humans are "a thing unshaped, raw material, a unworked stone that needs the sculptor's chisel" (*Ecce*, Zarathustra, 8).

Michelangelo portrayed sculpting similarly with the words, "Every block of stone has a statue inside it and it is the task of the sculptor to discover it,"[1] and thus the statue can emerge only when the sculptor gets rid of the excess stone. The excess, that we must discard in order to have a chance of being what we are, is massive and consists of layers of calcified thinking patterns, education, socialization, and religious indoctrination. Sculpting the self is an act of liberation: "The clearing away of all weeds, debris, vermin—that want to infringe upon the tender buds of the plant—an effusion of light and warmth, the gentle, quiet rustling of nocturnal rain" (*Untimely*, Schopenhauer, 1).

Intellectual Conscience

Self-creators, those who "want to become those we are—human beings who are new, unique, incomparable, who give themselves laws, who create themselves" have a developed intellectual conscience, and consequently, they do not take their immediate action tendencies on faith value or as morally justified; "it is up to us, whether to obey blindly our conscience, or challenge and ask questions" (*Gay*, IV, 335). Understanding the origin of moral judgments, they are skeptic about all moral conventions and ideas of sin, duty, salvation, conscience, or categorical imperative. Because our own judgments are colored by our heritage and culture, self-creators must develop a conscience behind the conscience (*Gay*, IV, 319), which will enable them to examine their choices (*Gay*, IV, 335). In order to become who we are, that is to say, become self-creators, we cannot believe in an almighty God, we have to recognize that the world is without any goal and we must understand our duality. On the one hand we are animals, part of nature; on the other hand we have a second nature, developed through living within human institutions (*Genealogy*, I, 6).

The nature and scope of societal and cultural detrimental influences on life, chief among them the anti-life values of Judeo-Christian morality, must be acknowledged and counteracted (chapter 4). It takes a special skill to identify them, as "these social values were erected over man to strengthen their voice, as if they were commands of God, as 'reality,' as the 'true' world, as a hope and future world" (*Will*, I, 7). In addition to the cultural-religious heritage, we should distance ourselves from wars and clashes between nations and religions, which are not our direct interest, but rather the agenda of powers that try to draw us in (*Untimely*, Schopenhauer, 1). Our education too must be examined critically, as it is basically a process of wiping out individuality, using reinforcements, to make persons more manageable, giving up their advantage in favor of "the general good" (*Gay*, I, 21). The next obstacle is not easier to overcome, as it is within us: our convictions, emotions, and own habituated ways of thinking, and specifically the Socratic intellectualism. "I want to understand what idiosyncrasy begot that Socratic idea that reason and virtue equal happiness—that most bizarre of all equations which is, moreover, opposed to every instinct of the earlier Greeks" (*Twilight*, Socrates, 4).

Being Our Own Experiment

Intellectual conscience implies self-examination; "great intellects are skeptical. Zarathustra is a skeptic." Skepticism is essential for those who wish to set their own values; it is the antidote to fixed convictions which imprison their holders, not letting them see what is far and around them. Self-creators examine their experiences as if they were a scientific experiment, seeing themselves as an experiment too (*Gay*, IV, 319). They are selective and know which conventions to adopt and use as means and short-cuts, without losing their sovereignty. Such strong emancipated spirits posit themselves as goals and decide on truth and untruth according to their own conscience (*Antichrist*, 54).

In addition to the examination of convictions and experiences, self-creators must be careful not to fall into the trap of "Trust in your feelings!" Feelings are not final or original inner truth as some see them. They descend from judgments, often from extraneous mistaken judgments. "Trusting in our feelings simply means obeying our grandfather and grandmother more than the gods within ourselves: our reason and experience" (*Daybreak*, I, 35). Now, when the excess layers are removed, the statue can emerge, or to use another of Nietzsche's metaphors, the pregnancy can complete its term.

A CATALOGUE OF GARDENS

There are no clear-cut borders between the following models or fashions of gardens, which can be mixed and modified. They are all possible life projects or different perspectives of "building palaces and laying out gardens." Each of them can become a final goal, or be a step towards higher ones, ultimately reaching for the Nietzschean palace of all palaces, the garden of all gardens, the Superman. The long shadow of Nietzsche's three meta-psychology themes (the Superman, Eternal Recurrence, and Will to Power) is felt here, in the discussion of higher selves. I will begin with the gardens of virtues, gods, and educators, continue with the garden of free spirits, and conclude with life-causes and tasks.

The One and the Four Virtues

Those who prefer gardens over wilderness can run their lives in light of guiding virtues and there are many of them to choose from. Virtues were extensively discussed in the ancient world—the Greek *arete* and Latin *virtus*, lauded excellence, the highest standard in any endeavor. A set of four virtues can be found in Plato's discussion of the good city "Clearly, then, it will be wise, brave, temperate, and just" (*Republic*, 427e). Cicero defined virtues as a habit of mind, in harmony with reason and nature, consisting of "wisdom (*prudentiam*), justice, courage and temperance" (*De Inventione*, II, 8). This tradition was continued by various Christian theologians, with some modifications, under the title of "the cardinal virtues." Nietzsche referred to virtues from a historical perspective, showing that in the first era of higher humanity courage was considered the noblest, after which came justice, temperance, and finally wisdom. He, the proponent of untimeliness, then asked his readers, "In which era do we live? In which do you live?" (*Human*, Wanderer, 64). Nietzsche criticized the common notion of virtue, arguing that what is called a virtue is often the outcome of indoctrination, an internalization of the Christian-slave morality, something that belittles individuality, making petty people believe they are masters; "they all preach submission and humility and policy and diligence and consideration and the long *et cetera* of petty virtues" (*Thus*, IV, The higher man, 3). The self-satisfaction of such virtuous persons is repulsive. "Arrogance on the part of the meritorious is, even more, offensive to us than the arrogance of those without merit: for merit itself is offensive (*Human*, VI, 332). Proclaimed virtues such as patience and forbearance, often serve only as a cover-up for lack of assertiveness and courage (*Human*, Wanderer, 251), and sometimes virtues are mentioned only to criticize their lack in others, rather than admit one's own shortcomings (*Human*, VI, 302).

Nietzsche's virtues were not carved in stone and we can change their composition and numbers at will. Zarathustra loved those who did not desire too many virtues. "One virtue is more of a virtue than two because it is more of a knot for one's destiny to cling to" (*Thus*, Prologue, 4). Furthermore, Nietzsche did not think that we should chain ourselves to virtues and make them a life commitment; we can change them and even take a break from them as "a sleep of virtues" can energize us. "When virtue has slept, it will arise all the more vigorous" (*Human*, II, 83). Nietzsche had his one virtue, but also a few sets of four virtues. His one virtue was being a master of his own virtues, to whom nothing is forbidden, "and if there be anything of virtue in me, it is that I have had no fear of any prohibition (*Thus*, IV, The Shadow). One of Nietzsche's credos was "to remain master of one's four virtues: courage, insight, sympathy, and loneliness." Nietzsche went on to elaborate and qualify these virtue-guidelines: living "with an immense and proud composure: always beyond," steadiness under stress, being attuned to one's feelings and being able to use their stupidity and passion. When necessary, a person ought to disregard, cover, and hide virtues from others, and "sit on them, as if on a horse, often as if on a donkey." In addition, he recommended adopting "that mischievous and cheerful vice, courtesy" (*Beyond*, IX, 284).

In this list, as can be expected from "the first immoralist," justice was discarded in favor of loneliness. It is noteworthy that Nietzsche who almost declared war on the feeling of pity included sympathy and courtesy among his four virtues. In another place Nietzsche offered another list of "the good four": honest towards ourselves and whoever else is a friend to us, brave towards the enemy, magnanimous towards the defeated, and always being polite (*Daybreak*, V, 556). Reader, you are entitled to compose your own list of virtues, and you are certainly permitted to change them tomorrow.

Gods and Educators

Nietzsche declared himself "the last disciple and initiate of the god Dionysus" (*Beyond*, IX, 295) and dedicated his book, "To him that has turned out well, who does my heart good, carved from wood that is hard, gentle, and fragrant—in whom even the nose takes pleasure" (*Will*, IV, 1003). This garden is built in a neo-pagan style, reminiscent of ancient Greek temples and rites. The god prominently positioned is made of wood, that is to say, he is a symbol and an icon. The disciples follow the god with a "compulsion to press themselves always closer to him, to follow him ever more inwardly and fundamentally" (*Beyond*, IX, 295).

Gods and goddesses are usually put on a pedestal, and their clay feet remain unseen. They can be mythological figures, historical dead persons or living ones, known in person or only through their writings and art. One can have one god, a trinity, or a whole pantheon of gods; one can also have in addition, a Satan, an anti-god to differ from and oppose. One can have a short time infatuation with such a god or a lifelong dialogue; one can also get rid of such gods and symbolically kill them. A disciple adopts the god's characteristics in a prolonged process of meditation, admiration, identification, worship, and sacrifice, and the god internalized or resurrected becomes the disciple's "genius of the heart" (*Ecce*, Books, 6; *Beyond*, IX, 295).

Nietzsche treated Christ (the Church's interpretation of Jesus the man) as the symbol of Christian morality and anti-life forces, and as the title of his book *The Antichrist* indicates, attacking them became a major part of his identity. Dionysus is Christ's antithetical god: "Have you understood me? Dionysus versus Christ" (*Ecce*, Zarathustra, 7). He had other such gods in different periods of his life, and seeing himself as Odysseus visiting Hades, he named "four pairs who responded to me in my sacrifice—Epicurus and Montaigne, Goethe and Spinoza, Plato and Rousseau, Pascal and Schopenhauer, who although dead, are for him more alive than many of his contemporaries: "With them I have to come to terms. When I have long wandered alone, I will let them prove me right or wrong; to them will I listen, if they prove each other right or wrong. In all that I say, conclude, or think out for myself and others, I fasten my eyes on those eight and see their eyes fastened on mine" (*Human*, Assorted, 408).

One such god, the demoted Wagner, to whom Nietzsche dedicated his first work *The Birth of Tragedy*, is not found in Nietzsche's Hades, although he continued to have an impact as a polemical object (*Nietzsche Contra Wagner*). Active and mighty persons, among them makers of history, need inspiration from "the exemplary men, teachers, and comforters." Living contemporaries are not usually equal the task, and thus encouragement and motivation can be found in prior examples of greatness, who ultimately teach in their own way "that the person lives most beautifully [is one] who does not care about existence" (*Untimely*, History, 2). Nietzsche described the role Dionysus and Schopenhauer had in his life, and he actually invited us to be like him and find our own "gods" or role models, to find our own "genius of the heart." By using Zarathustra as his mouthpiece, he offered himself as a god or educator for us.

The Dionysian Garden

We met Dionysus, in the discussion of the Dionysian-Apollonian dichotomy in Nietzsche's personality psychology (chapter 3). This god stands for a harmonious collection of "opposing currents" and celebration of life. Dionysus stands for exhilaration, independence, artistic creation, procreation, and resiliency. The Dionysian is about living passionately, taking chances, giving free reign to drives and intuitions; it also entails acceptance of all phases and aspects of life, including pain and suffering (*Will*, IV, 1003). Dionysus represents health and power, becoming "more comprehensive, more supranational, more European, more Near Eastern" (*Will*, IV, 1051). He also stands for wisdom, reflection, pensiveness, carefulness and discernment, lack of shame as well as fragility, tenderness, "new will," and hopes (*Beyond*, IX, 295). The Dionysian is a mode, a state of existence in which life is experienced intensively, with a special glow of poetic depth and fullness. In this state, the elements sexuality, intoxication, and cruelty are prominent, and when combined produce an aesthetic experience of perfection, "the extraordinary expansion of its feeling of power, riches, necessary overflowing of all limits" (*Will*, III, 801).

The Schopenhauerian Garden

While the core of the Dionysian is passion, the core of Schopenhauerian is truthfulness. The Dionysian garden was verdant and lush with a variety of plants; the Schopenhauerian garden is quite monotonous and arid. A person who adopts Schopenhauer as educator has a defined notion of the real meaning of life and lives with a longing for a secular "sanctification and salvation." Such disciples are unwilling to play the social game, and ready to suffer the societal consequences and personal hardships involved in being true to themselves. They live in the light of their own "blazing consuming fire" of convictions, far from the cold neutrality of scientists, and are willing, in the name of truth, to sacrifice themselves, clash with others, and be treated as enemies. A Schopenhauerian life-plan is based on the realization that "a happy life is impossible: the highest that man can attain is a heroic one"; moreover it agrees with Meister Eckhart that "the beast that bears you fastest to perfection is suffering," and indeed, despite great difficulties, sometimes the struggle succeeds and ends with a victory for the benefit of all. Living heroes usually go unrewarded, but in the end some of them are turned into noble impressive statues made of stone, and are remembered and celebrated as heroes (*Untimely*, Schopenhauer, 4).

The Dionysian genius of the heart is fluid, playful, and changeable. The heroic life in contradistinction is serious and demanding. One must insist on being loyal to oneself and therefore must be on guard, feeling as if "a kind of agreement exists to kidnap him out of his own cave." This fear leads to the resolution "I will remain my own!" Such a decision has painful consequences, of being preoccupied with unanswerable tormenting questions such as "Why do I live? Who am I? How do I become who I am? Why do I suffer from being who I am?" With these questions a gap is created between the "hero" and other people, who go on playing their social roles, "mindful solely of their comedy and not at all of themselves" (*Untimely*, Schopenhauer, 4).

The heroism of truthfulness consists of a refusal to be a toy in the "endless stupid game which the great child, time, plays before us and with us." Hence, a "hollow, deceptive, and shallow" becoming is rejected in favor of willful being, "in being thus and not otherwise, in the imperishable." This attitude leads to a continuous self-examination, identifying and destroying the upshots of false becoming (*Untimely*, Schopenhauer, 4). The Schopenhauerian, who does not care about personal happiness or unhappiness, and is only concerned with faithfulness to what is seen as the truth, walks in measured steps, the opposite of an adherent of the dancing, intoxicated Dionysus.

THE GARDEN OF FREE SPIRITS

The prior two gardens had each one word written on their gates—passion or truth. The one word to describe the present garden is freedom. Being a "free spirit" is a precondition for creation and carrying a mission in life. It is also related the Superman and to what I called earlier the Michelangelo principle. Nietzsche described the idea in simple terms: "The expression 'free spirit' in this book must not be understood as anything other than a spirit that has become free, that has once more taken possession of itself" (*Ecce*, Human, 1). Thus, freedom of spirit means self-determination of one's identity and a complete freedom from belief, schools of thought, fashions, "a god, prince, class, physician, father confessor, dogma, or party conscience" (*Gay*, V, 347). Free spirits embrace the "new freedom," freedom from "any system of purpose," realizing that good and evil have some meaning only from the perspective of a given community and reward and punishment are not in the essence of things (*Will*, III, 789).

Nietzsche hailed Goethe, who "disciplined himself to wholeness, he *created* himself," as the ultimate example of "a spirit who has *become free*" (*Twilight*, Skirmishes, 49). There were times, when Nietzsche saw the still-revered Wagner as a paragon of freedom, who taught us the way to emancipation by his personal example: "That passion is better than stoicism or hypocrisy; that straightforwardness, even in evil, is better than losing oneself in trying to observe traditional morality; that the free man is just as able to be good as evil, but that the unemancipated man is a disgrace to nature, and has no share in heavenly or earthly bliss" (*Untimely*, Wagner, 11).

Free spirits, similar to Goethe and Wagner, "will not be merely free spirits but something more, higher, greater, and thoroughly different" (*Beyond*, I, 44). Nietzsche named this total self-determination and freedom of will "free spirit par excellence," a spirit who "could bid farewell to every belief, to every wish for certainty, accustomed as it would be to support itself on slender cords and possibilities and to dance even on the verge of abysses" (*Gay*, V, 347). Yet, he realized that this picture is an idealized poetic invention, "phantoms and a hermit's shadow play" needed to cheer him up and serve as imaginary friends (*Human*, Preface, 2). More realistically, he saw freedom of spirit as a state of autonomy, a goal to strive to—not a permanent condition, but rather the "hardest test of independence" that must be repeatedly passed, always in independent and unique ways (*Gay*, III, 225).

Separated and Unbound

Independence is achieved by being unbound and separate from many things. "One must maintain the "voluptuous remoteness of the bird that ever flies further aloft in order to see more below it." It is necessary to keep away from other persons and even beloved ones—"everyone is a prison and a nook"—and it is essential to be separated from fatherlands, especially in times of victory, and from science, despite its achievements. Independence also calls for removing oneself from pity and sympathy, and for separation from one's own virtues and characteristics, including those that seem to be positive (*Beyond*, I, 41). People can be considered free spirits to the degree that they think "otherwise than would be expected" based on their origins, social economic status, or prevalent traditions and "political correct" views; they are not necessarily always right, but at least they examine things themselves and do not accept them on faith value (*Human*, V, 225). Bound spirits, on the contrary, have habitual views and handed down religious beliefs (*Human*, V, 226); are unaware of complexities and uncritical of conventions, easily take sides and act (*Human*, V, 230). Bound spirits do not see what is behind appearances, justify existing arrangements, and fulfill expectations, going so far as to support a war which began against their wishes (*Human*, V, 229). These spirits, who ask no questions, are the foundation which supports the survival of social institutions, class, marriage, education, and law (*Human*, V, 227).

Becoming a Free Spirit

Can bound spirits become free? Are free spirits made or born? Nietzsche's answer, as can be learned from his view of the "genesis of the genius," was that they develop through coping with hardships, in which one acts like a prisoner who uses every advantage creatively in order to escape. A handicap encourages using other organs in a new manner as compensation; becoming a free spirit is one such compensation (*Human*, V, 231). Another path to freedom of spirit is one of a deep emotional commitment to a cause, which leaves no room for efforts to conform; "when one firmly binds one's heart and keeps it prisoner, one can allow one's spirit many liberties" (*Beyond*, IV, 78). Freedom of spirit is a slippery goal which cannot be simply willed and can easily be missed, when part of us avoids struggles because we "would like to have things better, lighter, more loving, like a pleasing vice" (*Beyond*, VII, 227). Still, we can call on our resources—curiosity, courage, and Will to Power to overcome the world, and when needed, "come to the aid of our 'God' with all our 'devils'!" In any case, the results are not guaranteed since becoming a free spirit, like becoming who you are, is a process, the aggregate of many acts, not all of them voluntary or intentional.

Let us not strain ourselves. We must approach the issue of freedom of spirit with a grain of salt and avoid taking ourselves too seriously, so that we do not become saints or bores. "Every virtue tends towards stupidity; every stupidity tends towards virtue" (*Beyond*, VII, 227). We should know that virtues are no more than tools for a purpose, and we should not become their slaves; "all estimations have a perspective" (*Human*, Preface, 6). In order to be a free spirit, one must be free of all ends, including the end of being a free spirit and the very resolve to preserve independence (*Beyond*, I, 41). In his notes Nietzsche wrote about "the absolute necessity of the total liberation from ends" and that "only the innocence of becoming gives us the *greatest courage* and the *greatest freedom*!" (*Will*, III, 787).

CAUSES AND TASKS

We are dealing now with a topic that can be conceived in terms of Nietzsche's three meta-psychological themes of Eternal Recurrence, the Will to Power, and the Superman. I prefer however, to treat life's tasks in more down-to-earth empirical terms, as another psychological variable, a characteristic of some people, certainly not the majority, who live with a cause, who favor meaning in life over security or comfort. Nietzsche described their motivations and manner of operation and left it to his readers to decide whether to join the cause of having a cause. As a matter of fact, most people will find it very difficult to answer the question, "What is your life-task?" In his aphorism *Traffic with one's higher self*, he contended that they are afraid of their higher-self's demanding ideals, and will often try to avoid them. However, when in particular fortuitous moments they dare to transcend their routine workday's state of bondage and servitude, they gain power and are then at their best. "We should, for example, assess and honor a painter according to the highest vision he was able to see and portray." The problem is that this state cannot be reached voluntarily, as it appears and disappears in an unpredictable manner, and for this reason it is considered to be "a gift of the gods or chance" (*Human*, IX, 614).

I suggest that Nietzsche's essays on Wagner, Schopenhauer, and Jesus can be understood as case studies of persons with a life-task, and perhaps he had them in mind when he wrote about the "single task before each of us—to bring the philosopher, the artist and the saint, within and without us, to the light" (*Untimely*, Schopenhauer, 5). These figures, and also Socrates and Goethe (whom he did not treat extensively), can serve as role models, and he examined to what degree their actions, and in the case of Jesus and Socrates also their deaths, were true to their cause. Comparing Socrates and Jesus, he found the former to be much more intelligent, with a cheerful disposition and roguish wisdom, "the finest state of the human soul" (*Human*. Wanderer, 86) and yet, in his last moment he blundered and made a grim judgment of life as a sickness. Jesus, the passive and unassertive person that he was, "this 'bringer of glad tidings' died as he lived, as he *taught*—*not* to 'redeem mankind' but to demonstrate how one ought to live" (*Antichrist*, 35). Nietzsche's own writings could be read as a document of a person with a life-task, however, regrettably and ironically his own death was far from being true to his cause.

The Way of the Creator

Zarathustra dedicated a whole discourse to the creator, one who has a life-task. Creating is both an affliction and the way to oneself; a creator must be strong, "a first movement" and a "self-propelling wheel," not merely a person who escapes from a yoke or searches social power, but rather one with a ruling idea. The creator understands that "the question is not free from what, but free for what." Creators determine their own values and make their will their law, thus they become their own judges and avengers (*Thus*, I, The way of the creator). Creators transform their suffering into pieces of art; like God they create a world in their own image—"you want to create yourself a god from your seven devils"—and like God they can create as well as destroy. They are higher persons, who can live in a state of inner contradiction and conflict, who in creating combine their will to power and truth, who "have to be struggle and becoming and goal and conflict of goals" (*Thus*, I, The way of the creator).

Commitment and Sacrifice

Adopting a cause involves painful concessions and giving up other commitments, as one cannot have many causes and follow them all seriously—"no one can spend more than he has"—and people cannot spend themselves on politics, economy, and other worldly affairs and at the same time be true to their cause (*Twilight*, Germans, 4). A task calls for concentration, dedication, and sacrifices, in Zarathustra's words, "I love him who does not hold back one drop of spirit for himself" (*Thus*, Prologue, 4). Zarathustra talked about the creative process in terms of total commitment, death, and rebirth. "Ready must you be to burn yourself in your own flame; how could you become new if you have not first become ashes!" (*Thus*, I, The way of the creator).

Nietzsche rejected the *laisser-aller* ("everything goes") approach to creativity, in favor of limiting horizons and narrowing of perspectives, noting that "stupidity is a condition of life and development." Furthermore, he believed that any significant achievement depends on long time obedience to an idea and a mentor (*Beyond*, V, 188). Any achievement in the fields of virtuousness, intellectual development, art, music, and dance, which makes it "worthwhile to live on earth," necessitates being able to command and obey oneself over "a long period of time and in a single direction" (*Beyond*, II, 188). Giving up on one's life-task and not actualizing one's talents is a pathetic sight, and there is nothing more desolate than a person who "has broken away from his true genius, and does nothing but peer aimlessly about him" (*Untimely*, Schopenhauer, 1).

Life with a cause is a demanding life, turning creators into rare tyrannized individuals (*Philologists*, 6) who cannot allow themselves to waste time on their neighbors and must be on guard against their disturbances and influences (*Thus*, IV, The higher man). Nietzsche recommended realistic ambition: striving hard and knowing at the same time that causes cannot be fully actualized. Life-tasks cannot be completed because in the very attempt to do so, the person as well as the cause change: "Whoever reaches his ideal transcends it *eo ipso* [by the thing itself] (*Beyond*, IV, 73).

Happiness and Time

Creators, persons with a life-mission, have high expectations, strive for top achievements, and do not accept the given as satisfactory and sufficient. Current self-help, psychotherapy, and popular psychology books, what we termed "the new *psychologica*," preach self-acceptance and living in the "here and now," promising to the converted a life of pleasure and happiness. Nietzsche, in contradistinction, taught how to look forward, find a life-task, and live for a higher cause. Life with a cause is the antithesis of the "doctrine of happiness": One cannot want to be happy, as moments of bliss are the consequence of activity, of the Will to Power overcoming resistance, and a chance of happiness exists in far off ideals which take effort to be attained (*Philologists*, 181).

Life should be evaluated not by an amount or degrees of happiness, but rather by the degree of investment and heroic overcoming of obstacles in achieving life's mission. The trouble is that creativity is impossible without talent, and it quite probable that happiness as well cannot be experienced without a predisposition to have happy feelings. The animals asked Zarathustra if he seeks happiness, and he answered, "I have long ceased to strive any more for happiness, I strive for my work." Asked further if he dwells in "the blue lake of happiness," he admitted that his happiness is heavy, not like a fluid wave of water, but rather like molted pitch (*Thus*, IV, The Honey Sacrifice).

Life and Time

Time-perception is a central psychological variable in Nietzsche's writings, as was exemplified in his discussion of untimeliness, that is to say, living the past in the present, in order not to be sucked into the fads and conventions of the day. Life with a cause involves a different relation to time: seeing the present as an ephemeral self-annihilating nothing, the past as a source of inspiration, and the future as everything there is. "Existence really is an imperfect tense that never becomes a present" (*Untimely*, History, 1). Zarathustra similarly taught, "I love him who justifies the future and redeems the past: for he wants to perish in the present" (*Thus*, Prologue, 4). Zarathustra, who stands for Nietzsche, saw himself in this way, "I walk among men as among the fragments of the future: that future into which I look" and he added with a grain of sadness that he is "a seer, a willer, a creator, a future itself and a bridge to the future—and alas, still as it were a cripple on this bridge" (*Thus*, II, Redemption). Writing about the German soul (and for a change, in positive terms of powerfulness and overfullness as reflected in music), Nietzsche observed that "they are of the day before yesterday and the day after tomorrow—*they have as yet no today* (*Beyond*, VIII, 240). In his critique of modern culture he saw its present orientation as a defect. "One lives for today, one lives on the spur of the moment—one lives most irresponsibly: and it is precisely this that one calls 'freedom'" (*Twilight*, Skirmishes, *39).*

The idea of Eternal Recurrence was initially presented as a conjecture, as a thinking experiment, in which Nietzsche's readers were invited to consider the implications of switching from linear to a circular time dimension: "What, if some day or night a demon were to steal after you into your loneliest loneliness and say to you: 'This life as you now live it and have lived it, you will have to live once more and innumerable times more'" (*Gay*, IV, 341).

He suggested an additional related thinking experiment, again not as a geophysicist, but as a poet contemplating the fleeting moment, who wondered "whether some beings might be able to experience time backward, or alternately forward and backward (which would involve a different concept of cause and effect)" (*Gay*, V, 374). His point of departure, like the one of his genius confreres Qohelet, Marcus Aurelius, and Schopenhauer, was the fleeting of time, the vanishing of days, and consequently death. With the collapse of the sentimental comforts of divine origins and hopes for eternity through God, our "final corruptibility" has become our "new fundamental feeling." Nietzsche the poet found solace in envisioning a circular eternity: "Everything seems far too valuable to be so fleeting: I seek an eternity for everything: ought one to pour the most precious salves and wines into the sea?—my consolation is that everything that has been is eternal: the sea will cast it up again" (*Will*, IV, 1065).

Having a Why to Live

Those who have a cause do not ask themselves, in moments of decision, whether "it feels good," but rather how an issue stands in relation to their life-task. Devotion to a task, although not a guarantee for happiness and release from pain, grants passion, a sense of direction and something that makes life's hassles smaller. "A vocation is the backbone of life" (*Human*, IX, 575) and "he who has a why to live can bear almost any how" (*Twilight*, Maxims, 12). Moreover, living with a mission is a mark of greatness: "A great man? I always see only the actor of his own ideal" (*Beyond*, IV, 97).

Finding One's Cause

Do we choose our cause, or do they choose us or force themselves upon us? Nietzsche described a process of an exacting unfolding, "the hidden imperious something, for which we for long have no name until at last it proves itself to be our task" and this demanding part, "this tyrant in us," opposes and often punishes by sickness, any attempt to doubt, prevent, disturb, or avoid our life's purpose (*Human*, Assorted, 4). No one can tell others what their cause is; we cannot start the process of discovering it at will; but we can be lawgivers after the fact, decide to accept and respect what grows independently inside us, and disengage ourselves from what we cannot value anymore (*Contra*, How I broke away from Wagner, 2). All of us are doomed to discover our limitations of talent and our moral failings, a realization which fills us with sadness and a longing for the genius or saint in us (*Untimely*, Schopenhauer, 3). Such longing is the root of culture and, when joined with the Will to Power, it drives persons to find their own causes and ways to pursue them (*Beyond*, VI, 211).

This "hidden imperious something" is experienced in different ways, as something above us or something inside us or as our higher self. "Everyone has his good day, when he finds his higher self," a day that is different from "workdays of bondage and servitude." This is not a permanent state, but a peak that we later miss and try to imitate. It is also a frightening state. "Some regard their ideal with shy humility and would like to deny it: they fear their higher self because, when it speaks, it speaks demandingly." We cannot will this state directly, as it comes and goes as it wishes and we can at best avoid disturbing it (*Human*, IX, 614). Nietzsche used his favorite metaphor of pregnancy to describe the "ideal selfishness" necessary for developing a life-task: in this mysterious state, all actions are carried out in favor of what is "generated within us"; it is experienced with a mixture of joy, anticipation, apprehension, and the sense that "something greater than we are, is growing here" (*Daybreak*, V, 552).

People, with the presumptuousness "of the small human worm," concern themselves with the big questions—why the world exists or why humans are there. It would be much more beneficial to ask, at least once, a question that only the individual can answer, "why I am here," and thus try to justify one's existence by establishing even after the fact, a purpose, a final goal, a high and noble "to this end." The best purpose in life is to be "the great and the impossible, *animae magnae prodigus* [a great exuberant spirit]." One does not have to know explicitly what the task is; the main thing is to act passionately, and the cause will be named after the fact (*Untimely*, History, 9). There are no recipes and certainties here, and it is beyond the power of science, society, or introspection "to carry out the task of re-establishing the laws of life and action." Until the elusive cause is found, we should better have the ability to live in the *interregnum* [meanwhile], be our "own '*reges*' [kings], and run small experiments, for "we are experiments: if we want to be so!" (*Daybreak*, V, 453). In one of our experiments we might stumble upon our life task.

Seekers of life-causes and tasks, longing for "a stronger nature, for a healthier simpler humanity," could benefit from having a model to learn from. Schopenhauer the "educator," was Nietzsche's model for "longing for himself" and searching for one's "genius," and through him, "we are all able to educate ourselves against our age." The creative person is the "the highest fruit of life," one who can answer the crucial questions: "Do *you* affirm this existence in the depths of your heart? Is it sufficient for you? Would you be its advocate, its redeemer?" Life becomes free only if it can be thus justified. Nietzsche asked us this question directly, and then hinted at the answer too, "the answer of Empedocles" (*Untimely*, Schopenhauer, III). What was Empedocles's answer? It can be construed in many ways, as Nietzsche related to this founder of Western philosophy in different contexts. I suggest that Empedocles, who openly claimed to be divine, actually called humans to become divine like him, which is also the essence of the Will to Power, the will to be like God, to be a creator.

Questions and Qualifications

Life with a task is the opposite of the "doctrines of the sovereign becoming, of the fluidity of all ideas, types, and styles, of the lack of all cardinal differences between man and animal" (*Human*, IX, 614). Living with a cause is also the opposite of Nietzsche's distrust of idealism and his teachings on animality and the highly praised life according to instincts. Nevertheless, life with a cause is not for everyone and only the chosen few creators can take the challenge. Only a minority of persons living with a cause is a necessary counterbalance to the "frenzied instruction" on life of the senses, and without them people will "destroy themselves in egotistical trifles and misery, ossifying themselves in their self-absorption" ensuing with a cultural and social disintegration (*Untimely*, History, 9).

Nietzsche did not distinguish between different kinds of causes. It is not difficult to understand how humanity benefited from Dostoevsky, Beethoven, and van Gogh, all persons with a life's task. But did not Hitler, Stalin and bin Laden have a life-task too? The absolute conviction in one's cause, and the ability to see one's cause in positive terms, can easily become a recipe for a disaster. How does living with a cause influence one's immediate environment of friends, spouse, and children? Some artists betray the trust of their friends and families in the process of turning their life story into art; others are simply neglectful, always busy with their more important life-task. Lastly, what is the connection between having a life's cause and soundness of mind? The idioms "crazy, mad, or nuts about something," can in some cases be understood literally—the eccentric, feeding and hosting dozens of stray cats; the deluded, proclaiming the coming end of the world; and the highly esteemed author or composer might have something in common, and it is not clear what came first, the disorder or the passion. Nietzsche, I guess, would not have been bothered by these reservations, reaffirming that the good and the bad have a common origin and that chances must be taken. He could also argue that death and destruction are growth-encouraging elements of life (an idea which would be more difficult to stomach after the atrocities of the twentieth century). Finally he would have said that false Messiahs, mobs, and creative geniuses were always around and will also be part of the human scene for times to come.

NOTE

1. "Michelangelo Quotes," www.quoteauthors.com/quotes/michelangelo-quotes.html, accessed June 22, 2014.

Conclusion

I decided to delegate Nietzsche's themes of the Will to Power, Eternal Recurrence, and the Superman to his meta-psychology, that is to say, "speculative thought dealing systematically with concepts extending beyond the limits of psychology as an empirical science" (*Dictionary.com*), and then felt free from having to deal with them. I thus preferred one voice in Nietzsche, the one who cautioned about "giving a false reality to a fiction" (*Will*, III, 521), over another. Nevertheless, these themes were hovering in the background: the Superman in Nietzsche's social psychology; Eternal Recurrence together with *amor fati* in coping with pain and suffering; and the Will to Power, as we saw in the last chapter, in living with a mission.

NIETZSCHE CONTRA NIETZSCHE

As a psychological construct, the Will to Power is of limited value: there is nothing on heaven or earth that is not under its rule, it cannot be proved or disproved, and what explains everything does not explain anything. Besides, it is doubtful whether the Will passes Nietzsche's test of practically for life, as reading and talking about the Will, as uplifting as it might be,[1] is not going to change it in any way.

He chastised the "improvers of mankind" and the morality of breeding and taming, which use different versions of *pia fraus* [holy lie] (*Twilight*, Improvers, 5). Yet, he did not hesitate to suggest his own breeding ideas for higher persons, including making them immune to, heavens forbid, "blue eyes or heaving bosoms" (*Will*, IV, 877). The Superman (chapter 5) is a holy lie because it gave birth to the idea of the super race. It is also a lie as it is portrayed stereotypically, and it does not take much hammering to show that it is hollow: Is it possible to be a Superman, twenty-four hours a day, seven days a week, always dancing, laughing, and creating, without small talk, without a toothache? Besides, who in human history was a creator of new values? The names of Buddha, Socrates, and Jesus come to mind, all of them criticized by Nietzsche. Should Stalin, Mao Zedong, and Hitler be considered creators of new values? And should we wish at all for the arrival of such persons? In real life, trendsetters on such a scale as well as revolutionaries brought only havoc.

Eternal Recurrence was broken down to *amor fati*, the "highest wisdom" of acceptance (chapter 6), and the ideas of innocence and irresponsibility (chapter 4), which are important pillars in Nietzsche's psychology and psychotherapy. Of the three themes, it is the most poetic and inspiring, and its vision of interconnectedness offers spirituality to non-idealists, and a way out from a Socratic hyper-rationality, into the more adaptive and well-rounded non-dualism. His conceptions of wholeness and the unity of opposites converse with other giant thinkers, especially those probing non-duality. Nietzsche's words resonate with religious, pantheistic, and mystical thinkers, who taught that reality and life are non-dual: there are "no two things"; there is no separation between people and things, no separation between the self and the world. We or "it" are one, and in other words, there is no room for a subject-object relationship. The idea started in the Advaita-Vedanta tradition, which states that there is no difference between Brahman and Atman, and continued in Buddhism, various strands of Zen, Taoism, Sufism, and Kabbala. Now it is also found in Western culture, in modern New Age spirituality, sometimes under the banner of interconnectedness. Nietzsche was conversing with the "emperor" (Marcus Aurelius) who wrote:

> All things are implicated with one another, and the bond is holy, and there is hardly anything unconnected with any other things. For things have been coordinated, and they combine to make up the same universe. For there is one universe made up of all things, and one god who pervades all things, and one substance, and one law, and one reason.[2]

Zarathustra's poem, beginning with the line, "Everything goes, everything comes back; eternally rolls the wheel of being" (*Thus*, III, The convalescent, 2), corresponds with Heraclitus's circle of life and with the words of Ecclesiastes (Qohelet), "The wind goes toward the south, and turns about unto the north; it whirls about continually, and the wind returns again according to his circuits" (1: 6). In other words, the world, life, and we included, are one totality; what exists is necessary and could not have been otherwise.

HUMAN, JUST HUMAN

Reading and writing about Nietzsche's ideas on self-creating and life with a cause (chapter 8), I have repeatedly asked myself whether I am a gardener with a specific plan in mind, a person with a mission or a cause in life, and whether I wish to adopt the more positive traits of the Superman. I concluded that there are a few things in life I would like to accomplish (finishing this book will be one) and a few things I would like to change in me, but basically I am well contented, wishing just to continue, and hoping only that it will not get much worse. I accept my fate as

Nietzsche taught, but also accept humanity as it is, the good and the bad together. Although Nietzsche had Zarathustra say, "I love mankind" (*Thus*, Prologue, 2), he loved it not as it is, but as he believed it should be; not for the sake of the many, but rather for the sake of exceptional individuals. Humanity was for him "the breeding ground" for the Superman and he said, "not `mankind,' but *Superman* is the goal!" (*Will*, IV, 1001).

I am not the person who would have written *Human, All too Human*—but rather *Human, Just Human*: In other words, I do not have to like all human manifestations, but I should avoid generalizations ("shopkeepers"), respect the preferences of others (have vacations, buy luxuries, and go to church), remember that they are all part of what is human, and understand that contempt and hate would not change an iota. Although Zarathustra recommended to the highest persons to laugh at themselves and adopt the attitude of "what does it matter!" (*Thus*, I, The higher man, 15), he expressed it only once, and Nietzsche did not bother to repeat loudly enough that we are going to die anyhow.

IN *SACRE MONTE*

We were staying in Lago d'Orta, Italy, at a small hotel. I chose this vacation place because Nietzsche met Lou Salomé in May 1882 in *Sacre Monte*, which I could view from the room's balcony. At breakfast, Elanah, my life-partner, said that she wanted to understand my affair with Nietzsche and asked me: "Your Nietzsche-man, how does he live?" She continued, "He gets up in the morning, then what? Does he work? Is he worried occasionally? Does he have a family? Does he care about his spouse and children? What is so different and special about him?"

I answered that "Nietzsche-persons" have different personalities and backgrounds. They differ from each other, in their degree of involvement with Nietzsche and in the manner of understanding him, although most of them are convinced that their perception is the correct one. They can be rebels, recluses, adventurers, but also quite conventional people who know that everything is permitted and that they are their own and only lawmakers. Being a "Nietzsche-person" does not make them any better or worse, but, at least, true to themselves. They will know in their hearts that organized religion is folly and the state is a bully, but will keep this insight to themselves, not wanting to get into unnecessary trouble and strife.

"Nietzsche-persons" are graduates of the best school of suspicion; they are skeptics, who are alerted any time words like state, democracy, culture, morality, rights, duties, multiculturalism, equality, and other politically correct terms are voiced, rarely sharing with others their criticism, irony, and sometimes disdain. They avoid psychologizing and self-reification, seeing themselves as multiplicities in the process. Believing in innocence and irresponsibility, they try to avoid blaming themselves and others. They respect their body, listen to their instincts. Some of them have a defined mission and cause in life, but, in any case, everything in life for them is an experiment, nothing fixed, nothing necessarily so.

"Nietzsche-persons" are survivors, whose motto is *amor fati*. They justify and accept their life until now, knowing that they have only some influence on what the future will be. They are complex, with the snake and the eagle inside them; combine earthiness and shrewdness with a love of ideas and culture. "Nietzsche-persons" love reading and rereading Nietzsche—they continue to correspond with him, agree or disagree, but always find in him exhilarating gems and insights.

Finally, "Nietzsche-persons" are not really "Nietzsche-persons," as after all, they might have also other teachers of life, and being independently minded, they cannot agree with everything he wrote. Moreover, they can still admire Nietzsche despite some of his problematic ideas, which they disregard and forgive out of gratitude and compassion, knowing that he had an exceptionally tragic life. Nietzsche's first book was *The Birth of Tragedy out of the Spirit of Music*. His life's work was the birth of music out of the spirit of tragedy. Saying that I can now conclude my book and am going to be helped by Nietzsche's aphorism on *Knowing how to End*, and in so doing, quote him for the last time:

> Masters of the first rank are recognized by knowing in a perfect manner how to find the end, in the whole as well as in the part; be it the end of a melody or of a thought, be it the fifth act of a tragedy or an act of a state. The masters of the second degree always become restless towards the end, and seldom slip down into the sea with such proud, quiet equilibrium as, for example, the mountain ridge at Portofino where the Bay of Genoa sings its melody to an end. (*Gay*, V, 281)

NOTES

1. Jacob Golomb, *Nietzsche's Enticing Psychology of Power* (Ames: Iowa State University Press, 1989).
2. *The Emperor's Handbook: A New Translation of The Meditations.* Translated by C. Scot Hicks (New York: Scribner, 2002).

Selected Bibliography

APA Presidential Task Force on Evidence-Based Practice. "Evidence-based-Statement." *American Psychologist* 61 (2006): 271–85.
Aschheim, Steven E. *The Nietzsche Legacy in Germany, 1890–1990*. Berkeley: University of California Press, 1992.
Babich, Babette E. *Nietzsche's Philosophy of Science*. Albany: State University of New York Press, 1994.
Bernfeld, Suzanne. "Freud and Archeology." *The American Imago* 8 (1951): 107–28.
Breazeale, Daniel, ed. and trans. *Philosophy and Truth: Selections from Nietzsche's Notebooks of the Early 1870s*. Amherst, NY: Prometheus Books, 1990.
Carter, Elizabeth. *The Enchiridion*. South Bend, IN: Infomotions, 2001.
Clark, Maudemarie. *Nietzsche on Truth and Philosophy*. Cambridge: Cambridge University Press, 1990.
Cautela, Joseph R., and Albert J. Kearney. *The Covert Conditioning Handbook*. New York: Springer Pub., 1986.
Dunlap, Knight, ed. *The Emotions: Carl Lange and William James*. Baltimore: Williams and Wilkins Company, 1922.
Ellis, Albert. "Rational Psychotherapy and Individual Psychology." *Journal of Individual Psychology* 13 (1957): 38–44.
Festinger, Leon. *A Theory of Cognitive Dissonance*. Stanford, CA: Stanford University Press, 1957.
Freud, Sigmund. "A Short Account of Psycho-analysis." In *The Standard Edition of the Complete Psychological Works of Sigmund Freud (SE), vol. 19*. Edited and translated by James Strachey. London: Hogarth, 1953.
——— "The Interpretation of Dreams" In *SE, vols. 4 and 5*. Edited and translated by James Strachey. London: Hogarth Press, 1958.
——— "The Psychopathology of Everyday Life." In *SE, vol. 6*. Edited and translated by James Strachey. London: Hogarth Press, 1958.
——— "New Introductory Lectures on Psychoanalysis." In *SE, vol. 22*. Edited and translated by James Strachey and Anna Freud. London: Hogarth, 1964.
Gazzaniga, Michael, Richard B. Ivry, and George R. Mangun. *Cognitive Neuroscience: The Biology of the Mind*, 4th ed. New York: W. W. Norton & Company; 2013.
Golomb, Jacob. *Nietzsche's Enticing Psychology of Power*. Ames, Iowa: Iowa State University Press, 1989.
——— *Nietzsche and Depth Psychology*. Albany: State University of New York Press, 1999.
——— "Can One Really Become a 'Free Spirit Par Excellence' or an Übermensch?" *The Journal of Nietzsche Studies*, 32 (2006): 22–40.
Griffith, Samuel B. *Sun Tzu: The Art of War*. London: Oxford University Press, 1971.
Herbart, Johann Friedrich. *Lehrbuch Der Psychologie*. 1816. Rev. ed. 1887. Reprint. Würzburg, Germany: Königsh / Neum, 2003.
Hicks, C. Scot. Trans. *The Emperor's Handbook*. New York: Scribner, 2002.
Holbach, Paul Henri Thiry, and Denis Diderot. *The System of Nature or, Laws of the Moral and Physical World*. Kitchener, Ont.: Batoche, 2001.
Hollingdale, R. J. *Nietzsche*. London: Routledge & Kegan Paul, 1973.
Hollingdale, R. J., ed. *A Nietzsche Reader*. Harmondsworth, UK: Penguin, 1977.
James, William. *The Principles of Psychology*. New York: Dover Publications, 1950.
Jones, Ernest. *Sigmund Freud: Life and Work*. London: Hogarth Press, 1953.

Jung, Carl G. "Christ, a Symbol of the Self." In *Collected Works of C. G. Jung, Vol. 9 ii.* Translated by R. F. C. Hull. Princeton, NJ: Princeton University Press, 1970.

Kaufmann, Walter Arnold. *Nietzsche, Philosopher, Psychologist, Antichrist*. 4th ed. Princeton, NJ: Princeton University Press, 1974.

Kaufmann, Walter Arnold, ed. *The Portable Nietzsche*. New York: Penguin Books, 1976.

Kaufmann, Walter, trans. *Basic Writings of Nietzsche*. Modern Library Classics. New York: Random House, 2000.

Kelly, George. *The Psychology of Personal Constructs*. New York: Norton, 1955.

Kofman, Sarah, and Duncan Large. *Nietzsche and Metaphor*. Stanford, CA: Stanford University Press, 1993.

Kopp, Sheldon B. *If You Meet the Buddha on the Road, Kill Him! The Pilgrimage of Psychotherapy Patients*. Ben Lomond, CA.: Science and Behavior Books, 1972.

Laing, R. D. *The Divided Self: An Existential Study in Sanity and Madness*. Harmondsworth, Middlesex: Penguin Books, 1960.

Leiter, Brian. *Nietzsche on Morality*. London: Routledge, 2002.

Lemm, Vanessa. *Nietzsche's Animal Philosophy Culture, Politics, and the Animality of the Human Being*. New York: Fordham University Press, 2009.

Levy, Oscar, ed. and Anthony Ludovici, trans. *Selected Letters of Friedrich Nietzsche*. London: Heinemann, 1921.

Levy, Oscar, ed. and different translators. *The Complete Works of Friedrich Nietzsche.* 18 vols. Edinburgh and London: T. N. Foulis, 1909–1913. archive.org/search.php?query=nietzsche%20epub

Malkiel, Burton Gordon. *A Random Walk down Wall Street*. New York: Norton, 1999.

Matheson, P. E., trans. *The Discourses of Epictetus*. New York: Heritage Press, 1968.

Middleton, Christopher, trans. *Selected Letters of Friedrich Nietzsche.* Chicago: University of Chicago Press, 1969.

Minsky, Marvin. *The Society of Mind*. New York: Simon & Schuster, 1986.

Mullen, Edward J., and David L. Streiner, "The Evidence For and Against Evidence-Based Practice." *Treatment and Crisis Intervention* 4 (2004): 111–21.

Nassim, Nicholas Taleb. *Fooled by Randomness: The Hidden Role of Chance in Life and in the Markets*. New York: Random House Trade Paperbacks. 2nd updated ed., 2000.

Nehamas, Alexander. *Nietzsche, Life as Literature*. Cambridge, MA.: Harvard University Press, 1985.

Nietzsche, Friedrich. *Ecce Homo: And the Birth of Tragedy*. Translated by Clifton Fadiman. New York: Modern Library, 1927.

——— *The Will to Power*. Edited and translated by Walter Kaufmann. New York: Vintage, 1968.

——— *Daybreak: Thoughts on the Prejudices of Morality*. Translated by R. J. Hollingdale. Cambridge and New York: Cambridge University Press, 1982.

——— *Untimely Meditations*. Translated by R. J. Hollingdale. Cambridge; New York: Cambridge University Press, 1983.

——— *Human, All Too Human*. Translated by R. J. Hollingdale. Two vols. in one. Cambridge University Press, 1986.

Parkes, Graham. *Composing the Soul: Reaches of Nietzsche's Psychology*. Chicago: University of Chicago Press, 1994.

Pearson, Ansell, and Duncan Large, eds. *The Nietzsche Reader*. Oxford: John Wiley & Sons, 2005.

Pippin, Robert B. *Nietzsche, Psychology, and First Philosophy*. Chicago: University of Chicago Press, 2010.

Rand, Ayn. *The Virtue of Selfishness*. New York: Penguin, 1964.

Rawls, John. *A Theory of Justice.* Revised ed. Cambridge, MA: Harvard University Press, 1999.

Safranski, Ruediger, *Nietzsche: A Philosophical Biography*. Translated by Shelley Frisch. New York: W. W. Norton, 2002

Sarbin, Theodore R., ed. *Narrative Psychology: The Storied Nature of Human Conduct*. New York: Praeger, 1986.

Schachter, Stanley, and Jerome Singer. "Cognitive, Social, and Physiological Determinants of Emotional State." *Psychological Review* 69 (1962): 379–99.
Scheffauer, Herman. "Friedrich Nietzsche and August Strindberg." *The North American Review* 198 (1913): 197–205.
Seaver, Richard. *The Marquis De Sade: The Complete Justine, Philosophy in the Bedroom, and Other Writings*. New York: Grove Press, 1965.
Seligman, Martin E. P. *Authentic Happiness: Using the New Positive Psychology to Realize Your Potential for Lasting Fulfillment*. New York: Free Press, 2002.
Solomon, Robert C. *Living With Nietzsche: What the Great "Immoralist" Has to Teach Us*. Oxford: Oxford University Press, 2003.
Solomon, Robert C., and Kathleen Marie Higgins. *What Nietzsche Really Said*. New York: Schocken Books, 2000.
Sorell, Tom. *Scientism: Philosophy and the Infatuation with Science*. London: Routledge, 1991.
Stokes, Michael C., trans. *Apology of Socrates*. Warminster: Aris & Phillips, 1997.
Szasz, Thomas. *The Myth of Mental Illness: Foundations of a Theory of Personal Conduct*. New York: Harper & Row, 1974.
Taleb, Nassim Nicholas. *Fooled by Randomness: The Hidden Role of Chance in Life and in the Markets*. 2nd updated ed. New York: Random House Trade Paperbacks, 2005.
Thiele, Leslie Paul, *Friedrich Nietzsche and the Politics of the Soul: A Study of Heroic Individualism*. Princeton, NJ: Princeton University Press, 1990.
Valsiner, Jaan, "Integrating Psychology within the Globalizing World: A Requiem to the Post-Modernist Experiment with Wissenschaft." *Integrative Psychological and Behavioral Science* 43 (2009): 1–21.
Viereck, G. S., and Sigmund Freud. "*Interview with Freud*." In *Psychoanalysis and the Future*. Edited by Th. Reik, C. Staff, and B. N. Nelson. New York: National Psychological Association for Psychoanalysis, Inc., 1957.
Vitz, Paul C. *Psychology as Religion: The Cult of Self-worship*. Grand Rapids, MI: Eerdmans, 1977.
Weber, Max. *The Protestant Ethic and the Spirit of Capitalism*. Edited by Stephen Kalberg. London: Routledge, 2013.
Wernik, Uri. *Chance Action and Therapy the Playful Way of Changing*. Hauppauge, NY: Nova Science Publishers, 2011.
Whitaker, Robert. *Anatomy of an Epidemic: Magic Bullets, Psychiatric Drugs, and the Astonishing Rise of Mental Illness in America*. New York: Crown Publishers, 2010.
Whitman, Walt. *Leaves of Grass*. Philadelphia: David McKay, 1900.
Zerubavel, Eviatar. "Lumping and Splitting: Notes on Social Classification." *Sociological Forum* 11 (1996): 421–33.

About the Author

Uri Wernik, Psy.D is a senior clinical and medical psychologist and certified sex therapist. He is in private practice now, and his work experience includes heading a unit for autistic adolescents in a psychiatric hospital, working with staff and students in an art and design academy and facilitating groups for bereaved parents.

Dr. Wernik is a graduate of the Hebrew University of Jerusalem and of the University of Illinois at Urbana-Champaign. He is a founding member and former chairman of The Israeli Association of Sex Therapy and a member of the board of directors of Transtherapy.org. He has published *Chance Action Therapy: The Playful Way of Changing* (New York, Nova Science Publishers, 2010) and eight books in Hebrew, among them *I Qoheleth* [Ecclesiastes]: *Psychologist, Philosopher, Poet* (Jerusalem: Carmel, 1998) and books on sexuality, couple relationships, and self-help. He has published articles on psychotherapy, sexuality, psychology of religion, and creativity. Additional information can be found at his website: http://www.therapy.co.il.

www.ingramcontent.com/pod-product-compliance
Ingram Content Group UK Ltd.
Pitfield, Milton Keynes, MK11 3LW, UK
UKHW040154091026
15587UKWH00018B/229

9 781498 528672